Leisure Airlines of Europe

SCOVAL
PUBLISHING LTD

© 2001 Scott Henderson

Written by Klaus Vomhof

British Library Cataloguing in Publication Data

A catalogue record for this book is available from the British Library

ISBN: 1 902236 09 2

Published by:

SCOVAL Publishing Ltd

PO BOX 36

Ponteland

Newcastle-upon-Tyne

NE20 9WE

England

Tel: (01661) 820 838

Fax: (01661) 822 911

Printed by:

Kyodo Printing Pte Ltd

Singapore

Designed by Scott Henderson and typeset in 11 on 13pt Quorum by J.R. Taylor for SCOVAL Publishing Ltd

CONTENTS

CONTENTS

CONTENTS

CONTENTS

FOREWORD

At any time of day or night, Europe's leisure airlines — be they charter or scheduled — are carrying scores of holidaymakers to or from a multitude of destinations of their choice, be that somewhere in Europe, in the Mediterranean basin or in more exotic and faraway countries. More than half of all passengers in Europe use special flights arranged for leisure travel, testimony to a remarkable development which covers a period of fifty years.

For today's tourists going on a foreign holiday, travelling by air has become a matter of routine and convenience. This has largely been made possible by tour organisers offering package tours that have been perfected since 1950, covering air travel - to a large extent by charter aircraft - hotel accommodation and ground services at destination airports and holiday resorts. Mass tourism throughout Europe has become a well-established and essential part of our way of life. It is a prime factor in the social and economic structure of nations and in their increasingly close relationships. Many charter and scheduled airlines have made valuable contributions to the furtherance of the charter sector of European air transport. The spirit of enterprise of all the people who are, and have been, involved in this business, can only be admired. It is just as if there is no limit to a seemingly unstoppable enthusiasm for seeking out new opportunities. The charter airline business environment has progressed over the years beyond purely providing air travel. For many of the participating airlines, competitive pressure has been an incentive to go beyond just air travel as such. Efficient passenger handling on the ground as well as attentive and more sophisticated in-flight service are intended to make air travel as comfortable as possible and a memorable experience as part of an annual holiday. Several charter/leisure airlines have, in recent years, introduced a second class on board their aircraft used for long-haul operations, to meet the growing demand of passengers for a higher level of service.

Over the years, airports have seen the tremendous growth in the volume of holidaymakers, not to mention different strata of society. Terminal facilities and the general infrastructure of airports have had to be remodelled and expanded repeatedly, in an effort to keep up with ongoing traffic development and to provide the facilities necessary for handling the large variety in aircraft types, as well as the growing number of aircraft in service.

Nowadays, the choice of attractively priced holidays offered by tour organisers is impressive, easily meeting the requirements of discerning and demanding customers but the beginning of the package tour business in the fifties was rather more modest. The outstanding factor was that the 'package tour' based on charter air travel, as arranged by tour operators, was offered at such a reasonable price that it was widely accepted, almost instantly, by holidaymakers accustomed to venturing on foreign holidays by coach and/or train, if at all. One of the attractions of this new form of travel was, of course, the convenience of using the package tour

arrangements, and there was no hassle in so far as their journey by air was concerned. It is amazing that the package tour concept spread so easily not only within Britain, where it originated, but also to other countries across Europe and, in later years, to other parts of the world. It is, in fact, an ongoing development that is finding new opportunities, notably so in Eastern Europe and in the states which used to form part of the former Soviet Union.

In the fifties and early sixties, in the formative years of the holiday air charter business, the carriers involved often relied on piston-engined aircraft released by the scheduled airlines from front-line duty whenever more modern aircraft types were introduced. Gradually, this changed when the financial background of the charter airlines, not to mention competitive pressure, led to the introduction of jet aircraft, and new ones at that. At the present time, Europe's charter companies use the latest aircraft designs, thus setting high standards for the airline and tour operator industries alike.

The purpose of this book is to provide an overview of the remarkable development that has taken place in the field of IT charter operations since 1950. Efforts have been made to record the history of the large number of charter and scheduled airlines which have made a contribution to the evolution of Europe's leisure air transport. The air services under review are mainly those which form a part of a 'package' or 'inclusive tour', operated by both 'scheduled' and specialist 'charter' airlines under contract to a tour operator.

The geographical area covered by this book takes in all the countries of Western and Eastern Europe. The Baltic states, the western part of Russia and selected countries of the CIS nearer Europe are also included, taking account of the fact that, since the break-up of the Soviet Union, charter operations have seen such rapid development and their contribution to European air transport is of growing importance.

The adoption by the EC of more liberal policies towards air transport, especially since January 1993, has prompted numerous changes in the operating pattern and business acumen of airlines. Until the end of 1992, holiday charter flights were clearly identified as a special category in the international pattern of Europe's air services. Since then, this has no longer been such a clear-cut case. Airlines have, since 1 January 1993, been free to choose their mode of operation, be it 'charter' or 'scheduled' and, as a matter of policy, the EC does no longer differentiate between the two modes. Many air carriers have, however, retained their traditional charter mode of operation. Several airlines have chosen to continue operating in a dual 'charter' and 'scheduled' mode, while others still have switched entirely to the 'scheduled' sector. In turn, this has led to changes in the way member countries of the European Community nowadays publish their air transport statistics, traditionally a most valuable source of background information for students of air transport. Some

FOREWORD

countries continue to publish charter statistics as used to be the case before 1993, others combine scheduled and leisure operations as one category. It is feared that, in future, it will become more difficult for students of European air transport to obtain a balanced and factual picture.

Information about Europe's leisure air transport, and the companies involved, has been obtained from a large number of airlines as well as from airport and civil aviation authorities. Whereas historical records of past charter operations have been kept by many airlines, airport and civil aviation authorities proud of their contribution to this sector of air transport, just as many have failed

to do so. Securing data for a project of this nature, or finding support for the research undertaken, has often depended on a single individual in an organization who, because of his or her long-time career and personal interest in the subject matter, has been able and willing to assist.

For the fact that the author has managed to collect a great deal of data covering Europe's charter sector of air transport, it is intended to compile another book which specifically deals with its evolution beyond purely recording the history of the airlines as is the case in this current work.

ILLUSTRATIONS

Because of the large amount of illustrations contained in this work (900), it has been decided to list the photographers where known, by name in alphabetical order. For anyone who has not been acknowledged please accept our sincere apologies.

In view of space restrictions, and the fact that this work is intended principally as a history of the 468 airlines contained in this book, the illustrations are included by way of a guide to liveries carried over the years and have accordingly not been captioned.

Mike Axe, Colin Ballantine, Kevin Cobb, Peter J Cooper, George Ditchfield, Tony Eastwood, Clive Grant, Micheal Gilland, Mike Hooks, Scott Henderson, Peter R Keating, Dean Slaybaugh, John Stroud, N Shroder, Herward Schneider, Tom Singfield, Brian Stainer, Klaus Vomhof, John Veness, Ugo Vincenzi, Chris Witt, Airbus, BA Systems, Air Berlin, Boeing, Bombardier Aerospace, Crossair, George Ditchfield Collection, Scott Henderson Collection, Crossair, Scotpick, and a special thank you to Roger Jackson, for the black and white photographs from the A J Jackson Collection, used on pages 60, 62, 154, 156, 180 and 188.

ACKNOWLEDGEMENTS

I owe very special thanks to Henning K. Andersen, Robert Cook (UK CAA Library), Hélène Delacour (Air France), Marco Iarossi (jp4 Aeronautica), Erling Jensen (Sterling Airways, Sterling European Airlines), Erik Johansen (Maersk Air), Bo Kjellgren (Linjeflyg), Lis Klynge (Scanair, Premiair), Norman Hull, Peter Penica, Guy Pichot (DGAC Paris), Martin Stepánek (CAPC), Daniel Vasut (CAPC), Dietmar Wüthrich (BAZL Bern) — and last but not least Jacques Chillon, Björn Hellström, Charles Miller (Interavia Geneva), Francois Perthuis (Aviation Civile - DGAC Paris), Alexandra Wissen (Merscher Carrier Consult).

AIRLINES Selda Akgün (Istanbul A/L), Svend Andersen (SAS), Bodil Arveng (Braathens), Rimantas Baublys (Lithuanian A/L), Ferida Begunic (Air Bosna), Einar Birgisson (Islandsflug), V. Böhlen (Balair), K. Corbesi (Avioimpex), Richard W. Creagh (UIA), Colette Demeulemeester (Sabena), Jan Demulder (Air Belgium), Günter Eichinger (Austrian Air Transport), Eddie Farrell (Aer Lingus), Isabel Fernandez (Spanair), Darius Gedminas (Air Lithuania), Nevin Genc (Greenair), Peter Gluxmann (Austrian Air Transport), Andreas Görschen (Germania), Karsten v.d. Hagen (Deutsche BA), Martine Hanesse (Sobelair), Claudia Heckner (Condor), Andreas Heeger (Lufthansa CityLine), Ilona Káldy (Malev), Sofia Katsidou (Lufthansa CityLine), Anna-Liisa Katz (Finnair), Donal Kelly (Aer Lingus), Bo Kjellgren (Linjeflyg), Bodo Kruse (Germania), Caroline Lévy (Air Liberté), Valery Litansky (LATCharter), Usko Määtä (Finnair), Giuliano Martinelli (Volare), Alberto Menéndez González (Iberworld), Renate Moser (Rheintalflug), Simon Pfander (Air Engiadina), Hervé Pierret (Corsair), Ernst Preiswerk (TEA Switzerland), Licínio Rendeiro (Air Atlantis, TAP Air Portugal), Mirella Rossi (SunExpress), Anna Sacripanti (Meridiana), Karin Schneeweiss (Condor), Markus Seiler (Helios AW), Simone Spilker (Eurowings), M. Sponar (CSA), Tore Stenslie (Braathens), Thomas Storck (Eurowings), Frank Thiemann (Condor), Aby Thurmes (Luxair), Dirk Vanderweken (Constellation International Airlines), Alexander Vassiliev (Pulkovo A/L), Roland Voss (Hamburg A/L), Adam Wychowaniec (LOT), H. Zimmermann (Hamburg International).

AIRPORT AUTHORITIES Pascal Bigot (Lyon-Satolas Apt.), Carmen de Cima Suárez (AENA Madrid), Nicolas Claude (ADP Paris), Mark Evendon (Aer Rianta Dublin), Jan Kop (Amsterdam-Schiphol Apt.), Lutz Schönfeld (Berlin Apt. Authority), J. M. Sentenac (Toulouse-Blagnac Apt.), Rodolfo Vezzelli (Rimini), F. Weiss (Frankfurt Apt.).

CIVIL AVIATION AUTHORITIES Anders Andersson (LFV Stockholm-Arlanda), Christina Andersson (LFV Malmo-Sturup), Valeria Cicogna (DGAC Italy), Pirkko Eskuri (Ilmailulaitos Finland), Jessica Klangeryd (LFV Sweden), Astrid Lund (LFV Norway), Anders Molin (LFV Sweden), Marianne F. Johnsen (LFV Norway), Michel Noel (RDVA Belgium).

TOURISM AUTHORITIES Mine Belcher (Turkish Info Office London), Andrew Millis (Greek NTO London), plus Tourist Offices of Cyprus, Finland, Iceland, Ireland [Eire], Italy, Malta, Sweden.

LIBRARIES AENA (Madrid), Air France - Service Documentation (Paris), ANA (Lisbon), BAZL (Bern), Biblioteca Nacional (Madrid), Biblioteca Ministerio de Fomento (Madrid), Biblioteca Nazionale Centrale (Rome), Bibliothèque Publique d'Information - Centre Georges Pompidou (Paris), Bibliothèque Trocadéro (Paris), Koninklijke Bibliotheek / Bibliothèque Royale Albert I (Brussels), City Business Library (London), Civilavia (Rome), Ministerio de Fomento (Madrid), DGAC - Service Documentation (Paris), Dunstable, DVWG (Bensberg), Frankfurter Allgemeine (Frankfurt), Guildhall Library (London), Hovedbibliotek (Copenhagen), Ilmailulaitos (Helsinki), IPA (Athens), National Library (Athens), National Library (Dublin), Newspaper Library (London), Rijksluchtvaartdienst (Amsterdam), RDLW / RDVA (Brussels), Royal National Library (Copenhagen), Royal National Library (Stockholm), Staats- und Universitäts-Bibliothek (Hamburg), Schweizerische Landesbibliothek (Bern), Statens Luftfartsvæsen (Copenhagen), UK CAA Central Library and Information Centre (London-Gatwick Airport), Zentralbibliothek Koln (Cologne), Zentralbibliothek (Vienna), Zentralbibliothek (Zurich).

INTERNET Aer Lingus, Air 2000, Air Alfa, Air Atlanta, Air Malta, Air One, AOM, Balair/CTA, BMA, Britannia AW, Condor, Corsair, Crossair, Edelweiss Air, Falcon Air, Finnair, Fischer Air, Hamburg International, Islandsflug, JAT, LOT, LTU, Luxair, Maersk Air, Martinair, Meridiana, Monarch AL, Montenegro AL, Novair, Olympic AW, Onur Air, Portugalia AL, Premiair, SATA Açores, Sobelair, Spanair, Sterling European AL, SunExpress, Swissair, TAP Air Portugal, TransAer, Tyrolean AW, Ukraine International AL, Virgin Express, VLM, Widerøe.

AUSTRIA

AERO-TRANSPORT (ATF) FLUGBETRIEBSGESELLSCHAFT

The charter carrier ATF — Aero-Transport Flugbetriebsgesellschaft was formed in 1956 as an air taxi operator. Between late 1957 and February 1958, two Viking aircraft were acquired, the last one from LTU which allowed ATF to start IT charter operations in spring 1958. The carrier's pattern of ITC operations covered holiday charter flights from Vienna to Spain in summer, to Cairo, Beirut and Tel Aviv as well as to Kenya in winter, and from the UK to Austria throughout the year.

In the summer of 1959, ATF ran an ITC series from Vienna via Linz, Munich and Basel to Palma and, in Winter 1959/60, to Tenerife in the Canary Islands in co-operation with the German tour operator Transeuropa. In line with a policy change, Aero-Transport entered the long-haul IT market in 1961 using two Constellations. The first intercontinental flight was made from Vienna to New York on 18 August 1961, followed by other flights to Singapore, Tokyo and Nairobi. In summer 1962, ATF leased a Viscount of Austrian Airlines for holiday charter operations. For the summer 1963 season, one Viking and three Constellations were in service. Financial problems hit Aero-Transport in 1963, leading to one of its Constellations being impounded at Vienna Airport. The company ceased flying in October and was declared bankrupt in February 1964.

AIR SALZBURG

Since its formation in 1956, Air Salzburg concentrated on adhoc charter work until, in May 1996, the company ventured into the field of holiday charter operations. In co-operation with Touropa Austria and the Reiseladen tour operators, charters were operated from Salzburg to Dublin, Edinburgh and a number of island destinations in Greece, using a Dornier DO-328. The company went into bankruptcy in March 1997 and suspended its activity.

AUSTRIA FLUGDIENST (AFD)

Austria Flugdienst (AFD) was formed in March 1957 in association with the tour operator ÖVB (Österreichisches Verkehrsbüro), using two DC-3 aircraft and IT charters were flown to holiday destinations in southern Europe. When one of its DC3s crashed at Palma in May 1959, the carrier did not acquire any other aircraft as a replacement which rendered its activity precarious. Because of this, discussions were held with regard to the company's merger with Aero-Transport but this did not work out. AFD suspended operations in 1960.

AUSTRIAN AIR TRANSPORT (AAT)

Austrian Air Transport (AAT) was formed in February 1964 with Austrian Airlines (AUA), Aero-Transport and the tour operators ÖVB and Flugring Austria as major shareholders. In the early period, AAT used a dedicated Viscount on lease from Austrian Airlines. By 1966, Caravelle jets were handling 64% of its operations. The carrier's main activity consisted of outbound ITC flights to southern European holiday destinations, especially in Spain, and inbound flights from the UK and Scandinavia.

In 1966, AAT carried over 50,000 passengers, an increase of one third over 1964. A company restructure in March 1973 led to an increase in the AUA share to 80% and that of ÖVB to 20%. From the beginning, the aircraft used by AAT have been those of Austrian Airlines and this policy has been maintained ever since. The charter carrier has, therefore, used all the types of aircraft in the AUA fleet, from the Vickers Viscount turboprop to the latest jet, including the Airbus 340 for long-haul IT charters to the Caribbean since 8 August 1995.

On the commercial side, AAT functions as a completely independent unit but operationally and technically it is fully integrated with Austrian Airlines. The charter carrier's capacity requirements are given due consideration whenever AUA reviews future fleet programmes. All aircraft used by AAT for IT charters have the same seating configuration as on scheduled services of Austrian Airlines which is a marketing incentive for tour organizers. With the start of the Summer 1996 season, dedicated M82 aircraft were used for AAT charter operations. In Summer 1997, AAT had a fleet of five dedicated MD80 aircraft at its disposal. Passenger traffic increased from 139,276 in 1973 to 440,000 in 1982 and to over 600,000 in 1996.

LAUDA AIR

Lauda Air was formed in April 1979 as an air taxi company with a fleet of two F-27s. In April 1985, after the acquisition of two BAC 1-11-500 jets, Lauda Air ventured into the IT charter business, operating to a large extent on behalf of the tour operators ITAS, Paco Rabane, Belmondo and Topic. This led to continually expanding IT charter operations, with 450,340 charter passengers carried in 1994/95.

In line with the ongoing air transport liberalization process in Europe, Lauda Air was given approval also for scheduled services which commenced in May 1988. Long-range 767 aircraft came to be used for both scheduled and charter operations on intercontinental routes. Some charter services have, in recent years, been switched to a scheduled mode. In 1993 Lauda Air founded its subsidiary 'Lauda Air S.p.A.' in Italy, using Milan-Malpensa as its base for long-haul IT charters.

MONTANA AUSTRIA

Launched in October 1976, Montana Austria was Austria's first charter carrier to specialize in long-haul IT charters. Its fleet consisted of leased 707s, and operations started on 7 November 1976 on the Vienna ~ Bangkok charter route. The company had contracts with the tour operators Touropa (Austria), Meridian and Kuoni but nearly 60% of its business activity consisted of sub-charter work for other airlines, e.g. Alitalia, Air-India, Sudan Airways, Laker Airways and Germanair. There was co-operation with Austrian Airlines in the technical field.

By the Winter of 1979/80, IT charters were in operation to Mexico, Mombasa, Colombo and Bangkok, and US CAB approval was granted for New York operations from May 1980. The charter carrier's own tour operator, Montana Weltreisen, had an exclusive programme of long-haul tours on offer. Montana wanted to operate charters to India but, due to the protectionist policies of the Indian Government with regard to its flag carrier Air-India, permission was not granted. When the IATA member airlines introduced lower promotional fares to long-haul destinations, this undermined the charter carrier's business and increasingly caused financial problems. Gradually, there was a reduction in long-haul operations and flights to Bangkok, Colombo and Mombasa were suspended. In July 1981, the company started to drift into bankruptcy and only one regular IT service was still in operation, linking Vienna with New York. Montana's final service was on 27 July 1981.

RHEINTALFLUG

Rheintalflug came into existence as an air taxi company in 1973. In summer 1984, Rheintalflug became involved with IT charter work, running a series of flights to the island of Elba with 9-seat aircraft. Dash 8 aircraft have been used for holiday operations since 1989. Summer 1996 saw Rheintalflug extending its IT charters also from Germany, with departures from Frankfurt, Friedrichshafen and Munich. In the winter of 1996/97, the carrier was involved with charter operations for winter sports enthusiasts with special flights operated from Rotterdam, Hamburg and Frankfurt to Altenrhein for holiday makers heading for the Austrian Alps, using 50-seat Dash 8 aircraft. In 1996, Rheintalflug carried 48,393 passengers.

TYROLEAN AIRWAYS

Tyrolean Airways started scheduled operations from Innsbruck on 1 April 1980 then, in summer 1982, the carrier ventured into the business of holiday charter operations on behalf of a leading Austrian tour operator, with departures from Innsbruck and Vienna. The carrier's activity covers outbound charters from Austria throughout the summer season and inbound ski charters throughout the winter to Innsbruck, and to other Austrian cities as required, mainly from Britain and Scandinavia.

Tyrolean Airways has used a number of different types of aircraft in its fleet for holiday charter operations. The use of its Dash-7-8 aircraft has proved an advantage since some tour operators need the capacity of the smaller turboprop airliners for direct IT charters to some of the smaller islands in Greece.

BELGIUM

ABELAG AIRWAYS ~ AIR BELGIUM

Abelag Airways was formed on 3 May 1979 and Brussels was chosen as its main base. The tour operator Sun International and Abelag, a general aviation company, were the main shareholders. A 707 was acquired on 17 May 1979 but was leased to UTA from June until October before being leased to a Canadian carrier in December. The Abelag partner decided to withdraw its shareholding in the air carrier and this led to its name being changed to Air Belgium on 15 February 1980.

January 1980 saw the arrival of the first 737-200, followed by a second aircraft in March 1981 which allowed Air Belgium to expand its involvement with IT charter flying. A 737-300 was added to the fleet in March 1986 and replaced by a 737-400 on 29 October 1988. The acquisition of a new 757 in October 1989 enabled Air Belgium to start long-haul charters to the Caribbean and to South America, which proved a very successful venture. Charter flights to Ft Lauderdale, Florida, started on 29 October 1990. The 757 was leased out to Transwede on a three-year contract in 1995.

It was in summer 1983 when co-operation between Air Belgium and Sobelair started through the exchange of aircraft at peak times. In 1991 Sobelair acquired a 35% share in Air Belgium. In line with further air transport liberalization in the EC, effective January 1993, Air Belgium developed plans for venturing into the scheduled sector on a number of routes to top holiday destinations but this did not materialize. In addition to Brussels from where most of Air Belgium's IT charter flights originate, Liège and Ostend have periodically been used as departure cities. The air carrier handled 304,000 passengers in 1995.

In February 1998, Britain's tour concern Airtours gained a foothold in Belgium's tour market through the acquisition of the tour operator Sun International. This resulted in the buy-out of Air Belgium in April 1999 and the take-over of the 35% stake held by Sobelair. Subsequent to this, Air Belgium placed A320 aircraft into service.

AIRTOUR

The little known carrier Airtour had one Caravelle 6N in service from June until September 1971 for IT charter work on behalf of its owner tour operator of the same name.

AVIAMEER

The management team of the UK charter carrier Overseas Aviation was behind the formation of Aviameer in the early part of 1958. After acquiring one Viking aircraft from LTU on 28 April 1958, the carrier started IT charter operations from its Antwerp base. This continued until July 1960 when Aviameer suspended operations.

BENELUX FALCON SERVICE

In March 1993, Benelux Falcon launched IT charter services from Dusseldorf, Germany, to several destinations in Greece, Italy, Spain and Turkey, using a single 757 on lease from Air Europe Italy. Services were operated throughout the summer but were suspended at the end of the season.

BIAS — BELGIAN INTERNATIONAL AIR SERVICES

Formed by private interests on 1 July 1959, BIAS was initially based at Antwerp-Deurne airport. The initial fleet consisted of a DC-4 acquired from the defunct German charter carrier Trans-Avia and commercial operations commenced on 7 July 1959. Holiday charters to Mediterranean destinations were flown mainly from Brussels and expansion of this activity followed after the addition of a second DC-4 in December 1960.

When independence was granted to the Belgian Congo in 1960, there was, in the wake of this, urgent demand for the movement of passengers and freight, and this required the use of all the aircraft capacity which Belgian air carriers were in a position to make available. Consequently, BIAS sent its DC-4s to Africa and this necessitated the cancellation of all its IT charters. In March 1963, operations were resumed with a DC-6 on lease from Sabena. In subsequent years, several more aircraft of the type were acquired and the last DC-6B remained in use until December 1971. A Caravelle was added in March 1971, followed by two DC-8-32s registered to the air carrier's major shareholder Cie. Maritime Belge in March/April 1972. BIAS ceased operations in 1973.

CONSTELLATION INTERNATIONAL AIRLINES (CAI)

Founded by private investors in March 1995 to specialize in holiday charter operations, Constellation International Airlines (CAI) commenced flying in April 1995 with two 727-200s, joined later on by a 737-300. In summer 1996, the airline operated IT charters from Brussels and Liège to holiday destinations throughout Europe and the Mediterranean. Additionally, CAI made use of the provisions of the EC rules and based one of its aircraft at Palma de Majorca for inbound holiday charters from a number of cities in Europe to this popular gateway. For summer 1997, the CAI fleet consisted of two A320 aircraft introduced into service in May 1997.

CITY BIRD

August 1996 saw the foundation of City Bird, an airline intended to operate long-haul, low cost scheduled flights to North America and Africa. After taking delivery of its first MD11 aircraft, City Bird operated IT charter flights on behalf of the French carrier Star Europe from Paris, from December 1996 until March 1997. Effective 27 March 1997, the airline initiated its own scheduled services from Brussels to North American destinations. In addition, the airline has been involved with IT charter operations on behalf of the NUR tour operator.

DELTA AIR TRANSPORT (DAT)

Delta Air Transport (DAT) was founded by private investors in 1966 for general charter work using Antwerp-Deurne Airport as its base. In addition to its operations under contract to KLM and Sabena, DAT was involved with IT charter work from Brussels and Antwerp in the seventies and eighties. The company acquired the DC-8-33 jets of Pomair in October 1974. Since Sabena acquired all the company's assets, its activity has been focused on commuter-type operations on behalf of Sabena from Brussels.

EUROBELGIAN AIRLINES (EBA) VIRGIN EXPRESS

The charter carrier Eurobelgian Airlines (EBA) was formed by the City Hotels Group in November 1991 as a successor to failed TEA Belgium. EBA took over the TEA contracts with the Neckermann/Sunsnacks tour group, thus continuing the long standing relationship that was started by TEA. IT charter operations of EBA began in February 1992 from Brussels, at that time its only departure city, with a fleet of three Boeing 737-300s. The new charter carrier's activity proved a success and a considerable share of the Belgian outbound holiday market was won. The corporate strategy of EBA was in line with that of former TEA Belgium, in that it was aimed at expanding the company's activities beyond the limits of Belgium's relatively limited holiday charter market.

EBA was the first Belgian, and in fact the first Western European, charter carrier to broaden its sphere of operation under the new liberalization rules of the EC which became effective on 1 January 1993. The company set up a base at Paris-Roissy/CDG Airport from where IT charters were launched on 23 January 1993 on the Paris-Tenerife route. In April 1993, EBA started holiday charter operations from Milan and Pisa in Italy, later suspended because of unfavourable charter market conditions. In May 1993, EBA commenced operating from the German cities of Berlin and Cologne/Bonn. In recent years, expansion of such operations has taken place in France, with holiday charters operated from several provincial cities. To handle IT charter operations from other EC countries, EBA created subsidiary companies as EBA-France, EBA-Italia and EBA-Deutschland.

In the summer of 1993, EBA had a fleet of six aircraft including five 737-300s and one 737-400, all on short to medium term lease contracts. By 1995, the fleet had grown to 11 aircraft. EBA's passenger traffic grew from 323,000 in 1992 to 837,000 passengers in 1994 and 1,312 million in 1995. EBA has recorded profits from the start. Revenues from IT charter operations in 1995 stood at a level of 50.7% in Belgium, 17.6% in France, 5.7% in Italy and 9.4% in Germany. On 23 April 1996, the British Virgin Group acquired a 90% stake in EBA and the company was re-named Virgin Express effective 2 September 1996.

INAIR ~ TRANSPOMAIR ~ POMAIR

Inair was set up in 1969. The company then changed its name to Transpomair in March 1970, prior to starting operations in April, and finally adopted the name Pomair. The Ostend-based charter carrier Pomair acquired two DC-8-32-33 aircraft in May 1973 for long-haul holiday charter operations. Since this venture did not prove successful, financial problems forced the company out of business and the aircraft were sold in October 1974.

SOBELAIR

The history of Sobelair goes back to 30 July 1946 when the company was formed by ex-Sabena staff for general charter work and operations started on 15 October 1946 with a DC-3. Sabena took a 72 % majority share in Sobelair in 1949 and this was the start of a close partnership between the two companies. In April 1962, a new sphere of activity started when Sobelair ventured into the holiday charter business, initially using one DC-6 leased from Sabena, from its Brussels base.

In the sixties and for most of the seventies, the Belgian market for IT package tours was very much untapped and it was estimated that less than 15% of potential holidaymakers were travelling by air on the occasion of their annual holidays. Nevertheless, the subsequent boom in Belgium's outbound charter tourism helped Sobelair to expand in parallel to this development. March 1971 saw the introduction of three Caravelle jets followed, in May 1974, by two 707s on lease from Sabena. Close co-operation existed with the tour operators Centrair, Airtour and Suncomfort. Using 707s, Sobelair launched long-haul charters to Montevideo and Santiago de Chile in South America, and to the French West Indies and Mauritius. The oil crisis of 1974 and the subsequent increase in aviation fuel costs prompted considerably higher air charter rates. This affected Sobelair's traffic in a way that the end result for 1980 showed a loss of almost 30% in the number of passengers carried. The situation became worse due to the fact that two of Sobelair's major tour operator customers went bankrupt.

In 1977, Sobelair began to phase in 737-200s as a replacement for its Caravelle jets. By the end of 1979, the company's fleet consisted of eight aircraft, including five 707s and three 737s. By June 1986 when Sobelair had sold most of its fuel-hungry and noisy 707s, long-haul charter services were withdrawn. In July 1987, the first of several new 737-300 aircraft was delivered while one hush kitted 707 aircraft was retained until January 1990. In that same year, the first new-generation 737-400 was added to the fleet.

Sobelair's close working relationship with Sabena has led to the harmonization of the fleet and ancillary activities, and Sabena pilots also fly Sobelair aircraft under contract. The Belgian national airline held a 71% stake in Sobelair by 1988. Co-operation in various forms has also existed between Sobelair and Air Belgium since 1983 and aircraft have been exchanged at times of peak demand. In 1993, Sobelair secured a financial stake in Air Belgium and at the same time, a 37% share was acquired in the important Belgian tour operator Sun International. Plans in line with the European liberalization of air transport after January 1993 called for Sobelair to base some of its aircraft in Italy and Spain for ITC operations to third member countries within the EU.

On 2 July 1994, Sobelair introduced one 767ER and this made it possible to launch long-haul holiday charters, extending the carrier's network to the Caribbean (Puerto Plata) in Winter 1994/95 and also to Mombasa, Bangkok and Phuket. The company leases in aircraft for the peak summer period while, during the off season, its own surplus aircraft are in service with foreign airlines. In July 1996, Sobelair launched a joint service with BalairCTA on the route Brussels-Zurich-San Francisco after acquiring a second 767.

Holding a 50% market share in Belgium, Sobelair carried 390,000 passengers in 1985. In 1992, 914,938 passengers were carried and, during the peak summer period of that year, Sobelair had up to 14 aircraft in service. In 1995, the passenger total reached 1.2 million and the market share stood at 75% then, in 1998, Sobelair carried 1,609,513 passengers using a fleet of eight aircraft.

To broaden its sphere of activity, the airline planned to take a 40% share in the Swiss charter carrier TEA Switzerland but this did not materialize.

TEA — TRANS EUROPEAN AIRWAYS

Formed in October 1970, Brussels-based Trans European Airways (TEA) initially used one 720B from April 1971 onward. By October 1974, the carrier's fleet consisted of two 720Bs and three 707s serving an extensive network of holiday charter routes throughout the Europe/Mediterranean region, in co-operation with several Belgian tour operators, in particular with Sunsnacks. TEA was the very first European charter company to take delivery of a widebody Airbus A300B2 in November 1974, for use on the high volume charter routes linking Brussels with Palma, Malaga, Tenerife, Rome and Athens. In June 1996, 737-200s were introduced to replace the older 707 and 720B jets.

Under the leadership of Georges Gutelman, TEA devised ambitious plans for a pan-European charter airline group which eventually led to the formation of local charter airlines in Britain, France, Italy, Switzerland and Turkey. Furthermore, TEA also sought scheduled service rights from Brussels to a number of cities across Europe. In the end, approval was obtained for scheduled service only on the Brussels-London (Gatwick) route.

To be able to follow its far-reaching projects through, TEA placed very large orders for Boeing and Airbus aircraft. Unfortunately, in 1991, a number of events had a drastic impact on TEA. To start with, the Gulf War crisis caused a catastrophic fall-off in IT holiday traffic demand. Furthermore, the ambitious and extremely costly future expansion plans of TEA exerted a strain on the company's resources. To survive, the company requested financial support from the Belgian Government in July 1991 but this only met with refusal. The financial situation became so critical that, on 9 September 1991, TEA was forced to seek bankruptcy protection. Scheduled and some charter operations continued until 4 November 1991 when the carrier's liquidation was initiated by a Belgian court, and Sobelair and Air Belgium took over the failed airline's contracts with tour operators. In November 1991, the charter sector of TEA was sold to City Hotels of Belgium which immediately proceeded to form the new charter company EBA. The demise of TEA made it necessary for the carrier to divest itself of its financial share in all the other charter companies under its umbrella.

VLM — VLAAMSCHE LUCHTTRANSPORT MAATSCHAPPIJ

Formed on 1 February 1992, VLM chose Antwerp-Deurne Airport as its main base and using a fleet of F-50s, the airline initiated scheduled operations in May 1993. VLM has also operated seasonal IT charter services in summer from both Antwerp and Rotterdam, serving Shannon in 1997 and Jersey C.I. in 1998.

BOSNIA HERCEGOVINA

AIR BOSNA

In May 1994, Air Bosna was set up as the national airline of Bosnia-Hercegovina and plans called for essential air links between the capital Sarajevo and key cities in southern and central Europe.

Air Bosna commenced international operations on 19 February 1997 from Sarajevo to Berlin, Cologne/Bonn, Dusseldorf, Frankfurt, Munich and Stuttgart, using two Yak-42s on lease from Air Ukraine. In summer 1998, the airline operated in a 'charter' mode to German destinations and in a 'scheduled' mode to Belgrade, Istanbul and Vienna.

BULGARIA

AIR VIA — VARNA INTERNATIONAL AIR

Formed in 1990 by private investors, Air VIA was, for a time, associated with the Bulgarian airline JES Air. The airline's home base is at Varna, one of Bulgaria's Black Sea gateway airports. Air VIA has, in recent years, expanded its pattern of holiday charter services to numerous cities in Europe and the Middle East, having taken over from Balkan Bulgarian Airlines the ITC contract operations on behalf of the tour operator Balkan Holidays. On an annual basis, IT charters are operated in the summer season to the coastal resorts of Varna and Burgas whereas, in winter, special charters are operated to Sofia and Plovdiv for sports enthusiasts on skiing holidays in the Rhodope Mountain range. In summer 1998, the airline had a fleet of six TU-154s in service.

BULAIR

In the course of the sixties, Bulgaria gained importance in international tourism which helped to establish the country as one of the most popular destinations of the Black Sea region. To handle and further expand Bulgaria's share in an expanding international holiday charter business, Bulgaria's national airline TABSO formed its subsidiary company Bulair in 1968. This carrier existed until 1971 when Balkan Bulgarian Airlines took over the responsibility for IT holiday charters.

HEMUS AIR

Hemus Air was launched by the Government in 1986 for general charter work. In January 1991, the state holding was reduced to 40% and the rest was taken up by private investors. The Hemus Air fleet comprised a mix of TU-134, Yak-40 and TU-154 aircraft, some of them leased from Balkan Bulgarian Airlines and Air VIA. In 1996, Hemus Air also entered the field of holiday charter operations, linking cities in Germany, Austria and Eastern European countries with Burgas and Varna.

TABSO ~ BALKAN BULGARIAN AIRLINES

After the Second World War, the Bulgarian Government set up BVS as its national airline. On 29 June 1947, the carrier was, replaced by a jointly-owned Bulgarian/Soviet carrier named TABSO. This venture lasted until 1954 when the Bulgarian Government assumed full control of TABSO.

In the late fifties and early sixties when international tourism to Bulgaria began to develop, TABSO became involved in the operation of special holiday charter flights to Burgas and Varna on the Black Sea coast. Initially, IL-14 aircraft were used for charters from Austria and Germany to Bulgaria. TABSO's foreign charter passengers numbered 2,700 in 1958 and rose to over 23,000 in 1960 then the airline's charter activity expanded notably after the acquisition of IL-18 turboprop airliners in 1962. For summer 1964, TABSO was under contract to operate 137 IT charter flights from Ostend to Varna, believed to have been on behalf of a British tour operator. For the summer 1967 season, TABSO had a contract for 526 flights from six departure cities in West-Germany, providing a total seat capacity of 48,255. TABSO adopted the name Balkan Bulgarian Airlines in February 1968.

The popularity of Bulgaria as a tourist destination continued throughout the sixties and, by 1974, 521,000 foreign visitors arriving by air from Western Europe were recorded compared with 141,000 in 1965. In addition, 1,755 million visitors came from countries of the Soviet Bloc.

New TU-134s and TU-154s were added,which led to further expansion of IT charter operations. In addition to an extensive pattern of summer holiday charter operations to Burgas and Varna, winter tourism to Bulgaria has also been actively promoted in a way that special charter flights are operated in connection with skiing holidays in the Rhodope Mountains in southern Bulgaria. Sofia and Plovdiv serve as gateway airports.

The end of the communist era has seen a re-alignment of Bulgaria to a market economy since then which has also affected the country's air transport sector. Balkan Bulgarian Airlines lost its monopoly position in the field of scheduled and charter services when a new Government introduced an element of competition in Bulgaria's civil air transport, leading to the formation of additional airline companies. Bulgaria's tourism has been much affected by the disintegration of the Soviet Bloc and this has resulted in the loss of a very considerable amount of traffic from friendly socialist countries. In addition, there has also been a significant downturn in tourist numbers from western European countries since Bulgaria lost its attraction as a major holiday destination.

In the charter market where Balkan Bulgarian Airlines once enjoyed a strong and prominent position among all the other Eastern European air carriers, the company's charter traffic decreased from 652,581 passengers in 1990 to 408,651 passengers in 1995. Balkan has, in recent years, directed its efforts to regain its former eminent role in holiday charter traffic to Bulgaria and has contracts with tour operators in Western Europe, Russia, the Baltic states and the CIS. With regard to tourists visiting Bulgaria during the winter ski season, Balkan carried 13,000 passengers in the Winter of 1995/96, against strong competition from another Bulgarian airline, Air VIA, and from foreign airlines like Martinair, Transavia and Germania.

CROATIA

ZAGREB AIRLINES — CROATIA AIRLINES

Croatia Airlines was originally formed on 20 July 1989 as Zagreb Airlines and adopted its current name in 1990. Operations started on 5 May 1991 but had to be curtailed almost immediately because of the erupting ethnic civil strife in Yugoslavia. It was only in April 1992 when the air space over Croatia was re-opened for civil operations, and Croatia Airlines resumed commercial operations as the national airline of the new nation using 737-200s. Scheduled services have since been extended to cover important cities in Europe. In a parallel development, regular charter flights have since been resumed to Dusseldorf and Stuttgart where there is a large community of Croatian expatriate workers

The Adriatic coast of Croatia has traditionally been popular with holidaymakers from all over Europe. Since the volatile political situation of the early nineties has since stabilized, efforts were soon made to again attract foreign tourists to coastal resorts which had remained almost completely unscathed by the earlier civil war. Tourist charter flights to Croatian airports on the Adriatic coast were partially resumed in Summer 1994. Dubrovnik, the pearl of the Adriatic, could only be reached by scheduled services since the airport was re-opened on 25 October 1991 but holiday charter flights were resumed in the summer 1997 season.

CYPRUS

CYPRUS AIRWAYS

Cyprus Airways was established on 24 September 1947 with BEA as one of the co-founders. From the beginning, there was a close working relationship between the two airlines which lasted for many years, which also covered the joint use of several types of aircraft. The new airline commenced scheduled service on 18 April 1948 on the Nicosia-Athens route.

The use of Trident jet aircraft from September 1969 onward led to Cyprus Airways becoming involved with IT charter operations. Their scope was, however, limited because the Cyprus Government was opposed to any large-scale development of charter traffic to Cyprus which might prove detrimental to the scheduled sector.

The Turkish invasion of Cyprus in July 1974 brought all operations of the airline to an abrupt end. It was only on 8 February 1975 that Cyprus Airways was in a position to resume scheduled operations, not from the capital Nicosia but from Larnaca on the south coast.

For the fact that Cyprus became increasingly popular, especially with European tourists, a growing number of carriers started regular series of holiday charters from most traffic generating centres throughout Europe. To secure a share in this fast-growing traffic, Cyprus Airways formed its wholly-owned charter subsidiary Eurocypria in June 1991. To a limited extent, Cyprus Airways has continued to operate holiday charter flights.

EUROCYPRIA

Eurocypria has been in existence as a wholly-owned subsidiary of Cyprus Airways since 12 June 1991. The formation of this charter company was in line with strategic plans of the Cyprus Airways group to boost tourism to Cyprus and to compete more effectively with other carriers. Eurocypria was given the role of providing IT service from secondary cities in Europe, not forming part of the Cyprus Airways scheduled route pattern, the intention being to open up new markets and generate tourism to Cyprus. On 25 March 1992, Eurocypria commenced its inbound IT charter operations, initially only to Larnaca, from 17 cities in Europe. Its fleet consisted of two Airbus 320s leased from parent Cyprus Airways. The new charter carrier's activity proved a success and, by 9 August 1992, the 100,000th passenger had been carried. A market share of 9% had been achieved by the end of 1992.

For the Summer 1993 season, a third A320 jet was acquired and Paphos in western Cyprus was added as a destination airport. Due to the collapse of the UK tour operator Cypriana in 1995, Eurocypria lost much of its UK-originating traffic but was able to expand its operations in a burgeoning German market. The carrier managed to widen its pattern of service to 25 departure cities in Europe in Summer 1996.

HELIOS AIRWAYS

Ex-members of the TEA Switzerland management team formed Helios Airways in September 1998. It is claimed to be the first independent and privately owned charter company in Cyprus, with Cypriot partners holding a 90% stake in the company that has a share capital of CY£3 million. Based at Larnaca, IT charter services are planned to serve Larnaca and Paphos from cities in several European countries and the CIS. After delivery of its first aircraft, a Boeing 737-400, Helios Airways commenced operations on 26 May. Fleet expansion is planned to reach a total of four 737-800 jets by the year 2002.

CZECH REPUBLIC

AIR OSTRAVA

Set up in 1977 as a general charter company under the name of Air Vitkovice, Air Ostrava ventured into the field of scheduled services in 1995 and IT charters in 1996. For the latter, Air Ostrava leased F-28 jets from Fokker for the summer season but the aircraft were returned on 8 November 1996 which led to the suspension of all holiday charter operations.

AIR TERREX

The charter company Air Terrex was formed in 1992 to specialise in the operation of passenger charters. Three Boeing 727s were in use on charter routes to southern European and North African holiday destinations. The company suspended its activity in early 1995.

BEMOAIR

Set up as part of the Bemoinvest Group in 1991, Bemoair initially functioned as a school for pilots. In 1991, Bemoair started passenger and freight charter operations, using aircraft leased from the Czech Governmental fleet. An extensive pattern of IT charter operations was built up from Brno, Ostrava and Prague in co-operation with several leading Czech tour operators.

For Summer 1996, the fleet used for IT charter work consisted of two IL-62M and one 727. The airline was taken over by Egretta Air in 1996 but continued to operate under its own identity until the end of December 1996.

CSA - CESKOSLOVENSKÉ AEROLINIE ~ CZECH AIRLINES - CSA

CSA became the only state-owned airline of Czechoslovakia in 1945, resulting from the merger of the earlier CSA and CLS companies. From its base at Prague-Ruzyne, CSA commenced scheduled operations on 14 September 1946 and pursued a policy of expanding its network of domestic and international services.

In addition to its scheduled activity, CSA has periodically operated inbound charters from several western and northern European cities to Prague and Tatry. In 1965, West Germany's tour operator Neckermann had a contract with CSA to fly tourists from Hamburg, Dusseldorf and Frankfurt to Prague on a regular weekly basis, using IL-18s. In the course of the last decade, CSA services run on a charter basis have been switched to a scheduled mode.

Outbound holiday charter services have, since the sixties, been operated by CSA from Prague and Bratislava to southern European destinations, including Yugoslavia, Bulgaria and Greece. CSA used TU-134 aircraft for ITC operations until 1997. It is planned to retain TU-154s, built between 1988 and 1990 and released from scheduled service, for charter work for several more years.

Due to the break-up of Czechoslovakia into two separate states in early 1993, the name of the airline was adjusted to 'Czech Airlines - CSA' effective 27 March 1995.

CZECH GOVERNMENT FLYING SERVICES (CGFS)

The Czech Government Flying Services (CGFS) division has been involved in the operation of holiday charters from Prague-Kbely Airport to several destinations in the Mediterranean, using TU-154 aircraft during the Summer seasons until 1998. The carrier was disbanded on 1 January 1999.

EGRETTA AIR

The charter company Egretta Air was founded in November 1996 and took over two IL-62s from Bemoair in February 1997 for IT charter operations. The airline ceased trading on 31 December 1997.

ENSOR AIR

In 1991, Ensor Air came into existence and commenced IT charter flying on 11 April 1992 on the Prague—Dalaman route. A close partnership was later established with Air Terrex. TU-154 were leased from several Russian airlines and an IL-62M was in use for IT charters to the Canary Islands. At the end of March 1994, Ensor Air was disbanded and all its assets were taken over by Air Praha.

FISCHER AIR

Fischer Air was set up on 26 July 1996 by Fischer, one of the largest Czech tour operators, for the purpose of operating its holiday charter programme. With a fleet of two 737-300s, Fischer Air commenced IT charter flying on 1 May 1997.

GEMIAL AIR

Gemial Air was a Czech-owned airline which operated holiday charter services only in Summer 1991, using TU-154 and Il-62 aircraft leased from the Czech Government Flying Service.

GEORGIA AIR ~ AIR PRAHA

Georgia Air was set up as a charter company in 1992 and commenced commercial operations one year later. The company adopted the name Air Praha in 1994 and after acquiring two IL-62s, started IT charters in 1995 on behalf of several of the smaller Czech tour operators. Throughout that summer, holiday charter services were operated from Prague to popular holiday destinations in southern Europe using leased TU-154s, until the company suspended operations in late 1996.

IDG TECHNOLOGY CHARTER AIRLINE COMPANY

IDG was established in 1997 and initiated a program of holiday charter services in that summer from Prague and Brno. The carrier suspended operations in November 1997.

MOSTAREZ AIR (SKODA AIR)

This charter carrier was based at Brno and operated IT charter services to holiday destinations in southern and south-western Europe using a leased Yak 42. In Summer 1996, a leased TU-154 was introduced into service but the company suspended its operations in 1998.

TRAVEL SERVICE AIRLINES

In association with the Czech Government Flying Service, Travel Service Airlines was formed as a new charter carrier in September 1997. The capacity of its leased TU-154M aircraft is allotted to the tour operator Canaria Travel which owns a part of the airline, together with the Czech Airports Authority and former staff of CGFS. For the Summer 1999 season, two 737-400 aircraft were in use.

DENMARK

AERO-NORD

The Aero-Nord charter carrier was founded on 5 January 1965 by former staff of defunct Nordair with an initial fleet comprising three DC-7Bs acquired from American Airlines. The first DC-7B was delivered to the carrier on 2 April 1965 and operations commenced on the 15th from Copenhagen. It was planned to acquire a fleet of four Lockheed Electra turboprops but this did not materialize. The carrier's IT charter service pattern covered popular holiday destinations around the Mediterranean basin. It was privileged to be the first and, at that time, only Scandinavian air carrier to obtain a licence for charter flights to Israel, the first flight to Tel Aviv taking place on 11 October 1965.

On 30 November 1965, Aero-Nord entered into an agreement with the Swedish charter company Ostermanair in order to pool the two carriers' resources. This resulted in the formation of a new company named Internord whose crews and technical personnel were provided by the two original companies.

CONAIR ~ CONSOLIDATED AIRCRAFT CORPORATION

Set up by private interests in September 1964, Conair specialized in aircraft sales and leasing and held a 70% share in Flying Enterprise. In early 1965, three DC-7s were acquired for Flying Enterprise but this carrier suddenly stopped operating towards the end of March 1965. This placed Spies, one of Denmark's major tour operators, in a very difficult situation since it had Flying Enterprise under contract for its holiday charter programme throughout the summer 1965 season. Looking for alternative arrangements, Spies decided to buy Conair and re-establish the company as an air carrier on 1 March 1965. After obtaining a temporary operating permit on 2 April 1965, the final licence was granted on 23 April. Conair started holiday charter operations with a fleet of three 112-seat DC-7s. By early 1967, five aircraft were in service.

Fleet modernization plans in the late sixties came about due to holidaymakers' desire for jet travel. The delivery of the first of five 720 jets commenced in May 1971, and the first 720-operated charter flight took place on 15 May 1971 from Copenhagen to Palma de Majorca. The initial batch of 720s was replaced with a similar number of 720Bs acquired from Maersk Air and Monarch from January 1973 onward, which coincided with the withdrawal of the last DC-7. The last DC-7 IT charter was operated on 29 September 1971 on the Copenhagen-Genoa route.

The replacement of 720B jets began with the introduction of A300B4s purchased from SAS, and, on 26 February 1987, the first Airbus flight was operated on the Copenhagen-Malaga route. By November 1987, all the 720B jets had been phased out. Airbus A320 aircraft were introduced into service on 5 September 1991 and the fleet strength was eventually built up to six aircraft.

In the wake of a general shake-up of the Scandinavian charter scene, it was decided to merge Conair and Scanair and to set up Premiair which became operational on 1 January 1994. Both carriers initially retained the ownership of their respective aircraft. On 15 February 1996, Conair and its associated tour operator Tjaereborg Rejser were acquired by the British holiday concern Airtours and, subsequent to this, Conair ceased to exist.

FLYING ENTERPRISE

The UK charter carrier Overseas Aviation was involved in the formation of Flying Enterprise in July 1959. By June 1960, the carrier's fleet consisted of three Argonaut aircraft two of which were replaced in early 1961 with another two aircraft. In October 1963, Flying Enterprise took delivery of two DC-7s and a DC-6 leased from Svea-Flyg which led to the withdrawal of the Argonaut airliners from January 1964. On 26 March 1965, Flying Enterprise unexpectedly suspended operations and was declared bankrupt. Its successor company was Conair.

INTERNORD

Internord came into being as a partnership between Danish Aero-Nord and Swedish Ostermanair on 30 November 1965. With a combined fleet of eight DC-7B aircraft, operations commenced on 1 April 1966. To replace its ageing propeller aircraft, Internord wanted to lease in three World Airways 727s in the second half of 1966 but this did not materialize due to the US carrier's commitments in line with the Vietnam War. As an interim solution, a CL-44 turboprop airliner was leased from Loftleidir and three CV-990s were acquired from American Airlines, the first of

which was introduced on 1 July 1967. In October 1968, Internord encountered financial difficulties, resulting from the devaluation of the Danish currency and being forced to curtail operations to Greece on account of a boycott by Scandinavian tourists. Its efforts failed to secure more financial support for its future development and Internord ceased operations on 30 October 1968.

MAERSK AIR

Maersk Air was founded in August 1969 as a fully-owned subsidiary of the Danish shipping concern A. P. Møller/Maersk. International charter operations commenced in December 1970, with F-27 turboprop aircraft, on routes from Copenhagen to Munich and London.

December 1971 saw Maersk Air acquiring two of Denmark's major tour operators, Raffels Rejser and Bangs Rejser. Large-scale involvement with the IT charter business became possible by the acquisition of three ex-Northwest 720B jets, the first of which was delivered on 11 January 1973. The 720B jet was introduced on 31 March 1973 on the Copenhagen-Rhodes charter route. By December 1973, five aircraft of this type were in use, forming the backbone of the Maersk Air charter fleet until November 1987 when the last 720B was phased out.

In October 1975, Maersk Air was granted a permit by the US authorities for charter flights to the States and over the period 1976 to 1982, used its 720B jets on charter operations to North America, covering destinations both in the USA and Canada. In December 1976, Maersk Air first introduced 737-200 aircraft. From then on, the carrier has made use of several versions of the 737, starting with new 737-300s in May 1985. The first 737-400 was delivered on 16 September 1988, followed by 737-500s on 27 June 1990. The first 737-700 was delivered on 3 March 1998 and operated its first IT charter flight from Stockholm to Rhodes on 31 March.

In 1996, Maersk Air carried over two million passengers, and among its international passengers, 497,000 were carried on charter and 574,000 on scheduled flights.

NORDAIR

The charter carrier Nordair was founded by private investors on 1 September 1960 and commenced holiday charter flying on 4 February 1961 on the Copenhagen-Salzburg route. Its initial fleet consisted of three 73-seat DC-6 aircraft bought from American Airlines. SAS acquired a 45% share in the company in July 1963, which led to a working partnership between the two airlines. In August 1964, it was decided to disband Nordair and operations were suspended in October 1964. SAS took over the company's entire assets as of 1 November and Nordair's contracts with tour operators were taken over by Scanair.

PREMIAIR

In line with a general consolidation of the Scandinavian travel industry, SLG - the SAS Leisure Group - and Simon Spies Holding agreed, on 15 September 1993, to merge Conair and Scanair into a new charter carrier named Premiair. The ownership was equally divided between SAS and Spies. Operational from 1 January 1994, Premiair took over the existing contracts held with Scandinavian tour operators. The new company used a fleet of leased aircraft, including four A320s of Conair and four DC-10-10s of Scanair, with the original carriers retaining the ownership of their respective aircraft. The first services operated by Premiair on 1 January 1994 were from Malmo to Las Palmas by A320 and from Oslo to Las Palmas by DC-10. The merger proved successful and 1.2 million passengers were carried in 1994. The bulk of the airline's activity consists of IT holiday charter operations on behalf of Scandinavian tour operators, and the main base airports of Premiair are Copenhagen, Billund, Oslo-Gardermoen, Gothenburg, Stockholm-Arlanda and Malmo.

In July 1994, SAS sold its subsidiary Leisure Group to the British concern Airtours. This was followed, in February 1996, with the British leisure concern acquiring the Conair share in Premiair and all the aircraft involved. Subsequent to this, the two companies which formed the original component partners in Premiair were disbanded.

In November 1996, the replacement of the former Conair A-320s with Airtours A-320s commenced. For the summer 1998 season, Premiair had a fleet of four A300B4, six A-320 and four DC-10s in use, all of which were re-painted in Airtours colours.

SCANAIR

An investigation was started within the SAS organization in early 1961 with regard to the formation of a subsidiary air carrier to specialize in holiday charter operations. SAS was actively seeking a share in Scandinavia's charter traffic but, because of the IATA regulations at the time, was not permitted to operate ITC in its own right. This specialist company would be able to bank on SAS expertise and technical know-how, whilst providing additional work for its three maintenance bases at Copenhagen, Oslo-Fornebu and Stockholm-Arlanda.

Eventually, the charter carrier Scanair came into existence on 30 June 1961, registered in Denmark. SAS held a 45% stake through its three parent companies ABA, DDL and DNL, and the private sector companies SAAB, Det Ostasiatiska Kompagnie and Skibs Marina A/S of Norway holding the remaining shares. From the beginning, Scanair was intended to run its business independently from SAS. In addition to using its own dedicated aircraft, Scanair was able to make use of SAS aircraft in case of seasonal capacity requirements.

The arrival of yet another carrier on Scandinavia's charter scene caused great concern among the existing companies because it was generally expected that Scanair would adopt a policy of price dumping made possible, because of the ownership link, by SAS absorbing potential losses.

With an initial fleet of two ex-SAS DC-7Cs, reconfigured for 92 passengers, Scanair started holiday charter operations on 4 September 1961 on the Copenhagen-Athens route. The first jet service was operated on 11 February 1962, with a leased SAS DC-8-33, on the Copenhagen-Palma de Majorca route on behalf of its tour operator partner Stjernerejser. Throughout the summer 1962 season, a leased Caravelle was in use.

After the demise of Nordair in October 1964, Scanair took over all its contracts as of 1 November. The judicial set-up of Scanair was changed on 1 July 1966, retroactive to 1 October 1965, granting the company the charter licences for the three Scandinavian countries Denmark, Norway and Sweden as enjoyed by the founding companies of SAS, i.e. DDL, DNL and ABA. In the autumn of 1966, Scanair contracted with the Swedish tour operator Vingresor for the bulk of its aircraft capacity to be used, which covered a capacity requirement for 38,000 passengers at that time. On 23 October 1967, Scanair flew its final DC-7C charter service. On the same day, three 165-seat DC-8-33 jets were transferred from SAS, thus enhancing the charter carrier's competitive standing. As a result of an agreement with Transair Sweden, 727s came to be used from 1 October 1968 onward, an arrangement which lasted until 1975. Scanair started to phase in DC-8-55 jets in November 1970, followed by DC-8-62s in April 1976 and DC-8-63s in May 1980. In Winter 1986/87, a DC-10 was first leased from SAS for long-haul charters to the Canary Islands.

Scanair's traffic grew to such an extent that its annual passenger total reached 1.2 million by 1978/79. In 1986/87, the 25th year since its formation, the carrier held a combined 43% share in the Swedish and Norwegian holiday charter markets.

On 1 April 1983, Scanair introduced the first of three Airbus A300-B2 taken over from SAS and the phase-out of Scanair's DC-8-63 fleet was completed by the end of April 1989. Throughout the eighties and nineties, Scanair used SAS DC-9 series aircraft which proved advantageous since several of the gateway airports to southern European holiday destinations, especially in Greece, were unable to accommodate aircraft bigger than DC-9s or 737s. Scanair introduced its "Sun Class" in 1989 for passengers who preferred better and extra service, against payment of a supplement.

In April 1990, Scanair was established as an autonomous company, taking over the technical and operational responsibilities from SAS. A system-wide service improvement was the option of seat selection offered to passengers for both their outbound and return journeys and in an effort to improve efficiency and profitability, Scanair started a cost saving programme in the course of 1991. The Gulf War badly affected the carrier's activity, prompting large-scale flight cancellations and causing a substantial loss in revenue. The capacity of the DC-10 fleet proved too big and two aircraft were disposed of, however two MD80s were added to better serve destinations in line with reduced demand.

1992 was again a profitable year for Scanair although all of its Scandinavian competitors lost money. This was against the background of a decrease in demand towards the end of 1992 and lower traffic forecast for 1993 because of the overcapacity situation in the Nordic charter market. To handle this new situation, the decision was taken to form a new charter carrier which was intended to combine the operations of Scanair and Conair. The new airline was named Premiair which became operational on 1 January 1994.

STERLING AIRWAYS

The Reverend Krogager, MD of tour operator Nordisk Bustrafik — renamed Tjaereborg Rejser — pioneered Denmark's group travel when, in the post-war years, he began to offer package tours, by long distance coaches, to holiday destinations in central and southern Europe. In early 1962, Tjaereborg began using Nordair aircraft for the longer charter routes and it was at that time that the tour operator decided to form its own airline. Sterling Airways came into existence on 16 May 1962.

Sterling's initial fleet consisted of two ex-Swissair DC-6B aircraft. On 7 July 1962, its first charter flight was operated on behalf of Transair Sweden on the Copenhagen-Las Palmas route. IT charter operations on behalf of Tjaereborg commenced on 4 October 1962, with the destinations forming part of the initial network being Palma de Majorca, Milan, Rome, Athens and Salzburg. By mid-1963, the airline's fleet had grown to five DC-6Bs and, on 9 September 1963, the 100,000th passenger had been carried.

The announcement of an order for a Caravelle jet, in June 1964, and an option on a second aircraft, was greeted in the holiday charter business with surprise. Sterling took delivery of its first Caravelle 10B on 31 March 1965, introduced on the Copenhagen-Rhodes route on 3 April. Depending on payload, the Super Caravelle was capable of covering 3,700 km non-stop and was, therefore, considered ideal for Sterling's operations from Scandinavian cities to destinations in southern Europe as far as the Canary Islands. Initially, the Caravelle in Sterling service had a seating arrangement for 99 passengers, marginally more than the 97 seats in its DC-6Bs.

In early 1965, SAS made a take-over bid for Sterling Airways in line with its endeavour to win a larger share, if not control, of Scandinavia's burgeoning charter traffic. This plan however, did not go through. It was considered a diplomatic breakthrough for Sterling when, in 1965, overflying rights were granted across the western part of the Soviet Union for IT charters to Romania, reducing the journey time for the Copenhagen-Constanza sector by over one hour. Sterling launched IT charter operations from Billund, in western Denmark's Jutland province, on 19 March 1966 and at the end of 1967, Sterling's fleet consisted of seven DC-6B and three Caravelle aircraft.

In 1970, Sterling made the momentous decision to enter the IT holiday charter market ex Sweden, to be handled by its subsidiary Sterling Airways AB. In the course of the summer 1971 season, Sterling made use of Super Caravelle jets for long-haul operations between Copenhagen and destinations in the USA and Canada, the first time a twin-engined jet was authorized to cover longer flight sectors across the North Atlantic, with technical stops at Keflavik in Iceland and Gander in Nfld., Canada. 1972 turned out to be a milestone year in Sterling's history when the carrier had thirty Caravelle jets and eight DC-6Bs in use, and served a network of 58 destinations throughout Europe as far as the Canary Islands. IT charters were flown on behalf of all the major tour operators of Scandinavia and 2,391,804 passengers were carried, the largest total for any single year so far, making Sterling the largest charter carrier in Europe.

The airline's operating pattern was such that Copenhagen served as the focal point in its network, from where most of the holiday charter services radiated. In addition, non-stop ITC flights were operated from Billund, Stockholm, Gothenburg, Helsinki, Oslo, Bergen and Stavanger to holiday destinations which generated sufficient traffic to support independent services. Connecting flights to/from Copenhagen were arranged for Scandinavian cities which could not support non-stop operations and on selected days when lower traffic demand made such a pattern necessary.

On 26 April 1973, when the last DC-6B was withdrawn from service, Sterling became an all-jet airline. Delivery of the first 727-200 took place on 9 November 1973 and the aircraft's range capability made non-stop flights possible on the Stockholm-Las Palmas route. Sterling's Caravelle jets had a very reliable service record and played an important role until the last aircraft came to be withdrawn on 15 January 1992. Three ex-Thai International DC-8-63 jets, configured for 252 passengers, were placed into service on 15 May 1984 to Rhodes from both Copenhagen and Helsinki. They formed part of the fleet until October 1986 when they were replaced by more 727-200s. On 7 June 1991, Sterling took delivery of its own 757, having made use of Air Holland 757s since October 1989. Together with the 727s, this type formed the backbone of the fleet until the airline's demise.

Sterling drifted into a precarious financial situation in 1990, made worse by the Gulf War crisis of 1991 and aggravated by the loss of access to Finland's IT charter market. In early 1993, because of the worsening financial crisis, the owner of the French carrier EAS wanted to acquire the Danish airline for DKR 2.4 million, including all debts, while operations would continue under Sterling's name. This take-over did, however, not materialize. Sterling was declared bankrupt and all its operations were halted on 22 September 1993.

The company liquidators allowed Sterling to continue serving a limited charter pattern under bankruptcy protection. Operations were resumed on 30 October 1993 with a Copenhagen-Billund-Arrecife service and IT charters continued until the end of April 1994. During that period, 78,460 passengers were carried. A successor airline came into being as Sterling European Airlines.

STERLING EUROPEAN AIRLINES (SEA)

Sterling European Airlines (SEA) was formed on 14 December 1993 as a successor to Sterling Airways, taking over a select number of staff from its predecessor. With a fleet of six 727-200s, the new company commenced operations on 1 May 1994. The airline's operating pattern was very similar to that of former Sterling Airways, albeit on a much smaller scale, using Copenhagen as its base and the focus of its network. In addition to operating IT charters from cities in Scandinavia, the UK cities of Birmingham and Cardiff were also used as departure points in co-operation with British tour operators.

The Norwegian company Fred Olsen took a 95% share in SEA in November 1995. A fleet modernization programme began in February 1998 with the phasing in of two new 737-300 aircraft and on 11 June 1998, the first of five new 737-800 aircraft was delivered. SEA converted its 727 fleet into freighters for contract operations on behalf of TNT.

ESTONIA

ELK AIRWAYS

Privately-owned ELK Airways was formed on 23 October 1991 and commenced operations on 19 May 1992, using a fleet of two Let L-410 and TU-154 aircraft each. In addition to regional scheduled services from Tallinn, ELK Airways became involved with the operation of holiday charter services, starting in summer 1995.

ESTONIAN AIR

Estonian Air came into existence on 1 December 1991, taking over from the former Aeroflot Estonia Directorate. In its role as the national airline of Estonia, the airline has expanded its scheduled network to neighbouring Baltic, CIS and Scandinavian countries, and to leading gateway cities in western Europe. In 1996, a consortium led by Maersk Air acquired a 66% stake in the airline. To complement its scheduled operations, Estonian Air has also operated IT charters on behalf of Estonian tour operators since 1992.

FRANCE

AÉROMARITIME ~ AÉROMARITIME INTERNATIONAL

The name Aéromaritime was associated with an airline formed by the shipping company Chargeurs Réunis, in operation from 1934 until 1944. When, in February 1953, UTA decided to form a charter subsidiary, it adopted the name Aéromaritime. Operations included IT charter work with Caravelle and DC-6 aircraft from 11 January 1967 until December 1977. In subsequent years, specialist charter work was undertaken on behalf of Airbus Industrie.

UTA resurrected its subsidiary Aéromaritime in 1987 for passenger charter work, at rates some 30% lower than those charged by its parent company in compliance with IATA agreements. Aéromaritime re-started charter operations on 18 December 1987, using a 325-seat UTA DC-10 from Paris to the French West Indies on behalf of the tour organiser Nouvelles Frontières. On 29 March 1988, Aéromaritime initiated charter

operations in Europe with two 737-300s from Paris to Madrid, Frankfurt and Milan, followed by other destinations later on. It was intended to eventually switch these charter flights to a 'scheduled' mode as soon as the on-going liberalization of air transport in the EU made this possible. In summer 1988, four 737-300s, one DC-10-30 and one 747 aircraft were in use. Aéromaritime was 99% owned by UTA until May 1988 when Chargeurs Réunis acquired a 49% stake.

In line with its license for world-wide charter work, Aéromaritime started additional services to Réunion on 16 November 1988 and to Bangkok on 4 November 1988. Aéromaritime was carrying 410,000 passengers a year by 1989.

The company was renamed Aéromaritime International in April 1990 and close co-operation existed with the tour operator Club Air International. The first 767ER aircraft was delivered on 26 July 1990 and introduced on the Paris-Réunion route on 6 August 1990. However the charter carrier's role and activity changed completely when Air France acquired UTA. Flights to the French West Indies and Réunion were switched to a scheduled mode and the European IT charter activity was given up in favour of Air Charter. Aéromaritime finally ceased operations in October 1991 and its leased aircraft were returned and the 737-300s were passed over to Air Charter.

AÉROTOUR

Aérotour was formed by Catair in April 1976 and used Caravelle jets of its parent company for IT charter work. Although the company experienced financial problems in 1976/77, it managed to overcome this predicament and performed well later on.

Passenger traffic increased from 29,000 in 1976 to 287,600 in 1978. As an incentive to tour organisers, Aérotour offered different charter rates for mid-week operations. By 1979, the carrier had a fleet of seven Caravelles which it planned to replace with 737s starting in late 1981. Financial problems, however, again hit the air carrier in 1980 because Klattravel, its main tour operator client, faulted on its payments. A planned financial deal with Club Med did not work out and, on 3 November 1980, Aérotour was declared bankrupt.

AIRE D'ÉVASIONS

Registered on 14 December 1991, Aire d'Évasions aquired a DC-8-73 from AOM for international charter operations from its base at Paris-Roissy/CDG airport. Operations could only start on 27 February 1992 due to the authority's delay in granting an Air Operators Certificate. The company encountered financial problems after the bankruptcy of its tour operator partner Mediacom, prompting the suspension of operations on 2 December 1992.

AIR JET

Air Jet was founded in 1979 to specialise in general charter and express freight operations, covering the transport of passengers during the day and freight at night. The company has also been involved with holiday charter operations. With a fleet of three BAe 146QC jets, IT charters have been in operation since 1995, not only from France but also from other EC countries like Austria and Germany .

AIR LIBERTÉ

The tour operator Club Aquarius was involved in the formation of Air Liberté in July 1987 which was the first time in France that a charter airline had been directly linked to a tour organising company. Operations commenced on 26 March 1988 with holiday charters from Paris-Orly to Tunis and Athens. The new carrier's initial fleet comprised two MD83 aircraft, operating under contract not only to Club Aquarius but also to CIT, Go Voyages, Voyage Conseil and Aga Tours.

In addition to IT charter operations from Paris, Air Liberté subsequently expanded its operations from provincial centres, thus trying to exploit a sizeable market potential. To do this, for the Summer 1989 season, the air carrier based one of its MD83s at Lille from where IT charters were operated to numerous holiday destinations in co-operation with a local tour operator.

On 19 December 1991, the air carrier formed its own tour operating company under the name of Nouvelle Liberté. Plans were also made for the creation of subsidiary air carriers in the tourist receiving countries, notably in Tunisia, Italy and Turkey, but such plans were realised only in Tunisia with the creation of Air Liberté Tunisie.

Air Liberté was granted Government approval for IT charters to the French West Indies and Réunion on 28 February 1990 and thus came to be on par with other French carriers. The airline moved part of its operations from Paris-Orly Airport to Roissy/CDG Airport but its scheduled services continued to be focused on Orly. As a result of adopting a growing scheduled mode of operation, the airline's charter work had decreased to 30% of overall activity by 1994. In July 1994, DC-10 aircraft were placed into service on routes to the French West Indies. Then, in November 1995, it was announced that Air Liberté intended to acquire another French airline, AOM, but this did not materialize. Operating successfully and profitably from the beginning, Air Liberté continued to build up its fleet for its expanding scheduled services and charter contracts with tour operators.

By summer 1996, the airline's fleet consisted of 22 aeroplanes, comprising seven MD83, two Airbus A300/600, three Airbus 310, four DC-10/30 (on lease from Finnair) and six Boeing 737s. Passenger traffic increased from 200,136 in 1988 to 2,141,885 in 1994/95. Financial problems, however, hit Air Liberté in summer 1996 which caused the airline to go into receivership on 26 September. Temporary suspension of

operations followed on 1 October 1996. In line with a financial rescue plan, British Airways subsequently took over Air Liberté. In April 1997, the company was effectively merged with TAT, with the aim of a more rationalised approach to future operations under the BA banner. IT charter work has subsequently been resumed.

AIR LITTORAL

Since its formation in April 1972, this regional airline has notably expanded its domestic and international network and in recent years, the carrier has also become involved with seasonal holiday charter operations. Outbound charters link several provincial cities in France with destinations in the Mediterranean region and inbound flights serve destinations in Corsica. The carrier's fleet of Fokker 70/100 and Canadair CRJ jets is used according to traffic demand.

AIR MIDI BIGORRE ~ AIR MEDITERRANÉE

In February 1997, Antoine Ferretti who formed Air Toulouse, set up Air Midi Bigorre to specialize in the transport of pilgrims to Lourdes. The intention was to capture part of the niche market of pilgrim charters handled by foreign charter airlines, to the extent of 70%, and by rail companies. One 737-200 was delivered to the carrier at the end of July 1997 and, after its initial lease to Air France, the aircraft came to be used for pilgrim charter operations from November 1997. In February 1998, the company's name was changed to Air Mediterranée and, using a fleet of three 737-200s, the carrier has been involved with special pilgrim charters to Lourdes and IT charters mainly from Paris-Roissy/CDG.

AIRNAUTIC

In 1958, Airnautic commenced its activity, specializing in general charter and IT charter work from its base at Nice, initially using Viking aircraft. Outbound charters were flown mainly from Paris while inbound holiday charters were operated on behalf of British tour operators to Nice and Perpignan. When Air France took a majority share in the carrier in early 1962, Airnautic had one DC-6, five Vikings and two Boeing Stratoliners in service. Six DC-3s were acquired mainly for lease to other carriers. Financial problems affected the company and operations were halted in September 1965. Airnautic was finally wound up on 1 January 1966 and its air crews were taken over by Air France.

AIR OUTRE MER ~ AOM FRENCH AIRLINES

Privately owned Air Outre Mer was founded on 15 December 1988, based at Reunion. Operations commenced on the Paris-Reunion route on 26 May 1990 with a DC-10-30 acquired from SAS. In the early part of 1991, service was started to the French West Indies, then later the carrier was merged with Minerve to form AOM French Airlines on 21 January 1992. The fleet of the new company comprised five DC-10-30s, five MD83s, one 747 and three DC-8 aircraft. In 1992, two DC-10s were added as a replacement for the 747 and, in that year, over one million passengers were carried. At the end of 1992, the tour operator Club Med gave up its financial stake in AOM and, since 30 December 1992, 95% of AOM's shares have been subscribed by Altus Finance which itself is a subsidiary of Crédit Lyonnais.

Out of a 1998 passenger total of 3.5 million, 665,000 passengers were carried on IT charter flights. In 1999, two new long-range A340 aircraft were added to the fleet which consisted of three 737-500s, ten MD83s and eleven DC-10-30 aircraft. The ownership of the airline has meanwhile changed with the SAirGroup holding a 49.5% stake.

AIR PROVENCE INTERNATIONAL

Formed in 1978, Air Provence operated adhoc charters with a fleet of aircraft specially suited to this varied task. In 1991, the carrier commenced holiday charter operations with a fleet of Caravelle aircraft. This continued until the beginning of February 1992 when the company withdrew these services and resorted to its previous activities.

AIR TOULOUSE ~ AIR TOULOUSE INTERNATIONAL ~ AÉRIS

In 1969, Air Toulouse was set up as an air taxi operator. With its decision of 17 December 1986, France's CSAM granted Air Toulouse a licence to operate international charter services. This led to the acquisition of three Caravelles from Sterling Airways which had taken a 20% share in the French carrier. Passenger charter operations started on 8 December 1990 from London-Gatwick and Manchester to Toulouse, followed by a regular contract charter service between Toulouse and Bristol on behalf of Aérospatiale effective 10 December 1990. Financial problems, however, resulted in the company being placed under court order and its liquidation shortly after.

Subsequent to this, with financial support from an investor company which also owned EAS, the charter carrier reappeared under the name of Air Toulouse International. A close working relationship evolved between the two airlines which led to the take-over of two Caravelles from EAS in early 1992. 120,000 passengers were carried in that year.

Air Toulouse International continued to be involved in the operation of holiday charter flights on behalf of several tour operators which involved the operation of outbound and inbound charters. In Summer 1998, the airline had a fleet of six 737s in service. The carrier was declared bankrupt in June 1999 and placed under bankruptcy protection. Subsequently, efforts were made to re-finance the company and this was accompanied by a name change to Aéris in 1999. IT charter operations were launched on 1 July 1999 with four 737s.

BELAIR

Formed by private interests and ex-staff of Minerve and Air France in March 1995, Belair commenced charter operations on 4 September 1995. Since then, the niche carrier has successfully carried out its activities along the intended policies of its founders. In summer 1997, Belair used its two 727-200 aircraft for holiday charter operations on behalf of several tour operators from Paris-Roissy/CDG and also for adhoc and VIP flights. The aircraft were also leased out to other carriers to meet extra capacity requirements. Over 250,000 passengers were carried in 1997. Fleet changes involved the use of MD83 aircraft in 1998. The company was planning to build up its fleet in preparation for the new charter market set-up after the withdrawal of Air Charter in October 1998, but Belair faced financial problems in early 1999 and was placed under bankruptcy protection. IT charters were still operated throughout 1999 but the carrier's licence was withdrawn on 18 January 2000.

CATAIR ~ CÌE. D'AFFRÈTEMENTS ET DE TRANSPORTS AÉRIENS

Catair was founded in January 1969 and commenced holiday charter operations from Pontoise, near Paris, in May of that year. Initially, ex-Air France L-1049G Super Constellations were used then, in April 1971, the company acquired its first Caravelle. Its operating base was moved to Paris (Le Bourget) and, by 1974, the fleet had grown to five Caravelle jets and five L-1049Gs.

In 1976, as a separate division, Catair set up the charter carrier Aérotour and seconded two Caravelle jets to the new company. Financial problems forced Catair to terminate its operations on 3 January 1978 and other French charter airlines took over the IT contracts which Catair was holding with tour operators at that time.

CONTINENT AIR PARIS

The charter carrier Continent Air Paris was formed in April 1995 and initially used two ATR-42 aircraft for night air freight operations and daytime domestic passengers services. On 14 March 1997, the carrier commenced IT charter services with a 737.

CORSE AIR ~ CORSAIR

The company was originally set up in 1980 to play a role in the promotion of tourism to Corsica but since big investments were required to form an airline, the project was held over for a time. It was, however, re-activated on 28 January 1981 and the initial fleet comprised four Caravelle 6N jets acquired from the defunct Aérotour charter carrier. With strong support from the Chambers of Commerce and Industry of Ajaccio and Figari in Corsica, the company's commercial flying started on 21 May 1981 on the domestic route Paris-Ajaccio. Initially, the carrier specialized in working with some of the smaller tour operators then, in 1981, licenses were granted for IT charter operations to Mediterranean and European destinations.

According to an agreement with the national airline Air France, Corse Air undertook charter flights to the European Parliament in Strasbourg during the period 1982 to 1986. The company's operations came to be affected by a stagnant economy and this led to huge losses. In 1984, one of the Caravelles was leased out to the newly formed airline Air Calédonie International based at Nouméa, Caledonia.

The airline's turnaround came in 1985 when its activity again showed a profit. Meanwhile, it had become urgent to replace the ageing Caravelle jets, otherwise the carrier would have been forced to close down on 31 December 1986. The decision was taken to acquire two 737-300 aircraft on lease from GPA, the first of which went into service in 1987. Also in that year, the French tour operator Nouvelles Frontières (NF) took a 30% share in Corse Air, thus initiating a close working relationship between the two companies which led to NF buying out Corsair in 1990.

First attempts by Corsair to enter the long-haul charter market came in 1988 when a 747 was leased from Iberia for the period June 1988 until May 1989. With this background, the carrier applied for, and obtained, traffic rights for the French Antilles. It bought its own 747-100 (517 seats) which came on-line in June 1990 and services were initiated to Fort de France, Pointe-à-Pitre and St. Martin in June 1990. A second 747-100 was put into service in February 1991 and permitted the launch of service to Montreal, Dakar and Réunion in June 1991, followed by service to Bangkok on 25 October 1991.

Like most airlines, Corsair's activity was badly affected by the Gulf War crisis in early 1991, resulting in a significant downturn in traffic. The financial losses incurred in the medium-haul sector could partly be compensated for by profitable long-haul operations. In 1992 a third 747, fitted out with 530 seats, was added and put into service on the Paris-Los Angeles-Papeete charter route on 20 December 1992. Meanwhile, the two leased 737-300s were replaced by two 737-400s, and in early 1996, a 580-seat 747-300 was added to the fleet for use mainly on charter routes to the French West Indies. An important development was the start of service to Madagascar on 1 November 1996, the first time a regular charter series was permitted to serve this island nation which has traditionally been within the exclusive sphere of operation by Air Madagascar and Air France. Future plans call for service to Moroni in the Comores.

EAS ~ EUROPE AÉRO SERVICE

EAS came into existence in July 1965 as the successor to the carrier Aero Sahara, based at Perpignan. Later on, Paris-Orly was chosen as its main base and in 1966, EAS became involved with scheduled operations and contract flying on behalf of Air France. Two Herald aircraft were acquired in July 1968 from failed Globe Air. September 1971 saw EAS acquiring the assets of the failed carrier Trans-Union. Vanguard aircraft were introduced into service between April and November 1972 which enabled EAS to enter the holiday charter market. The need to remain competitive in this market led to EAS aquiring five Caravelles between 1975 and 1978. When the CSAM approved an increase in the Caravelle fleet later on, the gradual replacement of the Vanguard commenced. This had become more urgent since these turboprop aircraft no longer enjoyed their earlier appeal to the travelling public and in 1980, the last passenger Vanguard was withdrawn from service.

The airline carried 702,469 passengers in 1986, rising to 1.2 million in 1989. The EAS fleet comprised of fifteen aircraft, including six 737s and it was planned to acquire an Airbus A310 but this did not materialize. At the time, EAS operated a mix of charter and scheduled services and was involved in extensive sub-charter work on behalf of Air France, Air inter and Air Charter. In the wake of financial problems, EAS terminated its operations on 6 March 1991 and was declared bankrupt on 16 May 1991, and placed under law protection on 21 May 1991. The fleet at the time comprised six 737s, four 727s and four Caravelles. A court ruling in Perpignan announced the liquidation of the company on 3 March 1995.

EURALAIR ~ EURALAIR INTERNATIONAL

Euralair was formed in October 1964, initially concentrating on general charter work and later switched from its base at Toussus-le-Noble to Paris (Le Bourget) on 1 January 1965. IT charter operations commenced with F27s in early 1968 on behalf of CNRO (Caisse nationale de retraite des ouvriers) from Paris to Calvi, followed by charter flights for the Club Med to Olbia. IT holiday charter operations were expanded to cover other departure airports in France, made possible by the acquisition of two Caravelle jets in November 1971 and January 1972. In April 1978, a third Caravelle was added as a spare aircraft. By 1978, the airline was carrying 140,000 passengers. Due to the creation of the 'Group of Four', i.e. Air Charter International, Air Inter, EAS and Euralair, the company placed one Caravelle at the disposal of this group in 1978. Based at Lourdes, it was used by ACI for charter work from April 1979. At that time, Euralair was also working with the tour operator Montmartre Voyages which it subsequently acquired in 1981.

The new 737 jets which Euralair acquired to replace its Caravelles in 1979, could no longer be flown under contract to Air Charter since they only had a cockpit crew of two, a decisive factor not acceptable to the Air France Group. This conflict lasted for three years. During that time, Euralair operated holiday charters on behalf of various tour organizers in its own right until 1983 when, under a new contract with Air Charter, it again operated on its behalf. A 747 came to be introduced on services to the French West Indies in March 1989, in co-operation with Air Martinique and Air Guadeloupe. After the demise of Air Charter at the end of the summer 1998 season, Euralair again initiated charter operations in its own right. There was a special agreement with the tour operator FRAM and a number of other smaller tour operators, and for this, the carrier acquired two new 737-800 aircraft, the first French air carrier to use the type.

EUROBERLIN FRANCE ~ EUROBERLIN

Air France and Lufthansa set up the jointly-owned airline EuroBerlin France on 8 September 1988, Lufthansa holding 49% and Air France 51% of the share capital, with the company functioning according to French law. Using four 737-300s, EuroBerlin France commenced scheduled operations on 7 November 1988 and in addition, EuroBerlin initiated holiday charters from Berlin in April 1991, using spare capacity mainly over the weekend. In 1991, EuroBerlin carried 885,000 passengers of which 27,714 were carried by IT charter flights. The re-unification of Germany restored Lufthansa's right to serve Berlin and as a consequence, the carrier's purpose of existence changed entirely and prompting a termination of its own scheduled services. After changing the company's name to EuroBerlin, the airline was disbanded on 31 October 1994 after operating scheduled services on behalf of Air France and Lufthansa.

JET ALSACE ~ TRANS ALSACE

The owner of Minerve, F. Meyer, set up the subsidiary air carrier Jet Alsace in February 1988 as a successor to failed Point-Air, taking over its traffic rights. Initial plans called for Strasbourg to become its base but Basel/Mulhouse was chosen instead. In addition to a Europe-wide network of holiday charter services, Jet Alsace launched long-haul operations only in October 1988 since the French authorities did not grant the necessary approvals. This was influenced by the fact that the major customer switched to the charter carrier Aéromaritime. In the winter 1988/89 season, long-haul charter services were in operation from Mulhouse to Réunion, Miami, Lomé and Banjul, using DC-8-73 and MD83 aircraft of Minerve. On 27 July 1989, the carrier's first owned MD83 was delivered, followed by additional aircraft acquired from the defunct British charter carrier BIA. Because of financial problems, the second aircraft delivery was delayed until mid-1990.

As a solution to the carrier's financial situation, talks were held with Balair on 22 March 1990 and it was subsequently announced that there was a co-operation agreement between the two carriers. Balair also considered taking a financial stake in the French company and formed, for this purpose, Balair France but nothing happened. When Minerve merged with AOM, a way had to be found for subsidiary Jet Alsace to be disposed of. As a result, it was sold to the company Heli-Inter. For Jet Alsace to be able to operate its proposed summer 1992 IT charters, it had to lease in aircraft as required since it did not have any aircraft of its own. Only 20 of the planned 32 IT charter series could be operated. Financial problems caused Jet Alsace to be replaced in Chapter III on 17 February 1993. The carrier was subsequently bought up by the Egyptian-owned company Transcapital

Holding and its name was changed to Trans Alsace on 1 May 1993. Operations were resumed with two MD83s and IT charter services were operated from Mulhouse, Strasbourg and Stuttgart.

It was intended to merge Trans Alsace at the end of 1993 with the Egyptian charter carrier Trans Med and Trans Portugal to create a multinational carrier named Transeurope. Other carriers were planned to be formed in Brussels (Transcontinent) and in Beirut (Transorient) but none of these plans could be put into effect. When, in early 1994, Trans Alsace did not have any aircraft available, Shorouk Air supplied two A320s but the French authorities did not approve of this move. Trans Alsace also encountered financial difficulties and suddenly suspended its operations on 3 July 1994. Bankruptcy was declared on 8 July after the carrier unsuccessfully tried to gain financial support from various quarters.

MINERVE ~ CIE. FRANÇAISE DE TRANSPORTS AÉRIENS

M Meyer formed Minerve in June 1975. The company obtained its air operator's licence on 9 March 1976 and was granted rights for charter services within the Europe/Mediterranean region. With two Caravelle jets in use for IT charter operations commencing in November 1975, the carrier's progress was satisfactory. Additional business from defunct Catair helped boost the carrier's passenger total to 164,000 in 1978. By 1979, five Caravelle jets were in service based at Paris, Lyon and Toulouse. Some 80% of the carrier's flights consisted of holiday charters operated on behalf of leading French tour operators.

The owner of Minerve was one of the most vociferous to fight the monopoly of Air France in the French overseas territories' markets to which he sought access. An ex-JAL DC-8-53 was acquired in March 1981, intended to be used for the proposed long-haul operations. Finally, at the end of 1981, a licence was granted to serve the French West Indies on condition that all flights originate at Mulhouse, be routed via Brussels in Belgium, and with the additional proviso that a specified number of foreign nationals be carried on each flight. For the period 27 March 1981 until 31 December 1983, Minerve held traffic rights to serve Dakar, Mombasa, Asuncion and Lima. Furthermore, by the government decree of 7 December 1982, Minerve gained rights from France to a multitude of destinations in Canada and the USA, in South America, the Caribbean, Gabon and the Ivory Coast in Africa as well as in Nepal and Burma in Asia. The carrier was authorized to serve the French West Indies from European countries but not from France. In late 1983, Minerve won a permanent certificate for charter service between France and the USA. Minerve added DC-8-61 aircraft from 1 July 1986. It was in that month that the government finally gave its approval for charter operations to be arranged from Paris-Orly to the French W.I., in place of Mulhouse and Brussels. September 1986 saw the start of service on the route Paris-San Francisco-Papeete, in co-operation with the tour operator Nouvelles Frontières. To strengthen its traffic base, the airline created the two subsidiary air carriers Minerve Canada and Minerve Antilles/Guyane.

The carrier's first MD83 was introduced into service in April 1987, the first time this type was used in France. This, and the other five, MD83 aircraft were intended to replace the ageing fleet of Caravelle and DC-8-53 jets. A 467-seat 747 was introduced on 11 December 1987 between France and the West Indies, these flights being arranged in co-operation with the tour operator Nouvelles Frontières. The 747 was also introduced on the Paris ~ Réunion charter route on 6 January 1988. These long-haul services were termed 'public service charters' and were run with all the usual scheduled service commitments.

In 1988, traffic rights were held from Paris to the Europe/Mediterranean region, Canada and the USA, to the French West Indies, Central America including Mexico, Nicaragua, Panama, South America including Brazil, Peru and Paraguay, to Dakar, Banjul and Freetown in West Africa, to Bangkok, Kathmandu and Rangoon in Asia as well as to New Caledonia and Tahiti. In addition, Minerve held rights for service between the French West Indies, Canada and the USA, and between Papeete, Tahiti, and both Canada and the western USA. Minerve launched its Paris ~ Nouméa charter service on 17 April 1988, followed by a new service to Cayenne, Guyana, in the summer. Minerve then started service from Paris to Miami, Cancun, Mexico City and Acapulco on 22 October 1988 and, on 20 December 1988, holiday charters commenced to Bangkok and Phuket in Thailand on behalf of the tour operator Carrefour Voyages, a first for an independent airline of France. Service to Salvador in Brazil followed shortly after. In January 1989, Port-au-Prince in Haiti was added to the network, as were Barbados and Mombasa in April 1989. That month also saw the introduction of new DC-10-30 aircraft. A significant development was the launch of charter service on the Paris-Bamako route on 18 December 1989, co-ordinated with Uniclam Voyages, since this gave access to one of the most staunchly protected air transport markets.

In early 1990, the fleet of Minerve comprised five MD83s, one DC-10-30, one 747 and two DC8 aircraft. The airline formed its subsidiaries Minerve Tahiti/Nouméa, but the fiercely competitive situation in the Paris/French West Indies market prompted Minerve to suspend its charter operations to that region in July 1990.

Of significance was the fact that the tour operator Club Med took a 50% share in Minerve on 24 April 1990, which indicated a policy change for the air carrier as, beforehand, it had remained totally independent of any tour organizer. Because of Club Med taking a stake in Air Liberté, plans were muted about a merger of this new carrier with Minerve in 1991 but this did not work out. Club Med eventually gave up its share in Minerve and Credit Lyonnais took up a larger stake instead. Minerve finally disappeared from France's air charter scene when it merged with Air Outre Mer to form AOM French Airlines on 21 January 1992.

POINT AIR

P oint Air was formed in late 1980 by the tour operator Le Point-Mulhouse, to succeed the failed charter carrier SATT, and the company received its general operating licence on 14 April 1981. It was planned to operate low cost charter flights from Mulhouse to West Africa and other destinations but such plans immediately met with strong opposition from the established scheduled airlines Air France, UTA and Air Afrique. Using one ex-SATT 707, operations could only be started from Mulhouse and Lyon to Ouagadougou in West Africa in October 1981 but all potential

passengers had to be members of a travel club. A DC-8-61 was added in April 1982 and traffic rights were eventually granted for Lomé in West Africa. On 12 July 1983, Point Air was granted a licence to serve Réunion with one flight every two weeks, on condition that only a maximum 50% of the passengers held French passports. Service was later extended to Delhi, Athens and several Mediterranean destinations.

In November 1985, the start of low cost flights to New York was announced, with the French Transport Ministry setting a minimum price for the Paris-New York route at FF. 2,200. On 20 December 1985, a new DC-8-71 joined the fleet. Domestic charter flights were authorized and offered for the first time in Summer 1986 although the government imposed operating restrictions. A French ministerial decision opened the way for low cost charter flights to French DOM and TOM territories on condition that no flights be offered from airports in the Paris area. Point Air started a series of flights from Nice to Réunion on 30 June 1986, leading to a more extensive departure pattern from Marseille, Mulhouse and, eventually, Paris itself. Charter flights to Moroni, in the Comores, were advertised with a starting date of 21 December 1986. Other long-haul services operated during the Winter 1986/87 period were from Paris to Mombasa, New York, Los Angeles and San Francisco as well as from Marseille to Ouagadougou, Bangui and the Cape Verde Islands.

Point Air had three aircraft grounded by the French authorities in February 1987 for safety violations, making it necessary to lease in aircraft from other airlines to meet contractual obligations with tour operators. This caused a financial crisis that forced the company into bankruptcy on 3 December 1987. A number of interested airlines planned to salvage Point Air but it was Minerve which took a 60% stake in January 1988. Operations continued only until 24 February 1988 when the operating licence of Point Air was withdrawn.

ROUSSEAU AVIATION (RA)

In July 1963, Rousseau Aviation was set up at Dinard for general charter work. After the acquisition of a DC-3 in October 1964, the airline expanded its passenger charter operations and by 1970, two HS748s had been introduced into service along with eight Nord 262s. Because of the proximity of the Channel Islands and their traffic potential on account of the vast number of seasonal holidaymakers, the airline flourished and this continued until 1973 when the company was merged with TAT.

SAFA ~ SOCIETÉ ANONYME FRANÇAISE D'AFFRÈTEMENT ~ AIR CHARTER INTERNATIONAL (ACI) ~ AIR CHARTER

Formed on 7 February 1966 as a successor to failed Airnautic, SAFA was a wholly-owned subsidiary of Air France. Initially, aircraft of its parent company were used under a wet-lease agreement and operations started on 25 July 1966 with two Caravelle and L-1049G aircraft each. SAFA's activity covered outbound and inbound charter operations, mainly focused on Paris. The new company achieved positive results during its first year of operation, carrying 168,000 passengers.

On 14 May 1969, the carrier was granted the right to operate charter flights within the same geographical area of its parent Air France, i.e. on a world-wide basis. On 8 December 1969, the name Air Charter International (ACI) was adopted. Starting in September 1970, ACI had four dedicated ex-Air France Caravelles at its disposal and this was followed by the addition of two 727-200s in 1972. By 1971, ACI claimed a 60% market share in France and 420,000 passengers were carried. In 1977, efforts were made to boost the airline's share of charter traffic from provincial cities in France but, at that time, this proved only partly successful due to the carrier's equipment shortage.

February 1978 saw the signature to agreements with Euralair and EAS, then later with TAT, allowing Air Charter to use those carriers' aircraft for holiday charter operations. The French domestic airline Air Inter took a 20% share in ACI in 1978, enabling the charter carrier to avail of the domestic airline's aircraft during the weekend in cases of peak traffic demand. In 1978, ACI carried 848,010 passengers. For the first time in 1979, ACI used Air Inter and Air France Airbus A300 aircraft for weekend charter work, followed in 1981 by the use of Air Inter's Mercure aircraft. One of the carrier's Caravelle jets came to be based at Lourdes for inbound charters from Ireland [Eire], the UK and Italy.

In the summer of 1982 and 1983, ACI used Air France 747s for North American operations which supplemented its parent company's scheduled pattern. A similar operation in summer 1983 did not prove a success and only seven out of twenty-six planned flights between Paris and New York were operated. In the same summer season, Air Charter launched an extended programme of holiday charter flights from key cities throughout France, aimed at improving the charter capacity equilibrium between Paris and the provinces, this effort being co-ordinated with several leading tour operators.

In February 1984, the air carrier's name was shortened to Air Charter. A review of its commercial policies followed with the intention of improving fleet utilization overall and to develop charter programmes mid-week, by offering attractive and competitive rates to tour organisers. Air Charter succeeded in boosting France's share of the charter market to 46% for both outbound and inbound traffic. A contribution to this was achieved through greater participation in inbound charters to Lyon during the winter sports season and a greater share of pilgrim traffic to Lourdes. By 1985, 60% of the company's flights were operated mid-week, with 35% of all departures arranged from provincial cities. The total number of seats offered on inbound flights to France amounted to 120,000, focused on Paris, with Lourdes in second place. Operating in a totally deregulated market, Air Charter had as its principal competitors Royal Air Maroc, Tunis Air, Olympic, Nationair and Wardair. The new policy direction of Air Charter proved to be right as the increase in business was 112% over the period 1983 to 1985. The carrier was faced with the task of finding its proper place in the Air France Group without infringing on the activities of either Air France or Air Inter. The company did not seek a new future role once the common EC air transport market was in place.

In 1987, Air Charter acquired another three 727s from Air France and based one aircraft each at Lourdes and Mulhouse. Also in use were three 737s chartered from Euralair and four Caravelles from EAS. In November 1987, Air Charter commenced holiday charter operations to Dakar, Senegal, which proved very successful. For the first time, the passenger total reached beyond the two million mark in 1988 which, with a market share of 38%, made Air Charter the third largest airline company in France. Seven 727s, three 737s and one Airbus were in service, supported by five Caravelles and seven 737s of EAS, as well as three 737s of Euralair. Dedicated aircraft came to be based at Lyon and Nantes and in all, holiday charter flights were programmed to depart from 12 provincial cities including Bordeaux, Épinal, Lille, Limoges, Lyon, Marseille, Metz, Montpellier, Mulhouse, Strasbourg and Toulouse. The year 1989 saw a notable increase in long-haul operations to destinations in Canada, the USA and Senegal but 81% of the carrier's activity was still focused on medium-haul routes of the Europe/Mediterranean region.

The Gulf War crisis took its toll, causing considerable losses in both 1991 and 1992. By 1993, however, Air Charter's operations had again reached a profitable level. This was achieved partly by reducing the number of seats offered in markets with excessive capacity caused by the growing competition of additional French and foreign charter carriers. All long-haul charter operations were suspended to the benefit of Air France and ACI concentrated its activity on serving a medium-haul network. Scheduled services had, until that time, not formed part of Air Charter's activity but, for political reasons, the carrier was chosen by Air France to operate scheduled cargo services to Taipei, Taiwan, from September 1993 and passenger services from November of that year. Taipei services were combined with Nouméa in New Caledonia. By 1994, Air Charter's passenger volume had decreased to 1.266 million, and an average load factor of 75.8% was recorded. The carrier worked closely with some of France's biggest tour operators Jet Tours, FRAM, Club Med, Starter and Kit Voyage. To improve its competitive standing, Air Charter created a department to handle seat consolidation for smaller tour operators so that they could share aircraft capacity rather take on the commercial risk of chartering an entire aircraft.

Air Charter was re-capitalized in 1994, with Air France contributing an A300 valued at FF. 52 million and Air Inter FF. 13 million, then the airline began to replace its five 727s with new A320 aircraft. In February 1996, after consultation with seven of its main tour operator clients, ACI launched a new product intended to create a 'holiday atmosphere' right from the time when passengers get on the aircraft, with an enhanced inflight service and improved quality of food. At the same time, new uniforms for the crew were introduced and there was more emphasis on inflight duty-free sales.

In 1996 when Air Charter celebrated its 30 year history, the company was facing ongoing strong competition from other French and foreign charter carriers. Over a five year period, the airline lost a considerable share of France's outbound holiday charter traffic, especially from provincial cities, and saw its market share reduced from 75% to 25%. In the summer of 1996, the airline's base fleet consisted of two A300s, four 320s and four 737-200s. By using additional jets of Air France, Air France Europe and Aéropostale, Air Charter was able to offer greater flexibility in the type of aircraft made available to tour operators, with a seating capacity ranging from 102 to 500. In September 1996, in a policy change, it was announced that the carrier was to take over the scheduled services of Air France Europe linking Paris with the holiday destinations Malaga, Palma de Majorca and Seville effective from the summer of 1997. For the first time, in the Winter 1996/97 season, Air Charter based an A320 at Pointe-a-Pitre for inbound charters from North America to the French West Indies.

In recent years, Air Charter's activity has produced huge losses and its passenger traffic decreased to 1.1 million in the financial year 1996/97, with the average load factor dropping to 66.3. Air Charter's costs were, by comparison with its competitors, claimed to be about 30% higher. Since the prospect of regaining a profitable situation was very remote, the momentous decision was taken to disband the airline by the end of the summer 1998 season. Air Charter used an A320 for its final service on 24 October 1998 on the Paris-Tenerife route, and in its final year of operation, Air Charter carried 820,742 passengers.

STAR EUROPE SOCIÉTÉ DE TRANSPORT AÉRIEN RÉGIONAL ~ STAR AIRLINES

Star Europe was set up in 1995 in association with the tour organiser LOOK Voyages which held a 58.6% stake of in the airline. At the time when this company was formed, the partial withdrawal of Air Liberté from the medium-haul charter market proved an advantage. Working closely with LOOK Voyages, the carrier operated its first service on 20 December 1995 from Lyon to Tenerife. Paris-Roissy/CDG, Lille and Nantes are the main base airports. In the Winter 1996/97 season, two 737-400s were in use for the medium-haul network with a leased DC-10 of City Bird used for charter operations to the French West Indies. In February 1997, two new A320 aircraft were added to the fleet and, during the Summer 1997 season, a pattern of holiday charter services radiated from six cities in France. The company changed its name to Star Airlines in October 1997.

The Lille-based tour operator Aquatour took a share in the airline and its future was expected to be favourably influenced by the intended shutdown of the Air France subsidiary, Air Charter, at the end of the summer 1998 season. Closer co-operation with the Canadian charter airline Air Transat opened the door to a seasonal interchange of aircraft which placed a TriStar at the disposal of Star Airlines for the winter 1998/99 season.

(TAT) TOURAINE AIR TRANSPORT

The French regional airline TAT was established in 1968 to serve local and regional routes in France then, in 1973, it was merged with Rousseau Aviation. After expanding its activity with international services on a number of selected routes from Paris, British Airways which took a 49.9% share in the company in 1993. Due to a restructuring of Air Liberté, which was prompted in September 1996 by financial problems, it was decided to merge TAT and Air Liberté. This process was completed by April 1997 and also involved fleet rationalization of the air. TAT has in the past, operated holiday charter services to a number of Mediterranean destinations.

TEA FRANCE

With a majority shareholding of French investors and the remainder held by TEA Belgium, TEA France came into existence in September 1987. On 28 October of that year, the operating licence was granted by the CSAM but the Transport Minister who held the opinion that there were enough charter carriers in France, delayed giving his final approval. The company's plans called for one 737 each to be based at Lille and Lourdes airports which was in line with its policy of promoting IT charter operations from provincial cities in France rather than seeking access to congested airports at major cities, especially at Paris. In the case of Lille, TEA France was also hoping to attract those holidaymakers who, traditionally, had joined IT holiday charter flights offered from nearby Brussels. Eventually, on 6 October 1989, TEA France commenced its charter activity only from Lille with a fleet of two 737-300s. The original plan of using Lourdes as a base for inbound pilgrim charters from Ireland [Eire] and Italy did not work out since Irish and Italian tour operators did not respond well enough to support this venture. Furthermore, TEA France found it difficult to develop its outbound holiday charter business from France's provincial cities.

From 1990 until 1991, TEA France used an Airbus 310 which, in 1991, was jointly operated with TEA Basel. As a consequence of the demise of Brussels-based TEA in September 1991, TEA France ran into financial trouble and sought bankruptcy protection in October. According to a French court order issued on 20 January 1992, the company was due to be liquidated in that same month. Its staff did, however, manage to obtain an extension of the order on 30 January 1992 and the carrier was allowed to continue operating for another three months.

TRANSEUROPE AIRLINES

The Transcapital Holdings Group established Transeurope Airlines in 1993 through the merger of Trans-Portugal and Trans-Alsace, with Mulhouse chosen as its main operating base. In Winter 1993/94, one MD83 was used for IT charter work from Cologne/Bonn, Munich and Nuremberg, to destinations in the Canary Islands. Plans called for the acquisition of six 737-400 aircraft for 1994 but this did not materialise and the airline was disbanded.

TRANS ~ UNION

The charter company Trans-Union was formed in 1966, based at Nice. It had DC-6B aircraft in its fleet and also used two Caravelle jets for its own passenger charter operations and sub-contract work on behalf of other airlines. In September 1971, the company suspended all operations but re-appeared in 1974. Using a Caravelle leased from Sterling Airways, Trans-Union again operated IT charters from July to September. The company sought licences for long-haul charter work but permission was not granted and, in September 1974, all operations were terminated.

UNI ~ AIR

Founded in 1969, Toulouse-based Uni-Air specialized in passenger charter operations from April 1973 onward using two DC-3 aircraft. In November 1977, the first F-27 was acquired and the type subsequently replaced all DC-3s. The company was in existence until 1984.

FINLAND

AERO - FINNISH AIRLINES ~ FINNAIR

After World War II, the signing of the Treaty of Paris by the Soviet Union and the western Allies permitted Aero to resume international air services on 3 November 1947 which led to the restoration of the vital scheduled air link with Sweden. In subsequent post-war years, Finland's national airline expanded its international network to cover important gateway cities in Western and Eastern Europe.

To meet the latent demand for holidays in sunnier and warmer parts of Europe, Finnair commenced charter flights, in the fifties, to popular holiday destinations in southern Europe, using DC-3 and Convair aircraft. The acquisition of Caravelle jets from April 1960 onwards enabled Finnair not only to expand and improve its network of scheduled international services but also its charter activity to meet the demand for vacation travel fostered by improving standards of living and more discretionary income.

In 1962, Finnair adopted an operating pattern whereby its Caravelle jets, after completing their daily scheduled routine, would fly charter flights to holiday destinations in the Mediterranean region with evening departures from Helsinki. Returning holiday charter flights would reach Helsinki in the early morning, with enough time left for the jets to be prepared for operating their scheduled services.

In 1964, the Caravelle 10B, an improved version of the jetliner, was introduced which led to the gradual replacement of the earlier Caravelle types. Of significance was the fact that this "Super Caravelle" had a maximum range of 2,300 km, allowing Finnair to serve important European gateway cities and holiday destinations from Helsinki on a non-stop basis. Charter operations continued to expand yet, in a parallel development, Finnair also sought to provide scheduled service to more destinations of special appeal to tourists. This led to Finnair taking over, in April 1964, the operation of Kar-air's scheduled holiday route from Helsinki to Malaga. Because of the IATA policy covering charter work of its member airlines, Finnair was prevented from fully exploiting Finland's potential for holiday charters. This led to the creation of the subsidiary air carrier, Polar Air,

in 1961 which took over the responsibility of the parent company's holiday charter services. This arrangement lasted until November 1963 when Kar-air replaced Polar Air in this activity.

Demand grew for holidays in far-away destinations making it necessary to acquire modern airliners to replace the Kar-air DC-6B aircraft used for holiday charters at that time. There was also a growing requirement for the deployment of more modern aircraft for holiday charters out of Finland, for competitive reasons, since several foreign charter carriers were in the process of phasing in jet equipment. Finnair's choice fell on the Douglas DC-8-62 long-range airliner, the first of which was delivered in February 1969. Before being used on the first-ever North Atlantic scheduled service to New York in May 1969, the new DC-8-62s were used by Kar-air for IT charters from Helsinki to Las Palmas and Tenerife in the Canary Islands. This established a pattern for the use of DC-8s on long-haul holiday charter routes throughout the winter season. In the early seventies, DC-8s also commenced seasonal IT charter operations to North America, serving destinations in Canada and the USA where there was a sizeable ethnic population of Finnish origin.

A major change took place in April 1973 when Finnair signed an agreement with Kar-air, to again take over the responsibility for the operation of its own IT charters. A boom in holiday travel increased Finnair's charter passenger traffic share to reach two-thirds of Finland's total. To secure a larger share in Finland's outbound holiday traffic, Finnair took over, or acquired a share of, several tour operators. Its in-house tour operator became the country's largest travel company.

Long-haul charters in the form of air cruises were first operated by Finnair/Kar-air in April 1974 from Helsinki to Southeast Asia and the Far East, taking in Bangkok and Tokyo. Strong competition on North Atlantic routes prompted Finnair's decision to acquire widebody jets in the form of the Douglas DC-10-30. The type was initially used for ITC flights on the Helsinki-Las Palmas route from 14 February 1975. Finnair continued to use Douglas jet airliners throughout the seventies and eighties. In February 1976, delivery of DC-9-51s commenced, followed by DC-9-41s in 1980 and the Series 82 (later designated the MD82) in 1983, followed by MD87s in 1987, all types being extensively used for IT charter work.

Traditionally, most of Finnair's holiday charter operations have been arranged by tour operators to depart from Helsinki but occasionally also from larger provincial cities like Tampere, Turku, Oulu and Kuopio depending on traffic demand.

Although the major part of Finnair's ITC operations caters to the outbound market, inbound charters have periodically been operated during the summer season to Finnish destinations, mainly from Germany and Switzerland. In the last decade, charter flights have increasingly been arranged from major European cities to Rovaniemi in Finnish Lapland, during the pre-Christmas and New Year period, for day trips or short-term visits.

The economic downturn in Finland in the nineties caused a continuing reduction in Finnair's charter activity. Traffic decreased from a peak of almost 1.4 million passengers in 1989/90 to just about half the number in 1995/96. Finnair has switched the status of several holiday services from a 'charter' to a 'scheduled' mode. Another important development has been the designation as 'leisure' flights for all those services which Finnair offers to popular holiday destinations in addition to its regular service destinations. This has opened the way for tour operators and Finnair to sell seats directly to the public on a 'seat-only' basis without the obligation of traditional package tour arrangements.

The disbanding of the Soviet Union in December 1991 and the resultant emergence of various independent nations has proved a bonus for Finnair. The proximity of St. Petersburg and its surrounding region of Karelia, is prompting Russians increasingly to make use of Finnair's holiday flights, especially to the Middle East. In the financial year 1998/1999, Finnair made use of a dedicated fleet of four 757s and up to three MD80/83s, supported by MD11s during the peak winter season, for its special charter/leisure flights. The total number of charter passengers carried rose to 1.5 million.

FINLANTIC

The airline Finlantic came into existence in February 1961 to specialize in long-haul IT charters to North America. Operations started in November 1961 with two DC-6B/Cs and continued until early 1963 when financial problems forced Finlantic out of business.

FINNAVIATION

Finnaviation was set up in 1979, as a result of the merger of two Finnish air carriers, to provide third level service on short-haul domestic and international routes. Finnair took a share in the company and full integration took place effective September 1996. On a seasonal basis, Finnaviation has operated holiday charter flights from Finland, notably to Visby.

KARHUMÄKI AIRWAYS ~ KAR-AIR

Privately-owned Karhumäki Airways was formed in 1950 and operated a number of seasonal short-haul routes in its early years. The company was re-organized in the latter part of 1956 which led to the name Kar-Air being adopted as of 1 January 1957. The carrier initiated IT charters with 12-seat Lodestar aircraft in 1952, with service to a number of southern European holiday destinations. In order to further its involvement in holiday charter operations, Convair CV-440s were acquired for service from 1957 onward. Kar-Air formed the Swedish subsidiary company Kar-Air Sweden AB to gain a foothold in Sweden and to profit from that country's holiday charter potential. A DC-6B was purchased from SAS in May 1961 for long-haul charter flights.

The company's expansion in the field of scheduled and charter operations, and growing competition in Finland's holiday charter market, affected Kar-Air in a way that financial problems threatened the very existence of the carrier. This led to a co-operation agreement with Finnair, signed in November 1963, whereby the national airline took over the responsibility for all scheduled operations and Kar Air concentrated on IT charter work. The DC-6B fleet was boosted to three aircraft which helped Kar-Air's expansion into long-haul charter operations and over the period 1964 to 1968, a yearly mid-Summer round-the-World charter was flown. Due to Finland's favourable relationship with the Soviet Union, Kar Air was granted permission to overfly Soviet territory from Helsinki to south-eastern European destinations. Kar-Air continued to wet-lease Finnair aircraft throughout the sixties, using Caravelles on European charter routes from 1963 onward and from 1969, Finnair's new DC8-62 aircraft were also used. Keen to acquire jet aircraft of its own, Kar-Air decided on a DC-8-51 which was introduced in November 1972. An event of significance was the second Finnair/Kar-Air agreement of April 1973 — valid until October 1980 — which resulted in Finnair taking over the bulk of the IT charter operations formerly performed by Kar-Air, although the company continued to operate IT charter services in its own right. Two Airbus A300B4 were placed into service in December 1986 and they were in use until the end of March 1990. Finally, on 2 September, Kar-Air came to be fully merged with Finnair and the name disappeared from Finland's air transport scene.

POLAR - AIR

Finnair set up Polar-Air as a wholly-owned subsidiary in 1961, to take over the operation of its IT charter flights. This arrangement worked until Kar-Air took over this task in November 1963. It is reported that only the Helsinki-Tel Aviv holiday route continued to be served by Polar-Air until 1974 when the carrier was disbanded.

SPEARAIR

Finland's boom in foreign holiday travel in the early seventies prompted the tour operator Keihäsmatkat to form its own air carrier Spearair in 1972. With a fleet of two DC-8-32 aircraft, the carrier operated ITC flights from Helsinki to a total of 10 destinations in Summer 1973. When its parent tour operator went bankrupt, Spearair was forced to terminate its activity as of 5 August 1974.

GERMANY

AERO EXPRESS FLUG

Aero Express Flug was incorporated on 1 December 1955, and charter operations commenced on 1 February 1956 from Munich with a single Viking aircraft. The carrier was taken over by KHD in 1957.

AERO LLOYD ~ AERO LLOYD FLUGREISEN GMBH & CO.

Aero Lloyd came into existence in August 1979 and was granted its operating licence in June 1980. Due to financial difficulties, however, the carrier had to suspend its activity on 2 December. A second start was made with the formation of a new company called Aero Lloyd Flugreisen GmbH & Co. Luftverkehrs AG, registered on 5 December 1980, and operations resumed in March 1981 with two Caravelle 10Rs after the operating licence of the earlier company had been taken over.

Although the carrier's Caravelle aircraft were popular with tour organisers because of their 99-seat capacity ideally suited for short to medium-haul IT operations, it soon became necessary to replace the ageing Caravelle fleet in order for Aero Lloyd to remain competitive vis-à-vis other charter companies. Fleet renewal was initiated in May 1982 when the first of three DC-9-32 aircraft was phased in. MD83s joined in March 1986, followed by MD87s in 1988 whose range permitted non-stop flights, with a full payload, from German cities to destinations in Egypt and the Canary Islands. The overall business of Aero Lloyd grew to such an extent that, at the end of 1994, the fleet comprised 20 aircraft, made up of two MD82, fourteen MD83 and four MD87 jets. Results for 1994 showed that over 2.7 million passengers had been carried and, by 1995, Aero Lloyd had secured a share of about 13% in Germany's fiercely competitive holiday charter market.

An event of importance was the start of Aero Lloyd's scheduled operations on 31 October 1988 on German domestic routes, followed by service to international destinations on 1 April 1990. This venture did not turn out to be a success and all scheduled operations were suspended on 31 March 1991. From that time, Aero Lloyd has focused its activity entirely on IT holiday operations. Since 1 November 1992, the airline has been involved in 'seat-only' sales, making use of its experience with scheduled operations of earlier years. Close co-ordination with tour operators is required with regard to their seating requirements but 'seat-only' sales offer the guarantee that a planned flight is going to be operated. Most flights to popular holiday destinations have been switched from a 'charter' to a 'scheduled' mode and are bookable through various airline reservation systems. In addition to its contract work on behalf of various tour operators, Aero Lloyd also operates a pattern of regular services between Germany and several destinations in Turkey. In November 1995, for the first time, Aero Lloyd extended its sphere of activity to another EU country by launching operations from Linz in Austria. The airline began to introduce into service new Airbus aircraft in 1996, based on an order for six A320 and ten A321 aircraft as a replacement for the MD80 fleet. The first A320 was delivered on 17 January 1996 and, in summer 1999, the airline's fleet consisted of four A321, seven A320 and eight MD83 aircraft.

AEROTOUR

The tour operator Aeropa set up Aerotour in November 1958, taking over from Columbus Luftreederei, to handle its own holiday charter programme as well as that of a number of smaller travel organizers, having used the services of KHD since 1956. By August 1958, the Aerotour fleet consisted of two Viking and two DC-4 aircraft. Since the German holiday charter market, at that time, had entered a period of instability, Aerotour's business was badly affected. This was further aggravated by the fact that the DC-4s in use required costly maintenance. The company subsequently ran into financial difficulties and was forced to suspend operations due to bankruptcy in December 1959.

AIR BERLIN USA ~ AIR - BERLIN

The US-based Lelco company formed Air Berlin USA on 11 July 1978 as a charter carrier to take over from defunct Aeroamerica. With an initial fleet of two 707s, Air Berlin USA secured a five-year contract from the West-Berlin tour operator Berliner Flugring and initiated IT charter operations on the Berlin—Palma de Majorca route on 28 April 1979.

The company acquired two 737-200 aircraft in April 1981. This was followed, in 1983, by a 'first' in Germany, including West-Berlin, when 737-300 aircraft were introduced, followed by 737-400s in 1990. The new-design 737s allowed the airline to serve destinations in the Canary Islands and in Egypt non-stop from West-Berlin. Germany's re-unification in October 1990 led to a situation whereby those airlines which were serving West-Berlin in line with concessions granted by the Allies since the end of World War II, saw their operating licences withdrawn by the German Government. Air Berlin USA was re-registered as a fully German-owned company on 16 April 1991, trading under the name of Air-Berlin from then on. Under the rules of the Allies, the charter carrier had only been allowed to serve holiday charter routes from West-Berlin. The new political situation resulting from German re-unification enabled Air-Berlin to expand its sphere of operation and in 1991, IT charter services came to be operated for the first time from West German cities, in addition to its traditional pattern focused on West-Berlin. This has proved a very successful formula since Air-Berlin is essentially a niche carrier, with a favourable cost structure and aircraft of the right size, which fits in well with tour operator requirements. The carrier bases its aircraft at Munster/Osnabruck and Paderborn for holiday charter work on a year-round basis.

As part of an extensive fleet renewal programme, six new-generation 737-800 aircraft were ordered and the first aircraft was delivered in May 1998. In 1993, the company carried some 650,000 passengers and, by 1999, the passenger total had risen to over 3 million. In a policy change, Air-Berlin began to offer 'seat-only' sales for its holiday charter flights from the start of the Winter 1997/98 season. A notable 'first' in airline marketing in Germany was the innovative 'Majorca Shuttle' operation based on the 'seat-only' travel formula. The basic idea behind this concept is to make a wide choice of flights available to Palma de Majorca, operated to a consistent weekly schedule. The initial programme covered key cities like Berlin, Dusseldorf and Paderborn throughout the summer of 1998 but the success of this venture has led to Air-Berlin extending this system also to other cities.

AIR COMMERZ

Air Commerz was formed in June 1970 and started operations that same month with two Viscounts, followed by two 707s in March and May 1971. The carrier's activity was split between special flights for foreign workers and holiday charter work on behalf of smaller tour operators. The carrier began to face financial problems which prompted its operations to be cancelled as of 1st September 1972 and, by January 1973, Air Commerz had been liquidated.

ATLANTIS

Some staff of the former Südflug formed Atlantis in the early part of 1968. Using an ex-SAS DC-7C, Atlantis was initially involved with ferrying foreign contract workers from Greece, Spain and Turkey to West Germany, followed by holiday charter operations from several West German cities. A DC-8-32 was the first jet to join the Atlantis fleet on 1 November 1968. After receiving a permit from the US CAB on 30 September 1968 for IT charters to the USA, Atlantis set about preparing plans for the Summer 1969 season. From the US side, the company's proposed transatlantic charter programme was approved but this was not the case with Germany's Ministry of Transport (BVM). In fact, it delayed granting the necessary licence for a considerable time until Atlantis took recourse with a court and the Ministry's decision was declared illegal. Eventually, the BVM granted the airline an unrestricted licence which made it possible to commence charter flights to the USA on 24 May 1969 as per the original plans.

With a fleet of DC-8 and DC-9 jets, Atlantis was able to expand both its North Atlantic and European charter operations in 1970. A special deal with the Stuttgart-based tour operator Hetzel Reisen secured the exclusive use of two Atlantis DC-9s to handle that company's IT charter programme in Summer 1970. In that same year, Atlantis was granted the right to carry passengers also from the USA to Germany. The airline's North Atlantic operations were successful but they were a thorn in the eye of Lufthansa which countered this competitive threat by introducing low promotional fares between Germany and the USA. For Atlantis, this eventually became one of the contributing factors to an increasingly precarious financial situation. Further aggravated by under-capitalization and a policy of uneconomic charter price levels aimed at safeguarding the carrier's market share in a highly competitive environment, Atlantis was forced to terminate its operations in October 1972.

AVIACTION ~ HANSEATISCHE LUFTREEDEREI

In 1969, prospects for West-Germany's IT charter development appeared very favourable and a 40% future growth forecast appeared realistic. It was against this background that the air carrier Aviaction was set up in Hamburg on 22 December 1969 to cover a gap in the charter market in Northern Germany and to balance out the activity of the larger charter companies in West-Germany which comprised Atlantis, Bavaria, Condor and LTU. Aviaction chose 65-seat F-28 jets as the standard equipment for its holiday charter flights to some of the secondary airports in southern Europe, which could not be served with bigger aircraft at that time. The first F-28 jet was delivered on 26 February 1971 and holiday charter operations commenced on 28 March 1971 on the Hamburg-Palma route. An agreement was made with Braathens for the technical support of its fleet. In 1973, Aviaction sought investors to finance its proposed future expansion. Denmark's Sterling Airways was interested in acquiring the company, a move which would have given access to West-Germany's holiday charter market, but this did not materialize. A worsening financial situation eventually forced Aviaction to cease operations on 30 October 1973.

AVIACTION KASSEL FLUGTOURISTIK

The charter carrier Aviaction Kassel Flugtouristik, a subsidiary of Hamburg-based Aviaction, was set up in November 1971 in order to operate IT charters from Kassel. Operations started with one F-28 in early 1972 but the demise of parent Aviaction affected this subsidiary in a way that it was forced to suspend operations in October 1973 also.

BAVARIA ~ BAVARIA/GERMANAIR

In 1957, Bavaria came into existence as an air taxi company based at Munich. In May 1964, after taking delivery of a turboprop Herald aircraft, the carrier ventured into IT charter work on behalf of several tour operators, A second aircraft followed in 1965, and BAC 1-11 jets, ideally suited for medium-haul charter work, were introduced in May 1967. One year later, the Herald and DC-3 aircraft were withdrawn from passenger service and Bavaria's operations were focused on Munich until 1972 when holiday charters also came to be operated from other West-German cities. By that time, the carrier's fleet had grown to seven BAC 1-11 jets.

Bavaria and Germanair were both owned by the same financier. Striving to save costs in the area of maintenance and administration, closer co-ordination of the holiday charter operations of the two carriers began in December 1974, while the two carriers retained separate identities. For the summer 1975 season, the combined fleet stood at two F-28s and eleven BAC 1-11 jets.

On 1 March 1977, the two companies eventually merged and the name Bavaria/Germanair was adopted. Total passenger traffic in that year rose to 1,171,242. The principal departure cities for IT charter services were Dusseldorf, Frankfurt and Munich. Also in 1977, Hapag-Lloyd took a 100% share in the charter carrier but plans to merge Bavaria/Germanair into its own organization could only go ahead in January 1979 after Germany's governmental 'Kartellamt' carried out a lengthy investigation into this affair.

BERLINE ~ BERLIN-BRANDENBURGISCHES LUFTFAHRTUNTERNEHMEN

A rapidly changing political situation, which led to the sudden disbanding of Interflug, left a great number of qualified personnel out of work. They decided to pool their resources and formed a charter carrier in the autumn of 1991, under the name of Berline. After obtaining an operating licence on 1 November 1991, IT flying commenced the following day with a Berlin-Heraklion service. The carrier's initial fleet consisted of five IL-18 turboprop airliners which had formed part of the Interflug fleet since the mid-sixties.

Berline introduced Fokker F-100 jets in Summer 1992 to serve an expanding network of holiday charter routes. 66,000 passengers were carried in that year and the number increased to 355,000 in 1993. Meanwhile, new investors were being sought to facilitate future expansion but this did not prove successful. The company experienced financial problems and went bankrupt, prompting the suspension of operations on 31 March 1994. Plans were later announced for a re-start of the airline under the name of German European Airlines but this could not be put into effect.

BRITANNIA AIRWAYS GmbH

Formed by Britain's leading charter airline Britannia Airways in 1997, Britannia Airways GmbH uses 767 aircraft for its IT charter work. Operations commenced on 1 November 1997 and that winter season's holiday charter programme covered flights from Berlin-Schönefeld, Hamburg, Munich and Basel/Mulhouse to Caribbean sunspots on behalf of the tour operator FTi Touristik. The arrival of this new carrier on Germany's charter scene was watched closely by competing companies. Of special interest was the holidaymakers' acceptance of the 328-seat Britannia 767s with a notably higher seating arrangement than was customary in Germany, compared for instance with Condor's standard seating for 269. Britannia, however, emphasized that this factor allowed its tour operator partner to offer very attractively-priced holidays based on a notably lower cost level. Such a vital advantage could, however, be lost due to the extensive night flying restrictions enforced at most airports throughout Germany, which imposes rather severe operational constraints. As of 30 October 1998, FTi Touristik gave up its financial stake in Britannia, in line with preparations for the start-up of its own in-house charter carrier fly FTi.

CALAIR

Set up in Frankfurt on 17 November 1970, Calair acquired five Boeing 720B jets for its planned IT charter operations on behalf of several of West German tour operators. The operating license was, however, only granted by the BVM on 6 July 1971, and this lost the carrier a great deal of summer IT work. Subsequently, Calair drifted into financial difficulties towards the end of that year, which caused a termination of all operations in March 1972. The company was declared bankrupt and subsequently liquidated on 13 May 1972.

CDL ~ CONTINENTALE DEUTSCHE LUFTREEDEREI

Formed in early 1959, CDL obtained its operating license on 11 May. As a successor to failed Aerotour, it took over the two DC4s of the former company. Holiday charters were flown but CDL soon ran into financial difficulties due to the high maintenance costs for the DC4s. Coupled with a downturn in West Germany's leisure business, which had a devastating effect, CDL was forced into bankruptcy later in 1959.

COLUMBUS LUFTREEDEREI

Set up in July 1957, Columbus Luftreederei launched its commercial operations on 1 August, using two Viking aircraft from its Hamburg base. After an ownership change on 20 January 1958, the company's activity came to focus on holiday charter operations on behalf of the tour operator Aeropa, commencing in April 1958. By November of that year, the company was bankrupt.

CONAIR ~ VERTRIEBS GmbH für DEUTSCHLAND

The Danish partner of Premiair formed a separate company in 1994 to operate IT charters from Germany. With two A300B2 aircraft, Conair initiated service on 22 March 1994 from several German cities to destinations in Greece. Because of the bankruptcy of its tour operator partner Mit uns Reisen, Conair's venture lasted only until November 1994 when the Airbuses were returned to the carrier's Copenhagen base.

CONDOR BERLIN

In December 1996, the formation of Condor Berlin, a wholly-owned subsidiary company of Condor, was announced. This carrier was intended to specialise in holiday charter operations from secondary German cities, in line with tour operators' needs for lower capacity, a requirement that Condor was unable to meet because of the larger size aircraft in its fleet. The carrier's fleet consisted of eight A320s in the summer of 2000. With operating costs below those of its parent company, Condor Berlin is also able to offer lower charter rates, a vital factor that enhances its competitive standing vis-à-vis other German and foreign charter carriers. Condor Berlin commenced operations on 29 March 1998 and, on 7 July 1998, the 100,000th passenger was welcomed.

CONDOR LUFTREEDEREI

Founded on 26 September 1957 by the Oetker and Condor Group of companies, Condor Luftreederei started IT charter operations with two newly acquired Convair CV-440 aircraft from Hamburg on 12 July 1958. The carrier had a technical co-operation agreement with SAS. Since West Germany's charter tourism experienced a crisis at that time, traffic results turned out to be much less favourable than expected. An agreement with DFG resulted in the joint use of the Convair aircraft from August 1958 onward.

On 22 March 1961, Lufthansa acquired the company's CV-440 fleet and this subsequently led to a merger with DFG. Operations continued in Condor's name until 31 October 1961 when the last flight returned to Hamburg from Palma de Majorca. Lufthansa adopted the name 'Condor' for its charter subsidiary Condor Flugdienst.

CONTI - FLUG

Set up in 1987 for general charter work, Conti-Flug operated scheduled services from Berlin-Tempelhof Airport. The company ventured into the IT charter business in 1992, using a BAe 146 jet on routes from Berlin. It was this air carrier that was involved with re-starting holiday charter flights from Kassel to Majorca and Monastir from February 1994 onward. On 22 August 1994, however, operations suddenly came to an end due to the demise of the airline's parent company.

DELTA AIR ~ REGIONALFLUGVERKEHR GmbH

Private investors were behind the formation of Delta Air in March 1978. The company was set up to operate local and regional services which began on 1 April 1978 from Friedrichshafen, its base on Lake Constance. In addition to its scheduled activity, Delta Air also operated seasonal holiday charter operations with SF-340 aircraft from May 1991 onward, linking Friedrichshafen with holiday destinations in France, Italy and Yugoslavia.

On 13 March 1992, British Airways acquired a 49% share in Delta Air, leading to the formation of Deutsche BA on 5 May 1992. Full integration of Delta Air into the new airline became effective on 2 June 1992.

DEUTSCHE BA ~ DEUTSCHE BRITISH AIRWAYS (DBA)

The reunification of Germany created a new situation for British Airways which required the carrier to scale down its intra-German services. To be able to retain a presence in Germany, BA chose to take a 49% stake in the privately owned German regional airline Delta Air. This led to the formation of Deutsche BA (Deutsche British Airways) on 5 May 1992.

The new company took over the regional operations of Delta Air and also its holiday charter contracts for the Summer 1992 season. In subsequent years, Deutsche BA has greatly expanded its involvement with IT charter flying, using spare capacity in the course of the weekend. The success of this activity led to DBA deploying one 737 during the summer 1996 season exclusively for charter work. The airline carried more than 2.35 million passengers in the financial year up to 31 March 1997.

(DFG) DEUTSCHE FLUGDIENST ~ CONDOR FLUGDIENST

DFG was founded on 21 December 1955 by its shareholder partners Lufthansa, DBB (German Railways) and the shipping concerns Hapag-Lloyd and Norddeutscher Lloyd. The operating permit was granted by the Ministry of Transport on 8 March 1956 and IT charter flying commenced on 29 March with a fleet of four Viking aircraft in competition with LTU and KHD. Furthermore, a number of foreign carriers, several of them British-owned, were involved with IT charters from West-Germany as their licences were valid until October 1956, a leftover from the time when the Allies granted licences for such operations. Touropa was one of the principal tour operator clients in the beginning.

In October 1957, DFG started to take delivery of five pressurized Convair CV-240 aircraft acquired from KLM, and the aircraft were introduced into service from 6 December. This allowed DFG to offer the same standard of comfort and onboard service as the scheduled airlines of the time. In addition to securing charter work in West-Germany, DFG also sought work in neighbouring countries and for this purpose, had a co-operation agreement with Austria Flugdienst. The apparent protectionist policies of several neighbouring countries did, however, not favour any large-scale co-operation ventures of DFG with foreign charter carriers.

West-Germany's outbound holiday travel hit a downward trend in 1958 after an exceptionally high level of catch-up demand in earlier years had been met. A contributing factor to this was adverse publicity arising from the failure of several German charter carriers on account of low maintenance and operational standards. DFG was also affected by this trend, which resulted in a co-operation agreement with Condor Luftreederei in August 1958 leading to the joint exploitation of a combined fleet of five CV-240s and two CV-440s.

DFG encountered financial problems but, as a result of Lufthansa acquiring its assets in November 1959, the company's future was secured. From that time, the carrier's activity was carefully planned and supported by sound commercial policies. Its first Viscount was acquired from Lufthansa on 30 November 1960 and this initiated the phase-out of the ageing Viking and Convair aircraft in use until then. On 25 October 1961, DFG was re-named Condor Flugdienst, with full ownership retained by Germany's national airline Lufthansa. The tremendous passenger appeal of the Viscount, coupled with the fact that the West German IT charter market again experienced a significant upsurge in demand throughout 1962 and 1963, led to positive results for Condor, with its market share reaching a level of 70% in 1963. Condor's Viscount fleet was increased to four aircraft in March 1964.

Although LTU had been Condor's main competitor for a number of years, the situation changed when Südflug in 1963 and Bavaria in 1964 ventured into the IT charter business. Furthermore, there was growing competition from foreign carriers seeking access to the seemingly ever expanding West German holiday market. Palma de Majorca emerged as the most popular holiday destination for Germans, served by Condor with a daily service throughout Summer 1963. Whereas Condor carried 18,400 passengers to Palma in 1962, the passenger volume to that destination reached beyond 100,000 for the first time in 1965. Condor's passenger traffic overall increased from 25,705 in 1960 to 315,310 in 1965.

A significant event was the addition of the first 727-30 jet to Condor's fleet in February 1965, followed by two F-27s in February and March although not for IT charter work. The new 727s were placed into service on the busy holiday charter routes linking West-Germany with Palma, Barcelona, Tenerife, Rhodes, Athens, Pula and Dubrovnik. However the planned introduction of the 727 jet met with opposition, notably so in Greece where the concerned authorities initially refused permission for Condor 727s to serve Athens and Rhodes, as the privilege of jet operations was to be reserved for the two national airlines Olympic and Lufthansa. Condor operated an extensive pattern of regular IT charter flights throughout Europe, including the Canary Islands and North Africa. Its services to the Black Sea destinations of Constanza and Varna, however, came to be curtailed due to vacation traffic being increasingly captured by Tarom and Tabso/Balkan due to the lower charter rates applied by those airlines. The first 707 was added to the fleet in February 1967 for use on Condor's long-haul charter routes to Colombo/Bangkok, Nairobi and Santo Domingo. In December 1967, after lengthy negotiations, Condor won CAB approval for group charter flights to the USA. More competition in Germany arose through the emergence of the new charter carriers Atlantis, Germanair and Panair/Paninternational in 1968. In that year, fleet changes involved the sale of F-27s and Viscounts and the addition of more 727s, and Condor become an 'all-jet' carrier in December.

Condor's parent Lufthansa was deeply concerned about the success of the German charter carrier Südflug on North Atlantic routes and eventually acquired its assets which led to Südflug's merger with Condor on 2 January 1969. That summer saw considerable expansion of Condor's IT charter operations with Palma, its top destination, served by 60 flights/week. Condor also became more involved with running charter flights for foreign workers migrating to West-Germany. In 1971, the traffic development on many charter routes was such that a new operating pattern was adopted with more emphasis placed on the operation of non-stop flights from West-German departure cities, rather than by combining two departure cities as had often been the procedure in years past. Contract flying on behalf of the German tour operators TUI and NUR involved 85% of Condor's capacity. Meanwhile, IT charter work increased to 81% and special flights for foreign workers reached a share of over 12% of Condor's overall activity.

Condor made history with the introduction of a 494-seat 747 on 1 May 1971 on its busy routes to Palma de Majorca and Las Palmas. A second 747 was added on 28 April 1972 which enabled Condor to initiate charter flights to New York on 14 May. Of major concern was the progressive introduction of night curfew restrictions at several key airports in West Germany, which had an adverse effect on Condor's daily pattern of aircraft rotation and utilization. In 1974, the ABC charter rule was adopted for the North Atlantic and this mode of travel found instant favour with the travelling public. Over the period 1974 to 1975, IT charter traffic to Spain and south-eastern Europe showed remarkable growth, as did long-haul services. On the other hand, the political situation in Portugal adversely affected tourist traffic while operations to Cyprus were suspended in July 1974. In that year, Condor's fleet consisted of two 747s, two 707s, and thirteen 727-30 and 727-230 jets.

In 1975, it was intended to adopt easier booking conditions for West German travellers to Spain, similar to the ABC travel formula on the North Atlantic, because of the tremendous popularity of that country, having prompted many to buy property in various regions throughout Spain, including the Balearic and Canary Islands. A new travel concept could, however, not be introduced as hoped for and it took many years before 'seat-only' travel arrangements became the norm, similar to the developments taking place in Britain.

Although the recruitment of foreign workers by German companies had slowed down in the late seventies, new demand was created by the expatriate workforce, and their dependants, returning home to southern European countries on the occasion of their annual holiday. In 1977, Condor's traffic to the USA was influenced by the favourable Dollar rate and the carrier upped its US capacity by 50% for that summer season, all of which was sold out. In the late seventies, Spain somehow lost some of its popularity as a prime holiday destination due to political instability and strikes and also, increasingly, due to a notable increase in hotel rates and the cost of living. Condor's long-haul operations showed excellent traffic results, achieving an increase of nearly 21% in 1979. At that point in time, holidays to faraway destinations were still relatively high-priced and appealed mainly to higher income groups and Condor managed to carry nearly 80% of Germany's long-haul charter traffic. 1978 saw Condor reaching a passenger total of over two million in one year for the first time. New DC-10-30 widebody jets were added in December 1979 which led to the sale of the 747s as they proved too big for tour operators' capacity requirements of the time. Furthermore, the volume of charter traffic to North America was diminishing, caused by the scheduled airlines reducing their fares nearer the charter level. In the mid-seventies, a major problem arose from the sharp increase in fuel costs which could only partly be reflected in the final price charged to travellers.

Due to fierce competition not only from other German but also from foreign charter carriers, Condor's market share saw a decline to just under 19% by 1980. At the end of the Winter 1980/81 season, all 707s were withdrawn from service and a new commercial policy led to Condor's participation in the 'HIT' program for the first time in 1981. That year also saw the introduction of Condor's new 737-200s on short to medium-haul charter routes, starting with a Munich-Heraklion service on 9 May. Demand for 'seat-only' sales was particularly high for departures from North Rhine Westphalia and Condor's share of this business was recorded as 18% in 1982. At the end of that year, the fleet consisted of three DC-10-30, nine 727-200 and three 737-200 airliners. Condor's summer 1983 pattern of ABC charters covered 11 destinations in the USA, all served with the DC-10. In that year, Condor added two Airbus A300s, followed by A310s in 1985. Confidence of German vacationers in charter air travel increasingly came to be linked to the concept of a 'quality product', a combined effort of the tour operators and airlines with a good service and punctuality record.

Condor's prime medium-haul destination, Palma, recorded over 500,000 passengers in 1986 while Mombasa retained its top position as a long-haul destination. IT services to Turkey experienced tremendous growth, with more passengers from Germany choosing this country than Tunisia, Italy and Portugal. 1988 saw Condor's traffic increase to 3.1 million passengers. However, the Gulf War crisis of early 1991 took its toll on the demand for foreign holidays and adversely affected Condor's financial situation, an experience not unlike that of numerous other charter carriers. Meanwhile, Condor initiated an extensive fleet renewal programme which led to the acquisition of new 757, 767 and 737-300 aircraft. When 757s were acquired in 1990, the name 'Südflug' was resurrected, this subsidiary company being entrusted, on behalf of Condor, with the operation of these new aircraft with crews employed at lower salary levels.

The re-unification of Germany on 3 October 1990 opened up a considerably enlarged charter market covering the former German Democratic Republic and the eastern sector of Berlin. Condor initiated IT charters from Berlin-Schönefeld on 1 November 1990, from Leipzig/Halle and Dresden on 25 March 1991 and from Erfurt on 5 April 1993. By 1995, the airline was able to claim a 35% market share in the former East Germany and Berlin. For the fact that Condor's realm of activity was leisure air transport based on the charter mode, its statutes required to be changed so that it could operate a scheduled service from Frankfurt to Mahé in the Seychelles, starting 4 November 1991. Since that time, another scheduled long-haul route has been opened to Mauritius, which is presently run in co-operation with Air Mauritius.

Condor continued to profit from Germany's outbound travel boom which saw over 23 million Germans choose a package tour in 1994. 5.7 million passengers were carried by Condor and a profit of DM 126 million was recorded. Long distance travel by charter enjoyed tremendous popularity and some 8% of all Germans opted for a long-haul destination, often influenced by favourable US Dollar rates and the relatively low cost of living in those far-away resorts. The creation of a common air transport market within the European Community has offered new opportunities to Condor with regard to its market base. As a result, operations were started from Vienna, Austria, in co-operation with Lauda Air, on 1 May 1993, from Luxembourg City on 18 May 1994 and from Salzburg on 2 April 1995.

For the purpose of optimizing its modus operandi, Condor built up Frankfurt and Munich as hubs, with feeder traffic from other German cities for its medium and long-haul network. This involved not only Condor's own flights but also those of Lufthansa, thus opening a new marketing strategy. The carrier's operating pattern focused more on Munich during the winter season, by channelling traffic to many southern European and Middle Eastern destinations through this hub. A later development was the creation of a Condor hub at Cologne/Bonn beginning in Winter 1993/94, at Hanover in Winter 1995/96 and at Stuttgart in Winter 1997/98. Although it would have been more cost effective to concentrate all of Condor's long-haul services in Frankfurt and to make more extensive use of Lufthansa's domestic feeder flights, the non-availability of suitable slots at

Frankfurt has forcefully put a stop to such plans. In 1995, Condor took over Lufthansa's 40% share in SunExpress and subsequently forged a close partnership with this Turkish/German airline. An interesting development has been Condor's growing financial involvement with tour operators. Shares have been acquired in the tour operators Air Marin, Öger Tours, Fischer Reisen and Kreutzer which has helped to enhance Condor's chances of improved fleet utilization for the fact that these tour organiser partners tend to place the bulk of their capacity requirements with this airline.

Condor holds a special place within the Lufthansa Group, functioning in a distinctly complementary role within the framework of the parent company's corporate strategy, yet concentrating exclusively on service to holiday destinations world-wide. At the same time, Condor also enjoys the advantages of Lufthansa's existing sales and marketing facilities. Long-term marketing policy is aimed at providing quality air transport at a lower price level compared with that of a scheduled airline. Condor's activity and sphere of operation are taken into account whenever Lufthansa negotiates for traffic rights to foreign destinations take place.

Condor's Summer 1996 programme featured some 450 flights/week to destinations around the Mediterranean and in the Canary Islands, and an additional 40 weekly flights were offered to long-haul destinations. In Germany, Condor used 12 departure cities from where a total of 66 destinations was served. In early 1996, a fleet of 36 aircraft included eight 767-300ER, eighteen 757-200, four 737-300 and five DC-10-30 aircraft, at an average age of 4.6 years, offering a total capacity of 8,500 seats. This fleet mix is considered ideal as it allows Condor to serve holiday destinations economically and with flexibility, which gives its tour operator partners the chance to find a fair balance between capacity and traffic demand. 1997 saw Condor's passenger total reach beyond 7.2 million, with a market share of 25.4%. Condor's extensive fleet modernization and standardization programme was intended to reduce the fleet to two types of aircraft only, involving the 757-300 and 767. In turn its subsidiary company Condor Berlin had a fleet of six A320 in service by mid-October 1998, allowing the leased 737-700s to be returned to Germania. As a world's first, Condor introduced the first of thirteen new 252-seat 757-300 aircraft into service in March 1999. The last DC-10 was withdrawn from service in 1999.

The more recent affiliation with the tour concern C&N has undoubtedly been a contributing factor to Condor gaining a remarkably strong position in Germany's competitive leisure market. With an annual total of over 8.2 million passengers in 1999 and a noteworthy market share of 26%, Condor ranks top amongst the country's specialist air carriers catering for the holiday market. A noteworthy achievement was that, on 22 December 1999, Condor was able to welcome its 100 millionth passenger in its long history as a leisure airline. in summer 2000, Condor had a fleet of nine 767/300ER and 25 757 aircraft in service, supported by eight Airbus A320 aircraft of its affiliate Condor Berlin for service on routes of lower traffic density.

(DLG) DEUTSCHE LUFTTRANSPORT GESELLSCHAFT mbH

DLG was set up on 4 August 1954, with the British charter carrier Skyways holding a 30% share. The base airport chosen was Hamburg where Skyways had maintained a base for its charter operations since 1952. The carrier used a mix of Viking and DC-3 aircraft for its charter work until mid-1957 when its operations were taken over by Columbus Luftreederei.

EUROWINGS ~ EUROWINGS FLUG GmbH

Eurowings came into existence on 1 January 1993 through the merger of the two regional airlines NFD and RFG and serves domestic and international routes linking major German hub cities and regional centres. By early 1998, the Eurowings fleet consisted of 27 ATR42/72 turboprop airliners, supplemented by ten BAe 146 jets.

In addition to its scheduled services, Eurowings is also active in the field of holiday charter flights in co-operation with a number of tour operators. In summer 1995, for the first time, the carrier launched holiday charters from another member country of the European Union, linking Innsbruck in Austria with Palma de Majorca. In order to expand its charter activity, the subsidiary company Eurowings Flug GmbH was formed on 26 June 1996 and the new Airbus A319 aircraft, delivered in January and February 1997, came to be exclusively used by the new company. The range of the A319 makes non-stop operations to the Canary Islands possible from any airport in Germany. By summer 1998, the A319 fleet had grown to three aircraft which were in service on holiday charter routes both from Germany and Austria. In addition, turboprop aircraft and BAe 146 jets are used for IT charter work according to tour operators' requirements.

Because of Eurowings' growing involvement with holiday charter operations, 255,316 charter passengers were carried in 1997 which helped boost the airline's passenger total to a record 2.5 million in that year. In 1998, Eurowings initiated IT charter operations from Dortmund to Palma de Majorca, using BAe 146 jets.

FLY FTI

The German tour group FTi Touristik formed its own in-house charter airline Fly FTi in 1998. Using a fleet of three A320 and one 737, the airline initiated operations on 1 May 1999 on the Munich-Lamezia Terme holiday charter route.

GERMANAIR SÜDWESTFLUG ~ GERMANIA FLUGGESELLSCHAFT mbH

Germania was formed as a successor company to SAT and started its activity on 1 June 1986 with one Caravelle and two 727s. Fleet renewal was initiated with an order for three new 737-300s, the first of which was delivered on 5 November 1987 and entered service on the 29th, followed by two more aircraft in the winter season of 1987/88. This allowed the withdrawal from service of the last Caravelle and the two

727s by November 1987. One 737-300 was in service with Berlin European UK from March 1990 until February 1991 and other German air carriers have leased Germania aircraft intermittently since then. The replacement of the 737-300 fleet with new 737-700s started in 1998, with a gradual build-up of a fleet of fourteen aircraft by 1999.

Germania began to move its head office from Cologne to Berlin-Tegel Airport in the autumn of 1991 and this was completed by early 1993 with the transfer of its technical base. The Berlin-based British carrier Berlin European UK was taken over at the end of February 1991, and in that summer season, Germania operated its first holiday charters from Berlin. Germania took a 40% stake in the Stuttgart-based tour operator Hetzel-Reisen. In 1992, Germany's federal government contracted Germania to shuttle government officials between Cologne/Bonn and Berlin and, in October 1993, Germania carried its first millionth passenger. The airline's major tour operator clients are TUI, Berliner Flugring, LTT and LTU Touristik; In the summer 1999 season, Germania operated three 737s fully committed to TUI, in the tour operator's colours, and six 737s on behalf of LTU.

HAMBURG AIRLINES (HAL)

Hamburg Airlines, the successor to the Hamburg-based carrier Hadag Air, launched its operations on 15 April 1988. The addition of Fokker F-100 jets allowed the carrier to start holiday charter operations on 18 May 1990 but this activity was terminated in October 1990. Charter operations were resumed on 7 May 1991 with an extensive pattern of service to destinations across Europe. HAL was the first German airline to serve Kaliningrad since WW II when it started a charter series to that city in the summer of 1991.

The airline's owner Eugen Block was also financially involved with Saarland Airlines. When the latter's tour operator partner went bankrupt, Hamburg Airlines was equally affected which led to its liquidation in December 1993. Almost immediately however, a new company was formed using the same name and it was possible to continue scheduled operations as before, using a fleet of five Dash 8 aircraft. In summer 1995, three BAe 146 aircraft were in use for IT charters on behalf of numerous German tour operators, including NUR, Hetzel, DER and ITS. The airline was extensively involved with charter operations from Stuttgart during the closure of the airport's main runway since its BAe 146 jets were able to use the shorter secondary runway. Prompted by Hamburg Airlines' on-going unsatisfactory financial situation, its owner decided to shut down the airline on 21 December 1997. By that time, a total of 2.18 million passengers had been carried since the start of operations.

HAMBURGER LUFTREEDEREI

Formed on 1 June 1955, Hamburger Luftreederei commenced IT charter flights with a single DC-3 on the Hamburg-Munich-Klagenfurt route on 23 July 1955, followed by a service to Roenne on the Danish island of Bornholm shortly after. The carrier ceased trading at the end of 1955.

HAMBURG INTERNATIONAL

Hamburg International was founded in July 1998 and is majority-owned by the Schmider-Kleiser Holding company. The carrier intends to specialize in IT charter operations mainly from secondary cities in Germany and from Luxembourg, in co-operation with leading tour operators such as TUI and NUR. The carrier took delivery of its first 737-700 aircraft in Hamburg on 1 April 1999 and IT charter operations commenced to Heraklion from Luxembourg City and Lubeck on 26 April 1999. Future plans call for a fleet build-up to four 737-700 aircraft.

HAPAG-LLOYD FLUG

Hapag-Lloyd Flug was formed in September 1972 by its parent Hapag-Lloyd, one of Germany's largest travel concerns, and Hanover was chosen as its home base. Holiday charter operations commenced on 30 March 1973 on the Hamburg-Ibiza route with the airline's initial fleet consisting of three second-hand 727-100 jets. A close working relationship evolved with the Hanover-based tour operator TUI which, by 1974, was using about 70% of the carrier's capacity. In summer 1974, the first long-haul charter services started to Mombasa and, for cruise passengers, to Lomé in West Africa. Hapag-Lloyd welcomed its millionth passenger in 1975.

In April 1977, Hapag-Lloyd took over Bavaria/Germanair and, with a fleet of 17 aircraft, became West-Germany's third largest charter carrier. In addition to an expanding medium-haul network covering the Europe/Mediterranean region and the Canary Islands, the airline launched long-haul charter services to Colombo on 3 November and to Banjul on 21 December 1979.

The airline took delivery of its first 737-200 jet in June 1981. This started a process of fleet modernization which was intended to replace the early model 727 and the BAC 1-11 jets, with a completion date of October 1981. A second major fleet modernization programme started with the acquisition of A310s in January 1988. The type was subsequently used on routes to destination in the Canary Islands to boost winter capacity, the first service being run from Hanover to Fuerteventura on 18 February 1988. The first 737-400 was delivered in March 1989 for service introduction on 1 April 1989 on the Hanover-Palma de Majorca route.

Inter-continental charters with A310s were launched to the Dominican Republic in Winter 1989/90, followed by operations to Miami, New York-Newark, Philadelphia and Toronto in April and May 1990. Hapag-Lloyd's extensive fleet renewal covering the acquisition of four A310, six 737/400 and six 737/500 aircraft was accomplished by 1991.

Starting with the Winter 1990/91 season, the company became involved with 'seat-only' sales handled through the START reservation system. As a service improvement, Hapag-Lloyd had two A310-300 long-range aircraft fitted out with a two-class seating configuration which enabled the

airline to offer the 'Comfort Class' on long-haul flights to the Canary Islands and to the Caribbean from November 1991 onward. In a surprise move, beginning in Winter 1995/96, Hapag-Lloyd switched the bulk of its operations from a 'charter' to a 'scheduled' mode.

In line with the liberalization of air transport in the EC, Hapag-Lloyd based one 737 aircraft at Luxembourg City beginning in Winter 1993/94, followed by another aircraft at Basel/Mulhouse in Winter 1994/95. In 1995, Hapag-Lloyd introduced an innovation for its passengers by offering to transport their cars and motorbikes to selected holiday destinations served by A310s, for a nominal surcharge, in addition to the cost of a package holiday. This service has since proved popular with passengers spending long-term holidays in selected countries.

By 1980, over 5.5 million passengers had been carried by Hapag-Lloyd since the start of operations in 1973. This figure had increased to some 50 million in 1996. Another highlight was the fact that, on 19 December 1995, the millionth passenger in one year was carried from Hanover alone. The airline's passenger total in 1997 stood at over 4.9 million.

The summer 1998 season saw an increase in the number of departure cities to seventeen, and Vienna became part of the network for the first time. A fleet of 28 aircraft was in use, serving 38 destinations and Hapag-Lloyd became the launch customer for the new Boeing 737-800, first introduced in March 1998 on the Malaga route.

IFG ~ INTERREGIONAL FLUGGESELLSCHAFT

LTU set up IFG interregional Fluggesellschaft as a wholly-owned subsidiary on 26 August 1967, to take over from its parent the operation of a number of regional scheduled services focused on Dusseldorf. The IFG fleet consisted of F-27 and Nord 262 aircraft. Apart from its scheduled activity, IFG also operated regular summer services to Sylt, on a demand only basis, and holiday charters to Austria and Italy. However the international oil crisis of 1973/74 led to notable increases in the cost of aviation fuel, prompting a huge upsurge in the airline's operating costs. Although there was public funding for the scheduled service pattern at that time, the carrier's financial situation deteriorated and IFG was forced to terminate its activity on 25 January 1974.

INTERFLUG ~ GESELLSCHAFT FÜR DEN INTERNATIONALEN FLUGVERKEHR mbH

In 1955, the German Democratic Republic (GDR) formed its national airline Deutsche Lufthansa which started its first international service in February 1956 and domestic services in June 1957. A second air carrier named Interflug was set up on 18 September 1958 to handle charter work. Because East Germany's airline used the name of 'Deutsche Lufthansa' as well as West-Germany's Lufthansa, the case was taken up with the International Court of Justice in The Hague, and a decision in favour of West-Germany's national airline led to Interflug taking over the operations of Deutsche Lufthansa on 1 September 1963.

Interflug expanded its international pattern of service in Europe and to a number of countries in America, Africa and Asia, within the limits of diplomatic relations and the help of the airline industry of the Soviet Bloc. Because West-Berlin had become a very strong generator of international travel, the East German authorities looked for ways of diverting some of this traffic via Schönefeld Airport, their under-used base, to the south of Berlin. A border crossing point was subsequently opened to facilitate travel via Schönefeld with traffic developing steadily, mainly due to the lower air fares offered by Interflug and its Eastern European airline partners.

In addition to its scheduled operations focused on Schönefeld Airport, Interflug also became involved with holiday charter operations, under contract to West-Berlin based tour operators, to destinations in Romania, Bulgaria, Greece and North Africa. One of the main attractions was that Interflug's charter rates were lower than those applied by the US and British leisure airlines operating out of West-Berlin. The bulk of Interflug's charter traffic was outbound and flights could not be used by citizens of the GDR. In the sixties, in co-operation with local and foreign tour agencies, Interflug started to operate weekend charters to Dresden and East-Berlin from cities in Austria and Switzerland, and from Finland in 1972/73.

The political development in Germany in the late eighties, leading up to the unification of the two separate states in October 1990, prompted several airlines to make bids for acquiring Interflug's assets. Lufthansa's efforts in this regard were thwarted by the Bundeskartellamt on 30 July 1990. Subsequently, Interflug was taken over by the trust company responsible for the liquidation of East German state-owned enterprise which led to the airline being disbanded in 1992.

Throughout its working life, Interflug used Soviet-built aircraft almost exclusively, ranging from the IL-14, An-24, TU-124/134/154 to the IL-62. In preparation for future operations after German unification, Interflug acquired three Airbus 310 aircraft which were, apart from serving intercontinental routes, also introduced into IT charter operations in Europe.

INTEROT ~ AUGSBURG AIRWAYS

This airline was formed under the name of Interot in 1979. In September 1986, Interot started a scheduled air taxi service to Dusseldorf from the company's base at Augsburg. After the German BVM granted a full scheduled service license in December 1989, Interot gradually extended its network to include additional domestic and international destinations.

For the first time in summer 1993, in addition to its scheduled services, Interot became involved with holiday charter operations from Augsburg and Friedrichshafen during the weekend, in co-operation with local tour operators using Dash-8 aircraft. The airline's name was changed to Augsburg Airways on 1 January 1996 and, in that year, the carrier's passenger volume had reached 135,000, including 12,395 who used its holiday charter flights.

JET AIR

In May 1982, Jet Air was formed in Munich with the intention of securing a share in West-Germany's booming holiday charter business. Initial plans called for the use of three 737s on medium-haul charter routes covering destinations in the Europe/Mediterranean region. In the end, the carrier switched to two 727s but because of their late delivery, IT charter operations could not be launched before the autumn of 1984. At the end of the Summer 1985 season, Jet Air ran into financial problems and suspended operations.

(KHD) LUFTFAHRTUNTERNEHMEN KARL HERFURTNER

The Dusseldorf-based charter carrier KHD had a fleet of three Vikings and two DC4 aircraft in use during the 1956 summer season for contract IT charter work, mainly on behalf of the tour operators Dr. Tigges-Fahrten and Aeropa. In the course of 1957, Aero Express Flug was merged into KHD. However the crash of a DC4 in November 1957 caused financial problems which led to the suspension of the carrier's operations. The successor company to KHD was Trans-Avia.

LTS ~ LTU SÜD

LTU's subsidiary LTS was established in August 1983 to be based at Munich and the intention was to win a share of the regional holiday charter traffic potential of Bavaria. Operations were launched in June 1984 with one 757 and, from the start, the operations of LTS were closely integrated with those of LTU. On 1 November 1987, the company's name was changed to LTU-Süd while the well established pattern of co-operation between the two carriers continued as before. In 1996, plans were announced that LTU-Süd was to be merged with its parent company LTU, as a cost saving measure. This was finally put into effect as of 1 November 1997.

LUFTTRANSPORT UNION ~ LTU - LUFTTRANSPORT UNTERNEHMEN

Directors of the British charter carrier Overseas Aviation were behind the foundation of Lufttransport Union on 20 October 1955 and Frankfurt was chosen as the new company's operating base. In December of that year, two 36-seat Viking aircraft were bought and the first aircraft was delivered on 12 January 1956. The company was initially British-owned but, to meet local law requirements, German partners took over all its assets prior to the operator's licence being granted on 9 February 1956. The carrier launched its first IT charter service from Munich to Catania on 4 March 1956.

For the first summer season of 1956, the carrier had IT charter contracts with several West German tour operators for a series of flights from Hamburg, Dusseldorf, Frankfurt, Stuttgart and Munich. That summer saw a daily service operated to Palma de Majorca, with Southend, Naples, Catania, Rhodes and Tenerife in the Canary Islands among the destinations served. The year 1956 witnessed a great upsurge in foreign travel demand from West-Germany, long repressed during the period of reconstruction since World War II. In April 1958, the air carrier's name was changed to LTU — Lufttransport Unternehmen.

Another two Vikings were added in 1957, supplemented by a Bristol 170 converted to airliner standards and fitted out with 44 seats. When LTU began to phase out its Viking aircraft in 1958, they were acquired by charter carriers in Belgium (Aviameer), Austria (Aero-Transport) and Switzerland (Balair). A 72-seat DC-4 was placed into service in 1959. In that year, LTU moved its base from Frankfurt, first to Cologne then to Dusseldorf in 1960. Firmly established at Dusseldorf and, with the enormous hinterland traffic potential of North Rhine Westphalia, Germany's industrial powerhouse, LTU continued to develop satisfactorily. In 1961, it became the first charter carrier to introduce F27 turboprop aircraft, which helped to improve levels of productivity generally. Being surplus to requirements, the Bristol and DC-4 aircraft were sold off and LTU supplemented its F-27s with Caravelle III jet, the first of which was delivered on 5 February 1965. This made LTU the first West-German charter carrier to use this popular aircraft type, setting new standards of operation and passenger comfort. In December 1967, the advanced Caravelle 10R model was placed into service, its longer range making non-stop flights between West-Germany and the Canary Islands a possibility. LTU has the distinction of being the launch customer for the F-28 twin jet, the first aircraft joining the fleet on 17 February 1969, and regular IT charters with this type started on 1 April. The subsequent delivery of additional aircraft allowed the withdrawal of all F-27s and LTU became an 'all jet' airline in the latter part of 1969.

In the sixties, LTU operated exclusively from Dusseldorf, although there were requests from tour operators to cover additional departure cities in West-Germany. Focusing its operations on Dusseldorf, however, was claimed by the carrier to have the advantage of all aircraft returning to base at night, thus eliminating costs for overnighting aircraft and crews and also offering the opportunity to balance out possible delays in the course of an aircraft's daily operational routine. LTU was one of the few charter carriers to introduce the concept of 'regularity' for its holiday charter flights which were operated to set times throughout the week, similar to the scheduled airlines.

LTU carried over 500,000 passengers in 1971. A milestone event in the airline's history was the delivery of the first widebody jet in the form of a Lockheed L-1011 TriStar on 29 May 1973. The type was intended for service on high density charter routes, with the first flight operated on the Dusseldorf-Ibiza route on 14 June 1973. F-28s remained in service until the end of the Summer 1975 season. The availability of TriStars led LTU to expand into long-haul operations, with Miami becoming the first destination served from November 1976. LTU commenced ABC charter flights to New York and Los Angeles in May 1977, with Colombo and Bangkok added as the first Asian destinations in November 1977. It was a milestone event when LTU reached a passenger total of one million in 1978. The last Caravelle was sold off in October 1979, and the improved L-1011/500 TriStar version was placed into service from April 1980 onward, facilitating the expansion of long-haul services because of the type's extended range capability. In line with continuously growing demand for IT charter capacity, LTU built up its fleet of TriStars to eight aircraft by April

1982. There was also an agreement with Eastern Air Lines for the lease of additional TriStars for the peak summer season. 1988 saw LTU becoming West-Germany's 'number one' charter airline — ahead of Condor — with a passenger total of over 3.5 million. At that time, about 18% of LTU's capacity was allocated to long-haul operations, of which 49% covered the USA, the Far East 21%, the Caribbean 13% and Africa 12%.

August 1983 saw the formation of the subsidiary charter company LTS, followed by the creation of the Spanish subsidiary company LTE in April 1987. In 1990, plans were muted to set up LTU Italia but this venture did not materialize. For the purpose of co-ordinating the activity of LTU's tour operator partners, the holding company LTT Touristik was established in 1987. Eventually, this concern developed into West-Germany's third largest tour organizer, supported by LTU's subsidiary LTI specializing in the hotel business. The airline's seating capacity was, at that time, used to some 50% by affiliated tour operators of the LTU Group, 25% by smaller tour agencies and the rest allocated to the 'seat-only' sector which was to assume growing importance in later years.

With effect from 1 May 1990, LTU switched its services to the US destinations of Los Angeles, Miami, New York and San Francisco from 'charter' to a 'scheduled' mode. Starting with the 1993/94 winter schedule, service to a large number of destinations in Europe and the Canary Islands was also switched to a 'scheduled' mode. In line with LTU's expansion into long-haul markets, served mainly from Dusseldorf, additional non-stop flights came to be offered from Munich, effective 1 May 1992, to Los Angeles, Miami, Recife and Salvador do Bahía. Similarly, the service pattern for Frankfurt was built up for the Summer 1992 season. Good results were achieved in 1992 when 4.85 million passengers were carried. LTU's fleet for Summer 1993 comprised six L-1011/100/200, three L-1011-500, four 767ER, twelve 757-200 and four MD11 aircraft. On 23 January 1995, LTU started to introduce new Airbus 330 jets on the Dusseldorf-Larnaca route, followed by Faro on 18 February. The type was intended as a replacement of the TriStar fleet, with the last retiring on 7 May 1996.

By 1995, the bulk of LTU's activity was in the 'scheduled' mode. This was considered an advantage for the fact that it was easier to obtain traffic rights from foreign governments for scheduled services while, in the case of charter flights, the necessary licenses had to be requested on an ongoing basis for each new schedule period. On past occasions, LTU had experienced problems over foreign nations not granting traffic rights at the appropriate time.

LTU continued to expand its world-wide network and, as an additional service to its passengers, a joint tariff agreement was signed with Air New Zealand in 1995, intended to facilitate round-the-world travel on the two airlines' routes. Passenger traffic soared to 6.6 million in 1995 and the average load factor was given as 84.7%.

With the start of the Winter 1996/97 schedule period, LTU set up Abu Dhabi in the U.A.E. as a hub for its Asian operations. Passengers from/to several German cities were switched at Abu Dhabi to/from other LTU flights covering destinations on the Indian subcontinent and in Southeast Asia. A working relationship was formed between LTU and Hamburg Airlines whereby the latter's smaller aircraft could be used to provide a more appropriate level of capacity on lower density routes radiating from secondary cities. In line with a growing interest in eco tourism, LTU initiated summer-only service to destinations in northern Norway, a new destination area, in June 1997.

Swissair's SAir Group took a 49.9% stake in LTU Holding GmbH which controls the airline itself as well as LTU Touristik and LTU Catering, as on 1 November 1998, this move was intended to make LTU a partner in a Europe-wide group of leisure airlines under Swiss control. Fleet changes in 1999 involved the sale of four MD11s to Swissair and their replacement with more 757 and 767 aircraft.

LUFTHANSA CITYLINE

The main task of Lufthansa CityLine is to operate scheduled services on behalf of its parent Lufthansa on routes linking secondary cities. In addition, the airline also operates seasonal holiday charter services, in many instances during the weekend when there is less demand for scheduled services. The airline's fleet of medium sized Canadair and Avro RJ85 jets with a capacity of 50 to 85 seats offers the opportunity for further involvement in the charter sector since smaller tour organizers find this capacity range suitable for destinations where there is lower demand.

In summer 1999, Lufthansa CityLine operated IT charter flights to Naples from eleven German cities, the largest number ever, including Zweibrücken, a new departure point. Another 'first' was the operation of domestic charter flights in Italy, linking Milan and Turin with Naples.

NFD ~ NÜRNBERGER FLUGDIENST ~ NÜRNBERGER LUFTVERKEHRS AG

The history of NFD goes back to May 1974 when the Nuremberg-based Intro GmbH set up an air taxi project. The company received its operating license in 1976 which was then transferred to the newly formed Nürnberger Flugdienst and later, in April 1980, the carrier switched over to scheduled operations. In summer 1987, NFD ventured into the holiday charter business, using ATR 42 aircraft for the first-ever IT charters from Hof in north-eastern Bavaria, beginning on 9 May. In line with far-reaching plans for the creation of a pan-European airline, the British tour operator group ILG — owner of Air Europe — took a 49% stake in NFD in February 1989. An Air Europe 757 was subsequently seconded to NFD for IT charter operations from Germany, starting on 23 October 1989, supported by a second aircraft in summer 1990. This arrangement continued until the collapse of Air Europe in February 1991 when the leased 757s were returned to the UK. The immediate consequence was that the majority ownership of NFD reverted to German partners and scheduled and charter operations continued with a growing fleet of ATR 42/72 aircraft. The airline's ownership changed in 1992 in a way that the new owner, Dr. Albrecht Knauf held a majority stake in both NFD and RFG. It was subsequently decided to merge the two regional airlines on 1 January 1993 to form Eurowings.

PANAIR ~ PANINTERNATIONAL

Panair was founded by its owner, the tour operator Paneuropa, in 1969. Operations began on 15 June of that year with a BAC 1-11 jet, with two more aircraft added in March and May 1970. In line with ambitious expansion plans, the company's name was changed to Paninternational on 1 January 1970, and two 707s were acquired from American Airlines in February 1971 for use on long-haul charter routes from Dusseldorf and Munich. Operational and financial problems, however, caused the carrier to suspend its activity on 6 October 1971.

RATIOFLUG

Ratioflug was a well-established company that specialized in executive charter work and express parcel delivery. The decisive step was taken to enter the field of holiday charter operations and these were launched on 1 August 1997. using an Airbus A300 for services linking selected cities in Germany with destinations in Turkey. Financial problems forced the suspension of operations and the Airbus was repossessed. The company was declared bankrupt on 19 December 1997 and all flight operations were terminated.

RFG ~ REGIONALFLUG

Originally formed as Aero West in 1976, the company adopted the name RFG - Regionalflug in 1982. Initially from its main base at Dortmund, and later also from Paderborn, the carrier built up a network of regional scheduled services linking cities in West-Germany and in neighbouring countries. In Winter 1987, RFG started holiday charter flights on the Dortmund-Malta route. Since that time, the airline has periodically operated such services to a number of holiday destinations in Austria and Italy using its ATR42 aircraft. Most services were subsequently switched to a scheduled mode and RFG was merged with NFD to form Eurowings on the first of January 1993.

SAARLAND AIRLINES (SAL)

Formed in April 1992 and financed by Turkish interests, Saarland Airlines (SAL) succeeded the failed Turkish charter carrier Noble Air. Using leased 737-300 and Airbus A320 aircraft. IT charter operations commenced on 4 April 1992 on the Dusseldorf-Dalaman route. The carrier was successful and enjoyed a good reputation for outstanding punctuality and on-board service but events took a bad turn when SAL's principal tour operator partner, MP Travel Line, went bankrupt in July 1993. This caused serious financial problems and, since its shareholders were not prepared to further support the carrier, the demise of the carrier was precipitated. SAL was forced out of business in December 1993.

SAT ~ SPECIAL AIR TRANSPORT

In April 1968, the charter carrier SAT came into existence in Stuttgart, however operations only started on 5 September 1978 after an F-27 had been acquired, by which time the company's head office had been moved to Dusseldorf. SAT ventured into the holiday charter business after acquiring three Caravelle jets from LTU between November 1978 and October 1979. After less than two years of operations, the company experienced financial trouble, however SAT managed to pull out of this crisis and its first profit was recorded in 1981. SAT continued in its role of niche carrier operating charters on behalf of smaller tour operators for whom the capacity of the Caravelle, with increased seating capacity from 84 to 99, was ideally suited. SAT bought two 727-100s from Hapag-Lloyd in 1983 as a replacement for its Caravelle units and continued to expand and, by summer 1985, an operating pattern had been built up which covered eleven departure cities in West Germany. The passenger total in that year reached 233,509 and, in line with management plans for future expansion, an order was placed for new 737-300s. However, as part of an overall change of the company's image, SAT was replaced by the newly formed Germania charter carrier which took over all operations effective 1 June 1986. SAT subsequently returned its operator's licence and has, since that time, existed only on a nominal basis.

SÜDFLUG ~ SÜDDEUTSCHE FLUGGESELLSCHAFT

Set up as an air taxi company in 1952, Südflug became operational in May 1955 as soon as the Federal Republic of Germany regained its full aerial sovereignty. In July 1963, Südflug acquired a DC-7C from KLM and subsequently started IT charter operations from Stuttgart, in co-operation with the tour operators Scharnow and Touropa, both of which held a financial stake of 25% in the carrier. Two more DC-7Cs were added in 1964 which enabled Südflug to launch long-haul charters to the Far East, Central and South Africa. At the end of that year, Südflug applied to the US CAB for charter rights which were granted in early 1965, the initial permit being valid until 29 April 1968. Südflug launched charter service to New York in 1965, at a fare which was about half that charged by the scheduled airlines. Also at that time, foreigners were being recruited for work in West-Germany which led to Südflug becoming actively involved in ferrying these workers to several major cities in Germany. In summer 1966, the airline had a fleet of six DC-7C airliners and one F-27. For a time, Südflug became West-Germany's largest charter carrier, operating regular IT charter flights from nine West-German cities to twenty-two destinations.

The Frankfurt-New York charter service proved a great success, with a frequency build-up to four flights/week. To be more competitive, at the end of 1966, Südflug arranged to buy two DC-8-32 jets from Swissair but, due to their late delivery, it became necessary to lease in a 707 from Standard Airways and a DC-8 from Airlift for the summer 1967 season. Once the DC-8s had been delivered, Südflug worked out an operating pattern for these jets which involved their use from Friday to Monday for IT charters in the Europe/Mediterranean region and from Tuesday until Thursday for flights to the USA. Two DC-9-32s was acquired in 1967.

Although Südflug's charter activity proved successful, with passenger totals growing from 23,500 in 1963 to over one million in 1967, the costly fleet modernization programme involving the DC-8 and DC-9 jets placed a heavy financial burden on the company. Furthermore, the success

of Südflug's North Atlantic charter operations was considered a serious competitive threat by Lufthansa. This prompted Lufthansa to take-over Südflug as a fully-owned subsidiary on 2 January 1968. Subsequently, Südflug's operations were gradually integrated with those of Condor and this process was rounded off by the end of 1968.

The name Südflug re-appeared in 1990 when Condor acquired its fleet of 757 aircraft. As part of a cost saving exercise, the new company assumed the responsibility for operating the 757s with crews and personnel recruited at lower salary levels. Südflug was intergrated into Condor proper on 1 October 1992.

SÜDWESTFLUG ~ GERMANAIR

A property company set up the charter carrier Südwestflug in 1964 to fly prospective clients to selected destinations in Italy and Spain. A DC-6 was acquired in September 1965 but, by mid-1968, the air carrier had run into operational problems with its single aircraft and the name of the company was changed to Germanair on 1 September 1968.

After the delivery of its first BAC 1-11 jet on 16 October 1969, IT charter services were operated from several West-German cities. In 1970, 470,000 passengers were carried and contracts were held with all the major German tour operators. The fleet was supplemented by four new F-28s in 1971 and another two 1-11s in 1972 which put Germanair in second place after Condor with regard to its volume of operations and the number of passengers carried. From December 1974, Germanair's operations were integrated with those of Bavaria. On 1 June 1975, Germanair became West-Germany's first air carrier to introduce a widebody jet, an Airbus A300, for use on holiday charter routes to Athens, Gerona, Ibiza, Istanbul, Palma de Majorca, Tarragona/Reus and Tenerife. Germanair was merged with its partner Bavaria, on 1 March 1977, under the name of Bavaria/Germanair.

TRANSAER COLOGNE

In 1998, the Irish charter carrier TransAer formed its German subsidiary company TransAer Cologne for IT charter operations focused exclusively on Cologne/Bonn. Operations were initiated in March 1999 with one A320 aircraft but the carrier fell victim to changed market conditions and suspended operations on 8 April 2000.

TRANS - AVIA FLUGGESELLSCHAFT

Trans-Avia came into existence in December 1957 as a successor to the failed charter carrier KHD. IT charters were operated with a fleet of five Vikings and a DC-4 but the German authorities withdrew the company's operating license in December 1958 because of security violations.

GERMANY
WEST-BERLIN
US AIR CARRIERS

AEROAMERICA

After the demise of Modern Air in 1974, Aeroamerica took over the carrier's assets. Using three 720B and one BAC 1-11 jets, IT charter operations on behalf of several Berlin tour operators commenced on 27 April 1975. Such operations continued until November 1979 when, due to financial difficulties, Aeroamerica was forced to suspend its activity.

CAPITOL AIRWAYS

The tour operator Berliner Flugring contracted Capitol to operate its IT charter programme from West-Berlin for the period 1965 to 1967, using L-1049G aircraft.

INTERNATIONAL AIRLINES

International Airlines, a little known US carrier, operated DC-6 aircraft on holiday charter routes from West-Berlin from 1963 to 1964.

MODERN AIR

Berlin's tour operators wanted to use jet equipment for their IT charter programmes, starting with the summer 1968 season, and this led to Modern Air becoming involved with IT charter work from West-Berlin. Operations started on 24 March 1968 with an initial fleet of two CV-990s jets. Although popular with the travelling public, these aircraft later proved too costly to use in view of the sharp increase in fuel prices. This prompted Modern Air to terminate its Berlin operations in September 1974.

PAN AM

Pan American featured prominently in West-Berlin's history of air transport, serving a pattern of IGS and international routes. For the first time in 1974, the airline was contracted to operate IT charters on behalf of Berlin tour operators. This activity continued until October 1990 when, as a result of the company's financial difficulties and a changed political situation in Germany, Pan Am terminated its Berlin-based scheduled and charter operations.

RIDDLE AIRLINES

The US carrier Riddle Airlines operated holiday charters from West-Berlin during the Summer 1962 season, using DC-7C airliners. At that time, Riddle was the only air carrier involved in IT charter work from Berlin.

SATURN AIRWAYS

The West-Berlin tour operator Flug-Union contracted Saturn Airways to run its holiday charters, starting in Summer 1964, and two 96-seat DC-7s were based at Berlin for such operations until 1967. It was then that tour operators preferred to use jet aircraft for their IT charter programmes and Saturn subsequently withdrew from Berlin.

TEMPELHOF AIRWAYS

Formed in late 1981, Tempelhof Airways started scheduled regional services in October 1985, using Tempelhof Airport in the centre of town. In addition, the carrier also operated IT charter flights on the Berlin-Shannon route in Summer 1990, using SF-340 aircraft. At the end of the Summer 1990 season, all operations were suspended and the airline was disbanded in early 1991.

GREECE

APOLLO AIRLINES

In 1994, the carrier Apollo Airlines was formed by Greek and Swedish investors. In conjunction with the Swedish tour operator Apollo Resor, IT charter flights were operated to Greece starting in March 1995. Throughout that summer, a mix of scheduled and charter services linked Athens and Thessaloniki with London-Gatwick, Stuttgart, Hamburg and Paris using an Airbus A300. Throughout 1996, Apollo Airlines was operating more scheduled than charter services but financial problems forced the airline to close down in December 1996.

AIR GREECE

Formed in early 1994, based at Heraklion, Air Greece commenced scheduled domestic services from 16 September 1994 onward, followed by charter flights between Cairo and Heraklion with an initial fleet consisting of two ATR 72 aircraft. There was a delay to the start-up of international IT charter operations due to problems over the carrier's operating license until 1 May 1995. The company continued international charters until 1996 when it opted out of this activity

CRETAN AIRLINES

Formed in 1991 by private investors of Crete involving some 2,500 shareholders, the purpose of this company was to help boost tourism to the island. Cretan Airlines was one of the first Greek charter carriers formed after the Greek Government adopted more liberal rules in the field of air transport. International IT charter operations commenced on 2 April 1993 with a fleet of two A320 aircraft. Between April and December 1993, 88,717 passengers were carried and operations continued until January 1995 when the company folded.

CRONUS AIRLINES

Formed by private investors in 1994, Cronus Airlines launched IT charters to Greece in April 1995. Domestic scheduled services commenced in November 1995, followed by international scheduled services in July 1997. Since then, this mix of operations has continued and the carrier's fleet had increased to seven 737s by the summer of 2000.

GALAXY AIRWAYS

Set up in early 1999, Athens based Galaxy Airways commenced scheduled and IT charter operations with 737 aircraft on 31 August of the same year.

MACEDONIAN AIRLINES

Olympic Airways created its subsidiary Macedonian Airlines in 1992, for the purpose of operating IT charter flights to Greek destinations and thus increase Olympic's share in holiday traffic. The company, which uses Olympic Airways aircraft when required, did not become operational before 1999.

OLYMPIC AIRWAYS

The history of Olympic Airways goes back to 1951 when privately-owned TAE, Hellas and AME were merged into one airline company. On 30 July 1956, Olympic Airways was acquired by Onassis and this arrangement continued until 1975 when the Greek Government took over the airline. Since that time, in its role as Greece's national carrier, Olympic has sought to expand its scheduled operations throughout Europe, the Middle East, North America, Africa, Asia and Australia.

The Greek national airline has, for most of its existence, had to face extensive competition from foreign charter airlines which were granted access to the country in line with the Greek Government's open sky policy. This has continued to have a detrimental effect on Olympic, especially in financial terms. The airline has structured its international network in a way that the bulk of its operations is focused on the Greek capital Athens which also functions as the focal point of an extensive domestic network. Thessaloniki has, in the course of the last decade, enhanced its role in Olympic's international pattern of service. Although Olympic has built up a network of seasonal scheduled holiday routes mainly serving Athens, Corfu, Heraklion, Thessaloniki, Kavala and Rhodes, it has continuously had to compete with the large number of foreign charter carriers serving holiday resorts on numerous Greek islands, with attractively priced package tours.

Since the mid-sixties, Olympic has also been involved in the operation of holiday charters, yet only to a limited extent, apart from Summer 1982 and 1983 when the largest-ever IT charter patterns were in operation.

OLYMPIC CHARTER

The charter subsidiary Olympic Charter was formed in 1987 to specialise in the operation of international inbound charters from April 1988 onward, using aircraft of the parent company. However this project has not been put into practice.

PRINCESS AIR

This company is a successor to defunct Venus Airlines and started IT charter operations with 737s on 16 July 1998. In summer 1999, charter operations covered several cities in Germany but, due to the bankruptcy of Siokas Reisen, its tour operator partner in Germany, in July 1999, the air carrier was forced to suspend operations.

VENUS AIRLINES

In 1993, Venus Airlines was formed by private investors including the Swedish charter carrier Nordic East, to operate international holiday charters to Greece. Flying commenced in 1993 with two MD83s and the subsequent addition of two 727-200 and 757-200 jets allowed the carrier to expand its operations considerably. Throughout 1996, Venus had a contract with the Swiss tour operator Kuoni on whose behalf it operated an extensive pattern of charter flights between Switzerland and Greece. In November 1996, the carrier's operating licence was withdrawn by the Greek authorities, and although later restored, Venus Airlines did not resume its operations.

HUNGARY

MALEV

Malev Hungarian Airlines, the successor company to the Hungarian-Soviet joint venture Maszovlet, commenced scheduled operations in November 1954. Hungary, and in particular the capital Budapest, has always been a popular destination for visitors from East and West and has played a major role in international tourism. The tour company Ibusz started to promote tourism from western European countries to Hungary in 1964, actively involving Malev. In addition to an expanding network of scheduled services throughout Europe, Malev started to operate IT charter flights for foreign tourists to Budapest in the sixties, in co-operation with its own tour operator Malev Air Tours. This covered Finland, Scandinavia, West-Germany, France, Switzerland and Italy. In turn, foreign holiday tours have been arranged for Hungarians since 1975, Greece forming a particularly popular destination. In the nineties, the few remaining charter services from Cologne/Bonn, Dusseldorf, Hamburg and Stuttgart in Germany were switched to a 'scheduled' mode.

Political change at the end of the communist era lifted the last restrictions on foreign travel by Hungarian nationals. This has tremendously boosted the market potential for Hungarians' going on foreign holidays. Malev's outbound IT charter operations have meanwhile grown to cover numerous popular southern European holiday destinations, including the Canary Islands and North Africa. Both TU-134 and TU-154 were, prior to their planned phase-out, relegated to holiday charter work. The addition of long-range 767 aircraft in 1992 enabled Malev to commence intercontinental charter services. The first charters to North America started in Summer 1992, with Toronto and Cleveland as the major destinations. IT charter flights to Bangkok commenced in December 1993 but have since been switched to a 'scheduled' mode. Winter series of charter flights were initiated to the popular Caribbean destination Puerto Plata in November 1995, as were flights to Mombasa, East Africa, the first time ever that such destinations and countries were served by a Hungarian air carrier.

Malev has, since July 1992, operated inbound summer charter flights from Japan to Budapest in co-operation with the Japanese tour operator Sun Travel Agency. This Japanese operation is doubly beneficial to Malev in that Japanese visitors also use the airline's scheduled flights for regional travel within Europe. In 1996, Malev's charter traffic reached a total of 293,000 passengers.

ICELAND

AIR ATLANTA ICELANDIC

On 10 February 1986, Air Atlanta Icelandic was established by private partners to specialise in wet leasing of aircraft and to provide additional capacity to other airlines during periods of peak demand. The air carrier's involvement with outbound IT charter work commenced in April 1992, with a flight from Reykjavik to Palma de Majorca on behalf of the tour operator Flugferdir. Since May 1993, holiday charters have also been flown in co-operation with the tour organiser Samvinn Travel. June 1995 saw the start of Air Atlanta's inbound holiday charter flights from Germany to Iceland. Furthermore, the carrier commenced IT charters from Manchester, UK, to Mediterranean holiday resorts.

By 1996, the airline had built up a large fleet of aircraft comprising five 747s, four TriStars, one 737-300, and three 737-200s two of which are used only for cargo operations. Four of these aircraft are fully owned but the rest are leased. Most of the company's aircraft are operated under wet lease agreements on behalf of other airlines. In summer 2000, Air Atlanta operated IT charters with TriStar aircraft from London-Gatwick and Manchester on behalf of several smaller UK tour operators.

AIR VIKING

Between its formation in 1970 and spring of 1973, Air Viking operations were limited to adhoc charter work. In Summer 1970, a Vanguard was used for IT charters from Iceland to Spain, France and Ireland, and the season started with an IT charter flown in June from Reykjavik (-Keflavik) to Palma de Majorca. In 1971/72, a CV-880 jet was added and also in 1972, the company bought two 720Bs from United, used mainly for sub-charter work on behalf of other airlines. In June 1975, Air Viking initiated IT charters from Germany to Iceland with a series of flights from Dusseldorf to Reykjavik. By early 1976, however, the company had run into financial difficulties and was forced to close down, operating its final service on 12 March 1976. The planned Summer 1976 holiday charter flights from Germany to Iceland were taken over by Eagle Air (Arnarflug).

EAGLE AIR (ARNARFLUG)

Eagle Air was registered on 10 April 1976 by former staff of failed Air Viking whose 720Bs were taken over. IT charter flying started on 5 June 1976 from Reykjavik (-Keflavik) to Malaga, followed on 12 June 1976 with inbound charters from Dusseldorf to Reykjavik. This ITC operating pattern continued in subsequent years.

From 1978 onward, the carrier was also involved in leasing its aircraft to other airlines. Icelandair bought a 57% share in Eagle Air in 1979. In September of the same year, rights were granted for scheduled service to secondary destinations in Iceland. In 1981, preparing for the start of scheduled international services, Eagle Air acquired a 737-200 and the airline was granted licences to serve Amsterdam, Dusseldorf and Zurich. Financial problems, coupled with an uneasy relationship with the national airline Icelandair, its major shareholder, contributed to the company's demise in August 1990, followed by its liquidation in October.

ICELANDAIR

Flugfelag and Loftleidir, the two major airlines of Iceland, merged on 1 August 1973 to form Icelandair. The airline's international network is focused on the capital's major airport at Reykjavik-Keflavik and, since 14 April 1963, Icelandair has been involved with holiday charter operations. It was on that date when the first ever IT charter flight, with a DC-6B, was operated from Reykjavik to Tenerife for the Easter holiday period. The airline's first ever winter series of IT charters to Las Palmas, Canary Islands, started on 31 December 1970. The demise of Eagle Air in 1990 led to Icelandair taking over the licenses for the routes served by the former airline. At the same time, Iceland's Minister of Communications granted the national airline a general permit for holiday charters on all routes, in line with a more liberal air transport policy.

Icelandair's pattern of IT charter flying consists of service to a select number of destinations in southern Europe in summer and to the Canary Islands in winter. Eventualy, Icelandair formed its own tour operator Utsyn (Sun Vacations) to sell holiday tours to Europe.

ISLANDSFLUG

1991 saw the foundation of Islandsflug and, in addition to handling aircraft maintenance and running a flight school, scheduled services are now in operation from Reykjavik to 16 destinations in Iceland. The addition of a 737-200QC in early 1998 allowed the airline to operate holiday charter flights from Reykjavik to Manchester, Eindhoven and Rimini during the summer 1998 season. In addition, Islandsflug ran charters from Reykjavik to Kulusuk in Greenland throughout the summer season, using its ATR 42 aircraft.

IRELAND (EIRE)

AER LINGUS

Aer Lingus was formed in April 1936, and in its early years, the airline's sphere of operation was focused on scheduled links between Ireland and Britain. After World War II, the airline resumed these essential air services and embarked on a program of route expansion to additional destinations in Britain and to gateway cities across western Europe and in North America.

Since the early fifties, Lourdes in the French Pyrenées has been an important destination for Irish pilgrims visiting the holy shrine. Whereas Aer Lingus launched a scheduled service to Lourdes in May 1954, the growing volume of charter operations to that destination in subsequent years eventually replaced scheduled flights. At the peak of the pilgrimage season, Aer Lingus nowadays operates daily charters to Lourdes to meet demand.

From the late sixties onward, Aer Lingus has increasingly become involved with the operation of holiday charters to destinations across southern Europe, the Canary Islands and North Africa. All types of aircraft in the Aer Lingus fleet have been used for IT charter operations, ranging from 1-11, 707 and 737 jets to big capacity 747s to meet high season demand for selected destinations, especially Palma de Majorca or the Canary Islands. The airline has used its spare capacity mainly during the weekend.

In addition to outbound holiday charter flights, Aer Lingus has, for decades, also operated inbound charters to Dublin, Cork and Shannon from selected continental European cities during the summer season, working closely with the Irish tour operator CIE. This has been in line with the growing popularity of Ireland as a tourist destination. In recent years, most of these flights have been switched to a 'scheduled' mode.

AER TURAS

Since its formation in 1962, Aer Turas has specialised in air freight operations. However, a change in policy led to the company becoming involved with holiday charters in Summer 1997 from Ireland [Eire] and the UK, using a TriStar on behalf of other charter carriers.

CITYJET

CityJet was formed in early 1993 and commenced scheduled service on the London-Dublin route on 10 January 1994, initially under a franchise agreement with Virgin Atlantic but under its own brand from 29 July 1996 onward. The Swedish airline Malmo Aviation took a financial stake in CityJet in January 1997 but the airline reverted to being wholly Irish-owned in December 1997.

In addition to its scheduled operations, CityJet also became involved with IT charter work after winning a contract with the Irish tour operator Sunworld in February 1994, making use of spare BAe146 aircraft capacity over the weekend.

CLUB AIR

In August 1986, plans were under discussions to set up an airline to specialise in IT charter operations on behalf of several Irish tour operators. Club Air was formed to meet this requirement and holiday charter flying commenced on 6 May 1987 with a 727-100 and a leased 707, the first service operating from Dublin to Tenerife.

The company operated successfully and reportedly captured around 25% of the Irish package tour market, with over 120,000 passengers carried within a year. There were no IT charter operations in Winter 1987/88 but an extensive pattern of IT flights was again in operation throughout Summer 1988. Club Air, however, encountered financial problems by October of that year and was forced to close down.

HIBERNIAN

Throughout the Summer of 1967, Hibernian used DC-3s for IT holiday charters from Dublin to regional destinations until October. It was at that time that financial problems forced the carrier to terminate its activities, leading to its liquidation by December.

RYANAIR

In May 1985, Ryanair was founded for the purpose of providing low cost air travel between Ireland [Eire] and the UK. Scheduled operations commenced in July 1985 and, in addition to the destinations served in Britain, service has since been expanded to other countries in Europe. Complementary to its scheduled activity, Ryanair has also become involved with holiday charter flying on behalf of Irish tour operators. The first service started on 1 May 1987, with both 1-11s and 737s used for this work.

TRANSLIFT ~ TRANSAER

The Translift Group formed the charter carrier Translift in October 1991 and IT charter operations commenced in February 1992. Four DC-8-71 aircraft formed part of the fleet from February 1992 until March 1994, on lease from GPA and in October 1993 Translift became the first Irish air carrier to place Airbus A320s into service. A leased Airbus A300 was introduced on the Manchester-Malaga charter route on 27 June 1997, supplemented by a second aircraft later on.

Since 1992, Translift has operated IT charters on behalf of Falcon Holidays, Ireland's largest tour operator. Beginning in 1993, Translift expanded its IT charter work by starting operations from the UK, in line with the liberalization of air transport within the European Community. In 1994, the company formed its subsidiary TransAer Leisure responsible for the promotion and sale of flight programmes between Ireland and the USA. Translift changed its name to TransAer effective 1 May 1997. In recent years, TransAer has increasingly operated holiday charter services also from continental European countries like Germany and Italy and in 1998, 3.2 million passengers were carried.

ITALY

AERAL - AERONOLEGGI ALESSANDRIA

The charter company was formed in March 1958 as an air taxi carrier based at Alessandria and one of the initial major shareholders was Aermacchi. After a re-organization in 1977, when Aeral was fully taken over by a group of private investors, the carrier decided to expand into cargo charter operations. An Alitalia DC-8-43 was acquired on 15 December 1978, subsequently converted in the USA to DC-8-54F standards, and took off on 17 February 1979 from Rome-Fiumicino for the first time. After the acquisition of a second DC-8, Aeral commenced passenger charter operations on 1 May 1980. However, the company's first DC-8 was withdrawn in September 1980, followed by the second aircraft shortly after and the company was disbanded in 1981.

AERMEDITERRANEA

As a successor to failed Itavia, Aermediterranea came into existence on 20 March 1981, with Alitalia holding 55% and ATI 45% of the shares. Using DC9-32 aircraft leased from either Alitalia or ATI, Aermediterranea resumed scheduled operations on some of the routes formerly served by Itavia. IT charter operations were initiated on 1 April 1982, covering destinations in the Mediterranean region and the Middle East. In summer 1984, Alitalia announced the merger of Aermediterranea with ATI which became effective as of 1 April 1985.

AERO TAXI SUD ~ SAGITTAIR

The carrier Aero Taxi Sud was set up at Naples-Capodichino airport. The company's name was changed to Sagittair in 1990. The initial fleet consisted of two BAe146-300 jets delivered in June and July 1990 for IT charters mainly from Naples and Rome-Ciampino, and was officially presented to the press on 19 September 1990. The first MD83 was delivered on 21 March 1991, followed by another aircraft in May. Financial problems arose in September 1991, causing the shutdown of the carrier and all the leased aircraft had been returned to their lessors by November.

AIR EUROPE ITALY ~ AIR EUROPE S.p.A

In June 1989, the UK airline Air Europe established Air Europe Italy as its Italian partner in the 'Airlines of Europe Group', based at Milan-Malpensa. At that time, Fiat was the largest Italian shareholder in the company. IT charter operations commenced on 19 December 1989, with a fleet of 757s, to Mombasa, Male, Phuket and Cancun, mainly on behalf of the tour operator Alpitour with whom the airline held a major contract.

In the wake of the collapse of the UK company ILG and its affiliated airline Air Europe early in 1991, Air Europe Italy became wholly Italian-owned, trading under the name of Air Europe S.p.A. Since that time, it has developed into Italy's largest airline specializing in intercontinental holiday charter operations.

An interesting development was the operation of a series of charter flights from Japan to Italy in Summer 1996, bringing tourist groups to Rome and Milan from several major cities throughout Japan. By 1996, the fleet comprised five 767-300ER aircraft and another aircraft was added in April 1997. The first 777-200ER was delivered to the airline's home base at Malpensa on 21 July 1999 and introduced into service almost immediately. Air Europe's passenger total has more than doubled from 400,000 in 1994 to 890,161 in 1998.

AIR SICILIA

Air Sicilia was established by a private investor for the purpose of promoting tourism to Sicily and its neighbouring islands of Lampedusa and Pantelleria. The company structure comprises both the airline and hotel business and, throughout the summer season, Air Sicilia operates scheduled and charter services to Sicily and to the islands of Lampedusa and Pantelleria.

In addition to scheduled and charter operations within Italy, Air Sicilia has been involved in international IT charter operations in Europe, using various aircraft types, since summer 1994. A second 737-200 was ordered in August 1999 to reinforce not only the carrier's scheduled but also its charter activity.

ALIADRIATICA ~ AIR ONE

Aliadriatica was set up as a pilot training school in 1983, based at Pescara and the powerful construction and civil engineering Toto Group acquired a majority stake in the company in 1988. A 737-200 was acquired in June 1994 and scheduled domestic services were launched in April 1995. Then, on 23 November 1995, the company adopted the name Air One. The assets of the failed air carrier Noman were acquired on 1 March 1997.

Air One commenced IT charters in summer 1997, mainly on behalf of the tour operator Alpitour. Scheduled operations have, in recent years, been given priority but the volume of charter activity has nevertheless grown to be 15% of the airline's total. Air One was operating IT charter services in summer 1999 from Bergamo, Bologna, Milan-Linate and Rome-Fiumicino, with a mixed fleet of eleven 737 (200/300/400) aircraft.

ALISARDA ~ MERIDIANA

Alisarda was formed by the Aga Khan in March 1963 and its chosen base was at Olbia. Beginning in May 1966, Alisarda has provided scheduled service within Italy and, since summer 1978, also seasonal service to foreign destinations. Spain's airline Meridiana was merged into Alisarda and the new company adopted the name Meridiana on 1 September 1991.

In 1974, after the delivery of DC-9 jets, Alisarda also became involved with the operation of seasonal IT charters to bring foreign tourists to Sardinia. In later years, however, this sector has seen a large-scale switch to a 'scheduled' mode. In more recent years, Meridiana has operated IT charters to Greece, Turkey and Spain during the summer season and, in winter, to destinations in the Middle East. Due to the airline's commitment to offer extensive peak season scheduled services on domestic and international routes, there is only limited potential for IT charter work.

ALITALIA

In addition to the holiday charter operations of its subsidiary company ATI, Alitalia itself was active in this field, using its widebody aircraft for IT charters to a number of long-haul destinations including the Maldives and East Africa. On 30 October 1994, ATI was merged into Alitalia and, since then, the national airline has operated some IT charters which used to form part of ATI's realm of activity. However, in recent years, the bulk of this activity has been passed over to Eurofly in which Alitalia has a financial stake.

ALPI EAGLES

Formed in 1979, the carrier commenced air taxi operations in 1987 from its base at Venice. Alpi Eagles moved into the scheduled sector in March 1996, providing service on short to medium-haul routes, and a fleet of six F-100 jets was acquired between April and December 1996. This allowed the airline also to initiate IT charter operations in summer 1997 between major cities in Italy and destinations in Greece. Regular public charter services are maintained between Verona and Arad as well as Belgrade.

ALTAIR - LINEE AEREE S.p.A

Altair came into existence at the end of 1980 at Reggio Emilia and Venice was chosen as its operating base. After the delivery of the first Caravelle III jet in January 1981, the carrier decided on Rome-Ciampino as its base airport but switched to Bologna later on. Flight operations commenced on 1 March 1981 and a second Caravelle was added on 5 April 1982. Throughout that summer, IT charters were flown on behalf of Italian tour operations to Mediterranean destinations. It was at that time that Palma de Majorca became the most popular destination for Italian holiday-makers. 1983 saw Altair's growing co-operation with the UK tour operator Pegasus which resulted in 50% of the carrier's activity being focused on the UK - Italy market.

Financial problems arose in the latter part of 1983 which the carrier managed to overcome, and a fleet renewal programme was initiated with the acquisition of three Super Caravelles from Finnair, of which the first aircraft was delivered in March and the other two in June 1984. From October to November 1985, three Caravelles were withdrawn from service, leaving just one aircraft for charter work. The carrier was acquired by a building contractor firm in December 1985 and this led to the transfer of Altair's operating base to Ancona. The carrier, however, ceased operations and was declared bankrupt on 15 April 1986.

ATI - AERO TRASPORTI ITALIANI

The Alitalia subsidiary ATI was formed on 16 December 1963 for the purpose of building up a network of routes serving secondary cities in Italy. Scheduled operations commenced on 3 June 1964. The take-over of DC-9-32 jets released by Alitalia, and their introduction into service from November 1969 onward, initiated a decisive phase in ATI's development. The DC-9 fleet comprised twelve aircraft by mid-1970.

In order to streamline IT charter operations under the Alitalia banner, ATI absorbed the charter carrier Aermediterranea on 1 April 1985. It was from this date onward that ATI became involved with the operation of international IT charter operations, opening a new sphere for the airline. By 1989, IT charter operations accounted for 10% of its overall activity. ATI continued its scheduled and IT charter operations until 29 October 1994 when it was dissolved as a separate company and subsequently fully integrated into its parent Alitalia.

AVIOSARDA

Aviosarda was founded in 1993 as a flying school based at Olbia. The operation of short-haul scheduled services began in 1996 then, in summer 1997, the carrier also became active in the field of IT charter work, using ATR 42 aircraft. The carrier suspended its operations at the end of that year.

AZZURRA AIR

With an Air Malta shareholding of 49%, Azzurra Air was formed on 20 December 1995, based at Bergamo-Orio al Serio. Scheduled operations commenced on 10 December 1996, with two 92-seat RJ85 jets, joined by another aircraft in May 1997. One RJ70 jet was added in October 1997 and another two aircraft followed in March 1998. In line with the franchise agreement with Alitalia signed on 13 March 1998, the Azzurra Air aircraft were painted in the national airline's colours for scheduled operations under the Alitalia Express banner.

Since May 1999, two 737-700 aircraft have been specially dedicated to holiday charter operations, painted in the airline's own colours, this being the first time that an Italian carrier has used such an aircraft type in this field. Azzurra Air makes its fleet of RJ 70-85 jets available as a back-up to meet tour operators' seat capacity requirements. Throughout summer 1999, Azzurra Air operated medium-haul IT charters linking northern Italian cities with holiday destinations in Spain, Greece and North Africa.

BLUE PANORAMA AIRLINES

Formed on 3 September 1998, this charter carrier is associated with the broker firm Astra Associated Services owning 33% and the remaining shares held by private partners. Using two 737-400s acquired from Hapag-Lloyd, the carrier started IT charter operations on 26 December 1998 from Rome-Fiumicino, its main base airport, to Paris and Sharm el Sheikh. In the Winter 1998/99 season, IT charters were also flown to Vienna, Madrid, Luxor and Tel Aviv. The success of the initial phase of activity prompted the company to expand its operations for the summer 1999 season, with the use of four 737s.

COLUMBIA

October 1983 saw the formation of the charter carrier Columbia at Genoa. With the support of local businessmen with shipping interests, Columbia was intended to offer excursions by air to cruise passengers stopping over at Genoa and, in addition, IT charters to other destinations were planned. The carrier took delivery of its first Herald airliner on 10 March 1984 but was unable to commence operations before 1 September 1984, due to the authorities' long delay in issuing the relevant licence. A second Herald was added in December 1984 and Columbia continued its operations until October 1985, when the Heralds were leased out to the regional airline Aligiulia. After their return, the aircraft were ferried to the UK in August 1986 by which time Columbia had been disbanded.

EUROFLY

On 26 March 1989, Eurofly was founded in Turin with a 50% financial involvement of Alitalia, Olivetti and the Instituto Bancario San Paolo holding 10%. IT charter operations commenced on 26 February 1990 with two DC-9-51 aircraft and the carrier subsequently chose Bergamo as its main base. In April 1993, two DC-9-32s were added to the fleet. Eurofly served an extensive network of charter routes radiating from major cities like Bergamo, Bologna, Milan-Malpensa, Rome, Turin and Verona to holiday destinations in Europe, the Mediterranean basin and North Africa. On a seasonal basis, inbound charters are flown to Sicily from selected foreign cities.

As a result of a policy review, Alitalia changed its attitude towards the role played by Italy's charter carriers. After ATI was integrated into Alitalia on 30 October 1994, Alitalia's financial involvement with Eurofly led to Italy's national airline electing this carrier as its charter arm. To emphasize the charter carrier's part of the Alitalia Group, all Eurofly aircraft were repainted in Alitalia's colour scheme and, in recent years, Alitalia has been entrusted with maintaining the Eurofly fleet and training its pilots. After acquiring two 767-300ER jets in December 1998, Eurofly launched long-haul IT charters to the Caribbean and Central America. In 1990, the carrier's first year of activity, 141,252 passengers were carried, with the passenger total reaching 495,632 in 1996 and 849,933 in 1998.

FORTUNE AVIATION ~ NOMAN

Set up on 14 June 1979, Fortune Aviation initially functioned as an air taxi company and executive jet operator based at Rome-Ciampino. In a move intended to expand its activity generally, the company acquired two DC-9-15 aircraft in June 1961 from failed Unifly Express for cargo charter operations by a specially formed sub-division. By February 1992, however, this new venture had not yet started and the DC-9s were converted for passenger charter work instead. A 737-200 jet was acquired from failed Italjet on 1 July 1992 and Fortune launched IT charters on behalf of the tour operator Nouvelles Frontières on 16 July 1992, with its operations focused on holiday destinations in Greece and Turkey.

Due to a crisis in Italy's IT charter sector beginning around October 1993, caused by the growing involvement of Italy's scheduled airlines in the operation of holiday charters by making spare aircraft capacity available during the weekend, Fortune was adversely affected. They undertook a re-organization which led to a name change to Noman on 16 February 1994. In addition to the involvement with IT charter flying, Noman launched scheduled domestic service in December 1994, but financial problems eventually forced the airline to close down on 23 December 1996.

ITALJET

In February 1988, the charter carrier Italjet was founded. Sobelair took a 30% stake in the new venture and. in June 1990, sold one of their 737-200s to the airline. After obtaining its operating licence, IT charters were launched in September of that year, in close co-operation with the tour operator Turavia, focusing on Spain but also covering Austria, Germany and the UK. At that time, however, Italy's charter market experienced a decline and this had an adverse effect on the carrier's activity. Sobelair withdrew its stake in April 1991, but however, Italjet continued operating until February 1992 when financial difficulties prompted the single 737 to be impounded. The company was wound up shortly afterwards.

ITAVIA ~ AEROLINEE ITAVIA

Itavia was founded by private investors in April 1958 and launched scheduled domestic service on 15 July 1959. However services were suspended from 1961 until after the company had been re-organized in May 1962. In April 1963, Itavia put two Handley Page Herald aircraft into service for scheduled domestic routes, for seasonal IT charters from the UK to Italy and from Italy to Yugoslavia and North Africa. The carrier withdrew its last two Heralds in July 1973, after using a total of five aircraft since 1963.

On 23 April 1973, Itavia took delivery of two new F-28-1000 jets at Rome-Ciampino airport. At the beginning of 1974, the Itavia fleet consisted of four F-28s (65-seats) and three DC-9-10 series (90 seats) which allowed this regional airline to improve its scheduled operations and to secure a growing involvement with holiday charter operations on medium-haul routes. In 1980, the Itavia fleet consisted of five DC-9-14-15, three DC-9-30, and three F-28 jets, but the carrier ceased operations in December 1980 because of financial and operational problems. However in January 1981, it was announced that Itavia was to be re-started as a charter carrier but these plans could not be realized because of objections raised by Italy's civil aviation authority.

LAUDA AIR ITALY S.p.A

Lauda Air Italy S.p.A was founded by its parent Lauda Air in September 1990 and IT charter operations were launched from Milan-Malpensa on 1 November 1993. The carrier specializes in long-haul operations and leases a 767-300ER from its parent company. Its passenger total reached 227,362 in 1998.

MED AIRLINES

Set up in 1997, Med Airlines became operational in April 1998 using a Saab 2000 for scheduled local services focused on the Sicilian city of Trapani. In Summer 1998, the airline also operated holiday charter flights from Graz in Austria.

MEDITERAVIA

Mediteravia was formed in mid-1959 at Milan, and charter operations commenced in early July with one Viking airliner which was later replaced by a leased DC-4 in December 1960. However the carrier ceased operations in May 1961 and its failure was testimony to the fact that Italy's holiday charter market was not yet mature enough to support the existence of a specialist charter airline. Furthermore, the political and air transport regulatory set-up at the time did not favour private enterprise in the air transport sector.

SAM - SOCIETÀ AEREA MEDITERRANEA

Alitalia formed its subsidiary SAM on 1 December 1959, holding a 95% share. The carrier's commercial policy was directed towards securing a larger share of the charter traffic to Italy, the bulk of which was, at that time, handled by foreign airlines. SAM became operational on 1 April 1961 and IT charters were flown mainly from the UK, Germany and France to several popular holiday destinations in Italy, in particular to Genoa, Rimini, Rome, Naples, Palermo and Catania.

By 1966, a significant shift in the charter carrier's activity had taken place in that some 25% of the traffic carried by SAM was outbound from Italy to holiday destinations around the Mediterranean, as well as to Moscow, catering to the burgeoning demand of Italian holidaymakers in line

with signs of growing economic prosperity, to venture on foreign holidays. Of importance were special flights for pilgrims to Lourdes in south-western France. SAM used DC-6Bs initially, followed by Caravelle jets in1968, released by Alitalia when more modern aircraft were introduced into service. In Summer 1969, for the first time, SAM's service pattern also covered Belgium, the Netherlands, Austria and Switzerland. The carrier's charter traffic grew from 64,000 in 1961, its first year of operation, to 385,495 in 1967 and 657,000 in 1973. Although SAM made a valuable contribution to the furtherance of Italy's share in international charter traffic, financial results were not satisfactory and, in 1972, some eleven years after SAM started operations, Alitalia decided to gradually scale down the charter company's activity. Operations were suspended in January 1977 and the leased Caravelle jets, in use at that time, were returned to parent Alitalia.

SAV - SOCIETÀ AEREA VENEZIANA ~ AEROPA

Early 1969 saw the formation of SAV to carry flowers, fruit and vegetables from Italy to Northern Europe. The single 707, leased from 27 September 1972 onward, was used for IT charter services from Italy to the Middle East and Africa beginning in February 1973. Just prior to this, the company changed its name to Aeropa in January 1973.

After the addition of a second 707 on 8 April 1974, an expanded pattern of charter routes covered Mediterranean destinations and inbound charters were flown from selected European cities to Italy. Aeropa announced its intention to add another two 707s for future trans-atlantic operations but the company came to face financial problems. The US CAB did not grant the sought-after charter permit and Italy's Civilavia refused to give their approval for charters to Thailand. On 15 February 1975, Aeropa ceased flying because of the authorities' refusal to renew the operating licence.

TAS AIRWAYS

Using two BAe146 jets leased from British Aerospace from March 1992 onward, TAS Airways operated charters mainly from the UK to Italy, in addition to outbound IT charters from major cities in northern Italy. However the company experienced financial problems, causing its aircraft to be repossessed on 22 August 1994 and prompting the company's demise.

TEA ITALIA

The Belgian charter carrier TEA created its subsidiary TEA Italia in February 1990, with a 33.3% participation, based at Treviso. IT charter operations commenced on 22 December 1990 with one 149-seat 737-300 and, by April 1991, the fleet had grown to three 737 aircraft. The fact that these aircraft were able to use airports near popular holiday destinations, with relatively short runways, was claimed to be an advantage by the tour operators which chose TEA for their IT capacity requirements.

The demise of TEA Belgium in September 1991 created a crisis for the Italian charter company. In November 1991, however, the shares of TEA Italia had been acquired by Italian investors which made the company 100% Italian-owned. TEA Italia ran into financial difficulties, was forced to suspend operations early in 1992 and was subsequently liquidated in March. After another company restructure, the carrier resumed operations in July 1992, and an attempt was made in 1993 to combine operations with TAS but this proved unsuccessful. One MD82 leased from Meridiana was in use from June until November 1993 and a limited charter pattern was in operation throughout 1994. Plans were made to enter the scheduled sector with leased DC-9s but this did not work out. So in early 1995, the company folded because of bankruptcy.

TURAVIA

The company Turavia was originally set up as a flying school. However plans were made for IT charter operations to commence in summer 1968, with a fleet of DC-4 and DC-7 aircraft, but this did not materialize. A few months later, Fokker announced an order for two F-28s and one F-27, but in the end only one F-28 operated a few charter flights from Turin. Because of financial problems and little success with securing tour operator contracts, the company folded in September 1971.

UNIFLY ~ UNIFLY EXPRESS

Unifly was established in 1976 for general as well as executive charter work. In May 1984, the first F-28 was acquired and another three aircraft were introduced into service between September 1984 and October 1986, used also for IT charter operations. The company was then acquired by SEMA Eurofinance, underwent a re-organization and was renamed Unifly Express in January 1987. Three MD83 aircraft were added in May 1988, commencing service on 7 May 1988 with a Dusseldorf-Naples charter. The availability of this aircraft type facilitated a notable expansion of the carrier's pattern of service on short to medium haul routes which, increasingly, involved outbound holiday charters from several Italian cities. However the carrier's owner company SEMA went bankrupt on 9 October 1990 which prompted the demise of Unifly Express.

VICTORIA AIRLINES

With a fleet of two A320 aircraft leased from Onur Air, Victoria Airlines used the Air Operators Licence of Olbia-based Aviosarda for holiday charter operations effective from 28 July 1998. Throughout the summer season, the carrier operated from Bologna, Verona, Milan-Malpensa and Naples to Mediterranean destinations and Dublin. The company folded in October 1998.

VOLARE AIRLINES

Former staff of Alpi Eagles created Volare Airlines in 1997 as a specialist IT charter carrier. Two A320s were in use for IT charter operations which commenced on 3 April 1998 from Milan-Malpensa, Bergamo and Verona and the airline's route network covered medium-haul destinations in Europe and the Middle East. The Swissair Group took a 34% stake in the charter carrier in September1998, and the Summer of 1999 saw a notable expansion of the company's activity. In addition to holiday charter services, Volare launched scheduled domestic operations and inbound IT charters from central European cities, and the fleet was increased to five A320 aircraft.

LATVIA

LATPASS AIRLINES

Latpass Airlines was established to operate general and executive flights using a single TU-154 aircraft for IT charters to southern European holiday destinations.

LATCHARTER

LatCharter was formed as a privately owned air carrier in 1993, to specialise in general and executive charter work. Initially, the carrier's fleet was made up of Yak-42 airliners but these were replaced by the latest versions of TU-134B jets of which four were in use in 1996. With a range of up to 3,200 kms (1,730 nm), the TU-134s have been in use on holiday charter routes from Riga, Latvia's capital, to holiday destinations in southern Europe.

LITHUANIA

AIR LITHUANIA

Air Lithuania was formed on 13 September 1991 as a state-owned airline, replacing the Kaunas-based division of Aeroflot. The airline was allotted a fleet of six Yak-40s and, in April 1993, one TU-134A was added, followed by an ATR-42 in March 1997. Initially, general charter work was undertaken but, starting in February 1993, a network of scheduled services was developed, focusing on Kaunas, Lithuania's second largest city, and Palanga, a seaside resort in the vicinity of the leading seaport of Klaipeda. On 17 July 1995, Air Lithuania was re-organised into a joint stock company and became a subsidiary of Lithuanian Airlines in August 1997.

In addition to its scheduled international services, Air Lithuania has also operated holiday charters to Palma in Summer 1996/97 and to Varna in Summer 1997. In Summer 1998, outbound holiday charters were taken over by Lithuanian Airlines.

LITHUANIAN AIRLINES (LIETUVOS AVIALINIJOS)

On 21 December 1991, Lithuanian Airlines was established as the national airline, taking over from the Aeroflot Lithuania Directorate, based at the capital Vilnius. The airline has expanded its network of scheduled routes to key destinations in Scandinavia and in western Europe, while retaining some links with cities in Russia and the CIS. The airline's fleet comprises western and Soviet-built aircraft but the intention is to sell off its fleet of Yak-42 jets. In August 1997, Air Lithuania became a fully-owned subsidiary and in Summer 1998, the airline became involved with the operation of holiday charter services from Lithuania for the first time.

LUXEMBOURG

LUXEMBOURG AIRLINES ~ LUXAIR

Luxembourg Airlines was set up on 9 January 1948 and operated until 1949 when its commercial activity ceased. On 21 October 1961, the company was resurrected as Luxair, and the carrier started holiday charter services in May 1965 from Luxembourg City to Rimini, using F-27s. Since that time, the network of holiday charter routes has continuously been extended. The creation of the in-house tour operator Luxair Tours in 1968 has greatly helped to promote the airline's services to both scheduled and holiday charter destinations.

Luxembourg's national traffic potential is fairly limited due to the relatively small size of the principality and a total population of just under 400,000 (in 1993). It has, however, been enhanced over the years by the presence of a large contingent of nearly 100,000 foreigners on account of the country assuming a prominent role in the European Community.

Luxair's remarkable marketing efforts have, in recent years, been directed towards the promotion of its scheduled and charter services in neighbouring border regions of Belgium, France and Germany, thus extending its traffic base significantly.

The company Luxavia was established as a fully-owned subsidiary of Luxair, to operate flights on the South African route. Its operations continued as a separate entity until merged with Luxair. The combined service of Luxavia/Luxair and Icelandair provide en effective low cost way of travel between South Africa and North America.

MACEDONIA

AVIOIMPEX AIRWAYS

Formed on 15 May 1992, Avioimpex is engaged in charter operations between Skopje and Ohrid in Macedonia and a number of cities in central Europe. Initially, Tu-154 aircraft were leased from Balkan Bulgarian Airlines, Aeroflot and Albatros but, by Summer 1997, the carrier's fleet consisted of one MD81 and one DC-9-33 aircraft. The German tour operator Misir, in co-operation with Avioimpex, has offered package tours to Macedonia since Summer 1998, based on the airline's charter flights from Germany to Skopje and Ohrid, in a pilot project to restart and promote international tourism to Macedonia.

FALCON AIRLINES (MACEDONIAN AIRLINES)

Established in 1992, Falcon Airlines used 737 and TU-134 aircraft for charter operations from Skopje. The carrier suspended operations in October 1999.

MAT - MACEDONIAN AIRLINES

MAT was established in early 1994 and used a 737 (of Albatros) and a TU-154 (of Balkan). In August 1996, Palair Macedonian was integrated into the company, and a mix of scheduled and charter services is operated.

META

In 1992, META was set up for charter operations between Macedonia and central European cities, using TU-154 and Yak-42 aircraft on lease. However, the airline ceased trading in January 1994.

PALAIR MACEDONIAN

The charter carrier received its operating license on 20 May 1991 and commenced operations using two An-24s and one TU-154 on wet lease from Balkan Bulgarian Airlines. Service was launched to major European cities with a sizeable community of Yugoslav and Macedonian expatriate workers then, in August 1996, the airline was merged with MAT Macedonian Airlines

VARDAR MACEDONIA

Formed in early 1992, Vardar Macedonian operated a Yak-42 throughout the summer but its operations were suspended at the end of the season.

MALTA

AIR MALTA

Air Malta was formed on 30 March 1973 in the wake of Malta becoming an independent republic. The company was given the task of building up air links between the island state and important cities in neighbouring countries, in continental Europe and the UK. Close co-operation with Pakistan's national airline PIA got the new airline under way and, with two PIA 720B aircraft on wet-lease, Air Malta initiated scheduled service on 1 April 1974 to London, Birmingham, Manchester, Paris, Rome, Frankfurt and Tripoli. Travel to and from Malta is on a highly seasonal basis, with demand peaking between April and October. To better handle this seasonal traffic, the airline has leased in aircraft for the summer period, a policy that has been in effect up to the present time. Air Malta deploys both widebody and smaller capacity aircraft types ranging from A310s to 737s, 727s and RJ70s, providing suitable flexibility in line with demand. The growth in international tourism to Malta has been a vital factor in the development of the airline. In addition to an expanding network of scheduled services, Air Malta has been involved with the operation of IT charter services since 1983 from major traffic generating centres throughout continental Europe and the UK. This has proved highly successful and Air Malta's charter traffic reached 680,000 passengers in 1988.

INDEPENDENT MALTA AIRLINE

In 1968, Scandinavian and Maltese partners created this airline for IT charters from Scandinavia and continental European destinations to Malta, using a CV-990. The company was registered in Malta but did not become operational.

MALTA METROPOLITAN AIRWAYS

This charter company performed general charter work in 1963, using a single DC-4 which was the first aircraft to carry a Maltese registration.

MOLDAVIA

MOLDAVIAN AIRLINES

Registered on 26 July 1994, Moldavian Airlines commenced scheduled services from the capital Chisinau to regional destinations. Its fleet comprises Saab 340, TU-134 and Yak-40 aircraft and in Summer 1998, a regular charter service was in operation between Chisinau and Budapest.

NETHERLANDS

AIR HOLLAND (AHD) ~ AIR HOLLAND ~ AIR HOLLAND CHARTER

John Block, a former Transavia executive, initiated plans for a new charter carrier in 1978, and his official approach to the RLV in August 1979 was supported by ten Dutch tour operators. In September 1983, a licence was finally granted for holiday charters from Rotterdam and Maastricht, but this immediately met with strong opposition from the existing charter carriers in the Netherlands. After further negotiations with government authorities, Air Holland (AHD) was finally granted the right to operate from Amsterdam from where holiday charter operations commenced on 2 April 1985 on the Malaga route. The initial fleet consisted of two 727-200s, and the new company succeeded in establishing itself in the Dutch market and operated profitably. By 1987, 175,000 passengers had been carried and a market share of 22% had been won. High quality service was offered which was valued by the tour operators and holidaymakers alike.

For the summer 1988 season, Air Holland acquired three new 757s as a replacement for its 727s, since these technically advanced aircraft were considered more suitable for its IT charter operating pattern. In 1988, AHD announced plans for transatlantic operations as well as the formation of a subsidiary carrier in the West Indies, based at Aruba, under the name of Aruba Air Charter. These plans did not materialize however, and 1990 saw the signing of a co-operation agreement with Sterling Airways which led to the 757s being seconded to the Danish carrier. In Winter 1990/91, AHD leased a 767 from Britannia Airways and, in the fiscal year 1990/91, the airline carried a record 277,000 passengers.

Financial problems began to hit Air Holland in the course of 1991, prompted by the impact of the Gulf War crisis and economic recession. The generally difficult situation, at that time, in the holiday travel market caused a sharp downturn in travel demand and nearly led to the air carrier's collapse. AHD entered bankruptcy protection on 6 September 1991 but rescue efforts failed which led to the suspension of all operations on 2 October 1991, followed by liquidation of the carrier. On 3 November 1991, a successor company was formed under the name of Air Holland Regional which took over the assets of the former carrier, including one 757. The carrier's name was subsequently changed to Air Holland Charter trading under the name of 'Air Holland'.

1993 saw AHD form an agreement of co-operation with ELAL for the Amsterdam-Tel Aviv route. This is of importance to ELAL since, on a Sabbath (Saturday), Israel's national airline is subject to operational restrictions and AHD is able to operate on its behalf. Air Holland remained the only Dutch independently-owned airline. For its Summer 1998 IT charter work, AHD used two 737-300 and four 757 aircraft, offering departures from Amsterdam, its main base, as well as from Eindhoven, Groningen and Maastricht/Aachen. In 1999, easyJet made an unsuccessful take-over bid for the financially-ailing airline. Air Holland was forced to suspend operations on 4 November 1999.

BASE BUSINESS AIRLINES ~ BASE REGIONAL AIRLINES

Established in 1985, to provide feeder services in the Netherlands, BASE subsequently expanded into the international field with scheduled service on a number of secondary routes. In Summer 1995, BASE operated IT charter flights from Maastricht to destinations in Ireland [Eire].

KLM ~ KONINKLIJKE LUCHTVAARTMAATSSCHAPPIJ (ROYAL DUTCH AIRLINES)

KLM has the distinction of being one of the world's oldest airlines, using its Amsterdam Schiphol Airport base as the focal point for its world-wide network. From the sixties until the early eighties, KLM was also active in the field of holiday charter operations on behalf of several Dutch tour operators. The airline progressively abandoned this field as it began to build up a closer relationship with Martinair and Transavia both of which were in a better position to meet tour operators' capacity requirements because of their specialist role in the IT charter business.

MARTIN'S AIR CHARTER (MAC) ~ MARTINAIR HOLLAND

The airline's history goes back to 24 May 1958 when its founder Martin Schröder set up Martin's Luchtvervoer Maatschappij (Martin's Air Charter). The first DC-3 was acquired in February 1960 and a second aircraft in July. The first IT charters were operated in Summer 1960 under contract to the tour operator CTI — later known as 'Centouri' — from Amsterdam to Palma and Jersey, C.I. For the Amsterdam-Palma run, the DC-3 took 5:30 hrs. The success of these holiday charter operations required the leasing-in of a KLM DC-3 for the 1961 summer season, followed by the introduction of a DC-4 in 1962.

The leading Dutch steamship company Nedlloyd took a share in MAC in 1963, which eventually rose to 49% by 1971. On 1 February 1964, the small air carrier Fairways Rotterdam was acquired and another two DC-3s were thus added to the MAC fleet. A Convair 340 and a DC-7C were acquired from KLM and this led to closer co-operation with the national airline, not only with regard to clearly defined 'spheres of interest' in the field of IT charter work but also in MAC acquiring more piston-engined aircraft from KLM whenever they were due to be replaced by new jet equipment. This working relationship between the two companies was further cemented when KLM took a 25% financial interest in the charter carrier in 1964. The acquisition of additional DC-7C long-range aircraft allowed MAC to start transatlantic charters to New York and Vancouver in 1965, and 74 flights were operated in the course of that summer season.

In early 1966, MAC had its CV-340s upgraded to CV-640 standards with turboprop engines and an increase in seating capacity from 49 to 56, with the CV-640 being introduced on the IT charter route Amsterdam-Corfu on 23 April 1966. However the IT charter market in the Netherlands came under pressure in 1966 when the new charter carriers Transavia and Netherlands Airways joined the more established companies KLM, MAC and Schreiner Airways in the charter market. MAC and Transavia eventually survived as the principal IT charter carriers in the Netherlands and later, in 1966, the company's name was changed to Martinair Holland.

Competitive pressure prompted Martinair to replace its propeller aircraft with jets and, because of its close relationship with KLM, the charter carrier was guided towards selecting Douglas jet airliners. Its first jet was a DC-8-33 leased, and later bought, from KLM and introduced into IT charter operations on 25 March 1967 on the Amsterdam-Palma route. In February 1969, the first of several new DC-9-33s was delivered to Amsterdam and a KLM Electra was on lease for that summer's IT charter work. September 1969 saw the addition to the fleet of a new Fokker F-28 jet which was initially used for holiday charters to secondary destinations in Scandinavia, Austria and France, but later relegated to Government use. By September 1971, Martinair was an 'all jet' airline. DC-10 jets were also added from November 1973 and, by December 1978, four aircraft were in service.

The fiercely competitive situation on the North Atlantic prompted Martinair to withdraw from that market for the Winter 1978/79 and Summer 1979 seasons. In February 1983, the first of two MD-82 jets was delivered followed, in 1984, by two Airbus 310s. Then, in 1987, Martinair added a 747 to its fleet (with a second aircraft in 1988) and introduced its first 767 in November 1989. In the course of 1995, four new MD11 long-range jets entered service. All 747, 767 and MD11 aircraft offer two classes of service, the exclusive 'Star Class' meeting the high standard of business class.

In 1990, Martinair began to switch some of its intercontinental services from a 'charter' to a 'scheduled' mode of operation, a formula which has since been extended to all intercontinental destinations except for Canada, Mexico and Thailand. In 1992, 1.56 million passengers were carried. For several years, Martinair has made efforts to extend its market, beyond its home country, to include neighbouring Belgium and Germany where tour operators and its own sales offices promote the carrier's intercontinental services from Amsterdam with elaborate advertising campaigns. To facilitate access to Amsterdam Schiphol Airport, Martinair instituted special coach links in November 1993 from Brussels and Antwerp in Belgium, and from Cologne, Dusseldorf, Essen, Dortmund, Bielefeld and Munster in Germany, since replaced by the use of rail links.

Martinair's annual pattern of operation is characterized by IT charters throughout Europe in summer with emphasis on the Canary Islands in winter, as well as year-round scheduled services world-wide. In early 1998, the airline became a fully-owned subsidiary of KLM. A policy change of the Dutch Government abolished KLM's long-established monopoly for services to the Netherlands West Indies, which allowed Martinair to start charter operations from Amsterdam to Aruba, Bonaire and Curaçao in April 1999.

NETHERLANDS AIRWAYS

This company became involved in holiday charter operations in 1966 but its activity was, however, short-lived and the carrier ceased operations.

NLM CITYHOPPER ~ KLM CITYHOPPER

KLM created its subsidiary NLM - later named NLM CityHopper in 1966 to provide service on a network of short-haul domestic and international routes focused on Amsterdam. In addition to its scheduled activity, NLM has also been involved with holiday charter operations in the early eighties, for which F-28 jets were used. In April 1991, the airline became KLM Cityhopper as a result of the merger of NLM CityHopper and Netherlines.

ROTTERDAM AIRLINES

In 1977, Rotterdam Airlines was set up for general and IT charter work. In co-operation with its main shareholder, the tour operator Cristoffel, the carrier operated holiday charters with Boeing 737-200 and F-28 jets. The company was later disbanded in October 1984.

SCHREINER AIRWAYS

Formed in 1945 as Schreiner Aero Contractor, the company acquired a DC-3 for general charter work in March 1963, joined by a second aircraft in September. At that time, the name change to Schreiner Airways coincided with the start of a scheduled service linking Amsterdam with Groningen and Hamburg. IT charter operations started with a fleet of DC-7C and F-27 aircraft in 1964 and, for a time, the carrier had the distinction of becoming the Netherlands' largest ITC operator. Due to the arrival of Transavia in the Dutch charter market, in addition to MAC and KLM, it was generally felt that there was too much competition for the relatively limited holiday traffic potential of the Netherlands. A merger of Schreiner and MAC was discussed, which MAC favoured but Schreiner did not. The carrier subsequently decided to withdraw from ITC operations effective 1 October 1967 and the IT charter contracts signed for the Summer 1968 season were taken over by Martinair.

TRANSAERO ROTTERDAM ~ FAIRWAYS ROTTERDAM

Transaero Rotterdam was granted its operating licence in January 1961 and was based at Rotterdam using DC-3 aircraft for passenger charters. The carrier's name was changed to Fairways Rotterdam in mid-1961 and, in addition to adhoc operations, IT charters were flown until 1963. On 1 February 1964, the company was acquired by MAC and it ceased trading in January 1966 when MAC took over its assets and air fleet.

TRANSAVIA LIMBURG ~ TRANSAVIA HOLLAND ~ TRANSAVIA AIRLINES

The charter carrier was set up in 1965 as Transavia Limburg, having been granted approval for operations from Maastricht and Rotterdam effective 3 January 1966. It was planned to initiate IT charter flying in summer 1966 but this did not work out since the existing charter carriers Schreiner Airways, MAC and KLM sought to block the newcomer's access to the Dutch holiday charter market. It was only on 14 November 1966 that this problem was overcome and IT operations could be started.

Transavia's initial fleet consisted of DC-3 and DC-6B equipment. Contracts with Dutch tour operators for the summer 1967 season kept two DC-6s fully occupied, and 21,000 passengers were carried in that year, with traffic increasing to over 60,000 passengers in 1968. On 26 June 1968, the first 707 was delivered to Amsterdam for use on North Atlantic charter routes but the long-haul jets were returned to its lessor at the end of the 1970 summer season. In December 1968, a contract was made with the French manufacturer Sud Aviation for the lease of two Caravelle jets, the first of which was delivered to Amsterdam on 17 February 1969. The deployment of the Caravelle jets proved a success and, by 1970, six aircraft were in service. By that time, the volume of passenger traffic had risen to 270,000. It was an important development in Netherland's holiday charter business when tour operators were given approval to offer short-duration holidays in the autumn and winter of 1971/72. Although these tours proved a great success, the Dutch Government decided that they were to be stopped with effect from 3 January 1972.

The Dutch steamship company KNSM took a 40% financial stake in Transavia in 1972 and this move enabled the charter carrier to initiate a fleet renewal programme whereby the costly-to-run Caravelle jets were replaced with Boeing 737-200s. This move was all the more important since numerous European airports began imposing night curfews and noise restrictions which affected older jets like the Caravelle. The first 737 was introduced into service in May 1974. Dutch tour operators, at that time, had a requirement for widebody aircraft and Transavia ordered an Airbus A300 with a capacity for 300 passengers. Shortly afterwards, however, the Dutch holiday charter market experienced a downward trend, resulting from tour price increases in the wake of the oil crisis. This prompted Transavia to decide against the further use of the Airbus.

In 1977, KNSM acquired the entire stock capital of Transavia. Peter Legro took over the leadership of Transavia in 1979 and he succeeded in turning the airline into a successful and profitable undertaking. The merger of the shipping companies Nedlloyd and KNSM resulted in Nedlloyd acquiring all the assets of Transavia in 1981. Prompted by the economic recession in Europe of the time, and overcapacity in the vacation charter market, Transavia leased out several of its aircraft and commenced operations under contract to KLM. Transavia launched scheduled service on the Amsterdam-London (Gatwick) route on 26 October 1986 and, in subsequent years, scheduled service has been launched on a number of popular holiday routes. This move was supported by the notable change in the travel requirements of holiday-makers and the gradual move away from the traditional package tour.

The airline's fleet modernization programme continued with the delivery of the first 737-300 on 4 March 1986. Early 1987 then saw the company's name changed to Transavia Airlines. By the end of that year, over a million passengers had been carried, a very notable achievement. On 22 November 1989, an intercontinental charter route was opened from Amsterdam to Mombasa, subsequently also served intermittently during the summer season.

As a form of co-operation, Transavia began to pool its technical resources with its competitor Martinair, and an agreement was also worked out with Sterling Airways for the common deployment of aircraft in line with seasonal requirements. In 1990, over 1.3 million passengers were carried and Transavia's market share on Mediterranean charter routes reached beyond 50%, whereas its share in the Dutch market overall stood at 42%. By taking over from the shipping company Nedlloyd, KLM increased its financial stake in Transavia from 40% to 80% in 1991, which led to a closer working relationship between the two airlines.

NORWAY

BRAATHENS S.A.F.E.

The Norwegian shipping concern Braathens founded the airline Braathens S.A.F.E. on 26 March 1946 for the purpose of operating long-haul services from Norway. This was intended to be on a charter and/or scheduled basis, in support of Norwegian shipping companies, to countries not served by SAS, with emphasis on South America and Asia's Far East. The Oslo ~ Hong Kong route was served from 5 August 1949 until the Norwegian Government cancelled Braathens' license for this route, in favour of SAS, on 25 March 1954. To broaden its sphere of operation, Braathens commenced scheduled domestic operations on 18 August 1952.

In the late fifties, holiday charter operations in Scandinavia were expanding at a fast rate and Braathens sought to gain a foothold in this business. Its first holiday charter series, using a DC-4, was launched in summer 1959 from Oslo to Palma de Majorca on behalf of Saga Tours. The carrier's involvement with the holiday charter business progressed satisfactorily so that, by 1961, over 36,000 charter passengers had been carried out of an annual total of 161,000. Additional DC-6B and DC-4 aircraft were acquired to meet tour operators' growing capacity requirements for subsequent summer seasons.

In 1965, Braathens' charter passenger total reached 145,467. An agreement with Atlas Resor for ITC flights from Sweden, in 1968, led to a close and long-term relationship with this tour operator. Strong competition from other Scandinavian air carriers involved in IT charter work influenced Braathens' decision to order three 737-200s in 1967 and five F-28s in 1968, eventually using both for scheduled domestic and international holiday charter services. Delivery of the 737-200 jets commenced on 31 December 1968 and they were introduced on IT charter routes from January 1969 onward. On 22 March 1969, the F-28 jet was introduced on the Stavanger-Rotterdam-Palma route. In 1970, Braathens started to co-operate with the Swedish tour operator Paddans, followed by Norway's Solreiser. In that year, 258,849 charter passengers were carried out of a company total reaching beyond a million for the first time.

By 1971, the Braathens fleet had been modernized to comprise four 737s, five F-28s and three F-27s. The last DC-6B-operated IT charter flight took place on 18 September 1973 on the Malmo-Salzburg route. Strong pressure from tour operators prompted more use of Braathens' 737 jets, especially on IT holiday flights to the Canary Islands, an important and highly competitive winter season market. On 1 January 1979, Braathens became the owner of Saga Tours but, in spite of this, the airline's charter activity was focused on Sweden to about 80%, the remainder on Norway. It is reported that, by December 1979, every third passenger departing on an international holiday charter flight from Norway, used Braathens. In 1980, the airline's IT market share in Norway stood at almost 31% and in Sweden at 25%. The number of Braathens' ITC passengers had grown to 618,317 in 1981.

Braathens took delivery of the first of two 767s on 23 March 1984, intended for use on high volume holiday charter routes from Oslo and Stockholm. Strong competition among air carriers involved in Scandinavia's IT charter business and a general slow-down in traffic created overcapacity in the market, which prompted Braathens to withdraw its 767s by September 1986.

Effective 1 November 1986, charter services were banned from Oslo's Fornebu Airport which led to the transfer of such operations to Gardermoen Airport. Whereas the bulk of Braathens' IT charter operations has, traditionally, been 'outbound' from Scandinavia, a limited number of 'inbound' charters have also been operated to various destinations in Norway. An important development in summer 1987 was the start of inbound IT charter series from Genoa to Oslo on behalf of the Italian tour operator Giver Viaggi, which proved a very successful venture that has led to its continuation in later years. Inbound summer charters have increasingly been operated from more continental European countries, especially France, but the volume of this seasonal inbound holiday traffic is, however, only a fraction of Braathens' outbound charter traffic.

In the late eighties, there was a marked downturn in Scandinavia's economic activity which prompted a sharp decline in demand for foreign holidays, causing a notable drop in the volume of IT charter traffic. In 1989, Braathens made the momentous decision to pull out of Sweden's IT charter market completely which was a contributing factor to the airline's charter traffic declining to 358,000 passengers by 1990. An important development was the expansion of Braathens into the field of international scheduled services, the first of which commenced on 2 May 1989 on the Oslo-Billund route. Since that time, the service pattern has been expanded. Service on selected routes from Oslo, formerly part of the holiday charter pattern, have meanwhile been switched to a 'scheduled' mode. In 1998, the 'S.A.F.E.' part of the airline's name was dropped.

BUSY BEE

The charter company Airexecutive Norway adopted its new name Busy Bee in September 1982. One 737-200 was, at that time, in use for general charter work and IT charters were also flown on behalf of Norwegian and Swedish tour operators. Busy Bee had the distinction of being the first charter carrier to initiate IT charters to the Greek island of Chios, on 15 May 1988, after the new airport was opened for international traffic. By early 1992, Busy Bee was in financial trouble which led to its bankruptcy, and all operations were terminated on 17 December 1992.

FRED OLSEN ~ FLYSELSKAP A/S

The Fred Olsen charter company was set up in June 1946 and its initial fleet was made up of three DC-3s acquired from US war surplus stock. From 1946 until 1948, there was close co-operation with DNL/SAS and after this, only general charter work was undertaken. In summer 1959, IT charters were operated from Malmo in Sweden with C-46 aircraft, but plans to operate also from Stockholm in summer 1960 season did not materialize since the Swedish CAA did not grant permission. In 1961, the carrier's main activity reverted back to cargo charter operations.

MEY-AIR TRANSPORT A/S

Mey Air was registered in 1970 and had a CV-240 in service until 1973, along with two 737-200s which were added in September and October 1971 for IT charters from Norway and Sweden. YS-11 aircraft were used in 1971 before financial difficulties forced the air carrier out of business on 22 February 1974.

NOR-FLY - NORRØNAFLY

The charter carrier Nor-Fly came into being as an air taxi operator on 14 November 1953, and began passenger charter operations commenced in summer 1959 after the acquisition of a CV-240 aircraft. Two Ambassador aircraft were bought from BEA in mid-1960 but were never delivered to the carrier. Four CV-440 aircraft were in service, over different periods, from March 1975 until January 1984, and Nor-Fly was the only European charter company to use a Convair CV-580 from January 1980 until November 1980. Passenger charter work was undertaken from Norway and Sweden. However the company suspended its activity in 1984 and was subsequently disbanded.

NORWAY AIRLINES ~ AIR NORWAY ~ AIR EUROPE SCANDINAVIA

Private investors launched Norway Airlines in 1987 for IT charter operations from such major cities like Stavanger, Bergen and Trondheim in western Norway, initially using a single 737-300 delivered on 22 January 1988 and a second 737 which was added in November 1988. IT charter operations were launched on 19 February 1988 but, soon after, the carrier ran into problems when its tour operator partner went bankrupt.

The two 737s were re-registered in the UK after the British tourism concern ILG acquired a 33% stake in the company. To emphasize being a partner in Air Europe's pan-European airline alliance, the Norwegian carrier's name was subsequently changed to Air Norway. This was followed by another name change to Air Europe Scandinavia in June 1989 in line with the airline's responsibility for scheduled operations between London and Scandinavia.

The demise of Air Europe in early 1991 caused the Norwegian company serious problems and its name was changed back to Norway Airlines and the two 737s were re-registered in Norway in April 1991. During 1992 the airline leased extra capacity in the form of MD-83 and MD-87 aircraft, but later in the year, unable to overcome its financial problems, the company was forced to suspend operations on 14th October and was finally liquidated in February 1993.

POLARIS AIR TRANSPORT

The charter company Polaris was established in 1964 for adhoc work, using DC-3 aircraft. IT charters were also flown after the acquisition of the first CV-240 aircraft in September 1966, followed by another two aircraft in 1967. However operations were suspended in 1969.

TRANS-POLAR

Set up in 1970, the charter company Trans-Polar specialized in IT charter operations from Norway, Sweden and Denmark to southern European holiday destinations. Three 720B aircraft were in use, the first of which was acquired on 4 June 1970, but the company suspended operations on 18 May 1971 due to financial problems and was declared bankrupt on 24 June.

TROLLAIR

Trollair used two DC-6B for charter operations from January 1972 until mid-June of the same year when its activity was terminated as a result of financial difficulties.

WIDERØE FLYSELSKAP

Formed in 1934, Widerøe is one of the oldest airlines in Norway. In the seventies, the company's activity became focused on the operation of scheduled domestic services along Norway's long coastline stretching beyond the Arctic Circle. The airline has, on several occasions, been involved with IT charter work, using Dash-8 aircraft for special flights from northern Germany to Norway.

POLAND

LOT POLISH AIRLINES

The Polish airline's history goes back to 1929 when it was established as a Government-owned company. After the Second World War, Poland commenced the re-construction of its air transport industry and LOT was in a position to resume scheduled domestic services on 1 April 1945, followed by international services on 11 May 1946. In the following years until 1955, LOT had built up an extensive network of services and was one of the leading carriers in Eastern Europe. Holiday charter flights to southern European destination were also operated. The addition of IL-62 jets allowed LOT to initiate series of charter flights to US cities in summer 1972, where there were large communities of Polish emigrants. Summer 1987 saw Warsaw linked by regular charters with the US destinations of Boston, Chicago, Detroit, Hartford/Springfield and Los Angeles.

The changed political situation in Poland has boosted foreign travel by its citizens and LOT has, since the early nineties, increasingly become involved with holiday charter operations in the Europe/Mediterranean region, which reached a share of 30% of all passengers carried. Plans are under consideration to form a charter subsidiary, to respond to the notable increase in the outbound package tour business from Poland. LOT carried some 120,000 charter passengers on 650 flights in 1996, and over 200,000 were expected for 1997.

PORTUGAL

AIR ATLANTIS (AIA)

Air Portugal/TAP created its subsidiary Air Atlantis (AIA) in 1985, holding a 75% stake. At that time, TAP had managed to secure only 10% of the inbound holiday charter traffic and the new company's aim was to win a larger share by linking secondary cities in Europe with Oporto, Lisbon and in particular Faro, Portugal's gateway to the Algarve holiday region, where AIA established its main base.

Air Atlantis commenced IT charter operations on 1 May 1985 with two 737-200s and a 707 transferred from TAP. In the first summer season, contracts were held for 55 flights a week from 43 airports in Europe and North America to destinations in Portugal. Gradually, AIA succeeded in winning a sizeable share in the inbound IT charter traffic from the UK and West-Germany, and carried over 2 million passengers between 1985 and mid-1989. In the year 1991 alone, the passenger total reached 594,000. In summer 1992, Air Atlantis had a maximum nine aircraft in use and operated up to 220 charter flights per week.

In the wake of the Portuguese Government's adoption of a more liberal air transport policy, Air Atlantis considered launching scheduled services but such plans were never put into effect. The company found it increasingly difficult to operate profitably and the decision was made to suspend operations in early 1993. AIA was wound up on 30 April 1993.

AIR COLUMBUS

As one of the investors in Air Columbus, formed in 1989, Sterling Airways held a 34% share and one of their 727-200s was transferred to the new carrier which started operations on 5 October 1989 with a London (Gatwick)-Faro flight. Plans called for Air Columbus to provide charter capacity to Madeira in winter and to the Algarve in summer. For the company's summer 1993 charter operations between Portugal and Canada, Air Columbus leased a 757 from June until September. The airline's passenger total reached 239,430 in 1993, but the bankruptcy of the German tour operator MP Travel Line in 1994 caused financial problems for Air Columbus and prompted the shut-down of the carrier in December 1994.

AIR LUXOR

Owned by the Mirpuri Group, Air Luxor launched IT charter operations in 1997. The fleet comprises one 260-seat TriStar which is supplemented in peak summer by other aircraft leased in according to demand. Inbound charters to Portugal and Madeira are flown from several European cities whereas the outbound flights operated on behalf of Portuguese tour operators, cover destinations in North America and the Caribbean.

AIR SUL

The privately-owned carrier Air Sul came into existence as a consequence of the liberalisation of air transport adopted by the Portuguese Government in 1988. Operations commenced in December 1989, with 737-200s, flying Portuguese expatriates working in Switzerland and other western European countries home for Christmas. Inbound IT charters were subsequently flown to Faro and Lisbon until January 1992

when the carrier was forced to suspend its activity for financial reasons, having tried unsuccessfully to secure additional financial support from its shareholders for future expansion. Its contracts with tour operators were taken over by AIA.

PORTUGALIA

Launched on 25 July 1988 as a joint-stock company, Portugalia started scheduled operations on 7 July 1990, after the Portuguese Government adopted its deregulation policies for air transport. The initial pattern of service covered the routes Lisbon/Faro and Oporto, followed by regular charter flights on the Lisbon — Funchal route from 28 July. In subsequent years, Portugalia operated regular IT charter services on several international routes prior to switching such operations to a scheduled mode, however IT charters are still operated on a limited scale. Portugalia's initial fleet consisted of two F-100s leased from GPA, used both for scheduled and charter services and, in 1993, 447,000 passengers were carried.

SATA

A company policy change in 1994 led to SATA Açores becoming involved with international holiday charter operations which led to the adoption of the name SATA International on 19 March 1998. The carrier obtained its AOC on 17 June and was granted rights for both international charter and scheduled operations in line with EC rules. In January 2000, the carrier launched charter operations between the Azores and both Canada and the USA, using its single A310 and, for the summer 2000 season, SATA International leased in three 737-300s.

TAP - AIR PORTUGAL

As Portugal's national airline, TAP has primarily been concerned with building up a pattern of scheduled services between Portugal, Europe and countries in Africa and America. In addition, since the late fifties, holiday charter work has been undertaken although the scope of this activity has been relatively limited. To secure a bigger share in the holiday charter traffic directed to Portuguese destinations, TAP founded Air Atlantis in 1985, which took over from its parent company all holiday charter operations. After Air Atlantis terminated its activity in early 1993, TAP again resumed holiday charter operations.

ROMANIA

JARO INTERNATIONAL

Jaro was founded on 1 August 1990 and commenced general charter operations on 5 August 1991. Using two 707 jets, Jaro serves a network of scheduled and charter services throughout Western Europe as far as Cyprus.

LINIILE AERIENE ROMANE (LAR)

In order to handle its growing inbound charter traffic to Romania, Tarom formed LAR as a subsidiary company using a fleet of BAC 1-11 jets. LAR became involved in some IT charter work but never actually took over the operation of such flights from Tarom.

In recent years, LAR has operated regular series of IT charters from a number of cities to Constanza during the Summer season and ski charters to Bucharest in Winter.

ROMAVIA

The Romanian Government created this company on 3 April 1991 for the purpose of operating flights for government officials as well as scheduled and charter services to a selected number of cities in Western Europe. Its fleet of transport aircraft consisted of three BAC 1-11 jets and one 707 in Summer 1996.

TARS ~ TAROM ~ TRANSPORTURILE AERIENE ROMANE

In 1946, the Romanian and Soviet Governments created the joint venture airline TARS, and this company functioned until 1954 when the Soviet participation was relinquished and a new national airline was formed under the name of Tarom.

Beginning in 1954, Tarom extended its network of scheduled services across Europe in line with the political ambitions of the Romanian Government which sought closer co-operation with western countries. At that time, plans were put into effect to develop the Black Sea coastal region near Constanza for international tourism. Since Europe was experiencing a tourism boom in the late fifties and early sixties, Tarom also became involved in the operation of holiday charter services to Romania which, similar to Bulgaria, also emerged as a popular new international tourist destination.

Tarom initially used IL-14 aircraft for its holiday charters, but after the addition of IL-18 turboprop airliners in 1962, charter traffic began to soar. Romania became a very popular holiday destination, especially for West-German nationals and, for the summer 1970 season, Tarom held tour operator contracts for a total of 1,200 flights from ten West-German cities to Constanza. The airline has made use of all the different types of aircraft in its fleet, including BAC 1-11, 707, IL-62 and TU-154 aircraft, for a widespread charter network across Europe.

Since the fall of the communist regime in December 1989, Romania has struggled to establish a market-orientated economy. A great impact has, however, been the fact that Romania lost some of its attraction as a holiday destination and this has had a general adverse impact on the inbound holiday charter market. Tarom's international charter traffic had declined to 50,626 passengers carried in 1998.

In October 1997, Tarom was re-organized as a commercial enterprise, the Romanian Government (through its Ministry of Transport) holding a 70% share, the rest being held by private investors. Tarom's fleet renewal is under way although, reportedly, there will be no financial support from official government sources.

RUSSIA

AEROFLOT

In the early sixties, the Soviet Government initiated a programme of tourism development aimed at attracting foreign visitors to the few selected 'open' cities of the country. Aeroflot became actively involved in this tourism promotion. Being able to use its new TU-104 jet and IL-18 turboprop airliners, Aeroflot arranged charter flight programmes from Western European cities to Moscow, Leningrad, Kiev and Sochi. These destinations in the Soviet Union came to be served on a regular basis throughout the summer season in subsequent years. The charter flight pattern was later on extended to take in departure cities in Britain, Ireland (Eire), France, Scandinavia, Italy and Switzerland.

AEROFLOT — RUSSIAN INTERNATIONAL AIRLINES (ARIA)

The vast organization of state-owned Aeroflot was dismantled in 1992 in the wake of the dissolution of the Soviet Union. A successor company was formed under the name of ARIA - Aeroflot Russian International Airlines which became the official international airline of the Russian Federation.

In addition to a growing network of world-wide scheduled services, Aeroflot is also involved with outbound holiday charters from Moscow have been developed in recent years, arranged by a growing number of Russian tour operators. Regular series of charter flights now serve popular resorts in Turkey, Greece, Italy and Spain but the switch from a 'charter' to a 'scheduled' mode is under way. Aeroflot works closely with Russian tour operating companies under the trade banner of 'Aeroflot Tour Group'.

AJT AIR INTERNATIONAL

AJT was established in 1991 and operates holiday charter services mainly to Italy and Turkey with IL-86 and TU-154 aircraft.

ALAK

Established in 1991, ALAK operates holiday charter services in co-operation with a number of Russian tour companies. Services cover popular destinations in southern Europe, including Bulgaria, Greece and Turkey using TU-154 aircraft.

AVIAPRIMA SOCHI AIRLINES

Aviaprima was based at Sochi-Adler Airport on the eastern Black Sea and came into existence in October 1992. Operations started on 3 March 1993 with a fleet of TU-134 and TU-154 jets. The scheduled network covered destinations in Russia, the Ukraine and Germany and, in addition, regular charter flights were operated to Turkey and the Middle East. The carrier ceased its activity in 1998.

DOMODEDOVO AIRLINES

Operating a mix of scheduled domestic and international services, Domodedovo Airlines has also operated IT charters from Moscow. The bulk of its international operations, however, consists of 'shopping' charter flights to destinations in China, Pakistan, India, the Middle East and Turkey.

KALININGRAD AIR

Kaliningrad Air is based at the Russian port city of Kaliningrad on the Baltic Sea. The carrier started to operate international holiday charter services in summer 1991, and its operations have since been extended to cover several cities in Germany with TU-134 and TU-154 aircraft in use.

KARAT

Karat is a Moscow-based company which operates scheduled domestic and international charter services with a fleet consisting of seven Yak-42 aircraft.

OREL AVIA

Orel Avia is the successor to Aeroflot's regional Orel Division and was set up in 1992. Using a fleet of Yak-42 and TU-204 aircraft, the carrier also serves holiday destinations in southern Europe.

PULKOVO AIR ENTERPRISE (AVIAPREDPRIYATIYA)

Pulkovo AP has succeeded the former Aeroflot Leningrad Directorate and is based at St. Petersburg (-Pulkovo) Airport. As one of Russia's largest airline companies, nation-wide services are in operation to numerous key cities in Russia and CIS member states. The international services have been run under the banner of Aeroflot but are increasingly taken over by Pulkovo AP in its own right.

The airline is also involved in the operation of holiday charter flights on behalf of local tour operators and the list of charter destinations is growing from year to year. In use are TU-134, TU-154, IL-86 and IL-96 aircraft.

ROSSIYA (RUSSIA)

The Government-owned airline Rossiya specializes in air transport operations for government departments throughout the Russian Federation and has a very large fleet of aircraft at its disposal, some of which are also used by ARIA. In recent years, seasonal holiday charter services have been started to destinations in the Mediterranean region.

TRANSAERO

Transaero has been in existence since December 1990 and its operations started in November 1991. The carrier is engaged in scheduled domestic and international operations. IT charter flights are operated from Moscow to popular holiday destinations in the Mediterranean region, reaching as far as the Canary Islands.

TRANSEUROPEAN AIRLINES

Transeuropean is a new company set up in 1997, to operate holiday charters with TU-154 aircraft from Moscow-Sheremetyevo to southern European destinations.

TYUMEN AIRLINES

As one of the successor airlines to Aeroflot's Tyumen Directorate, Tyumen Airlines has the task of providing service within the oil and gas rich region of Tyumen and maintaining services with important cities throughout Russia and the CIS. International charter services were in operation in Summer 1996, using Moscow as a technical stop on routes from Tyumen to southern European holiday destinations.

URAL AIRLINES

From its home base at Yekaterinburg-Koltsovo Airport, Ural Airlines operates regular charter services to European and Asian destinations, using TU-134, TU-154 and IL-86 aircraft.

VNUKOVO AIRLINES

Vnukovo Airlines came into existence in March 1993, succeeding one of Aeroflot's largest directorates. From its base at Moscow-Vnukovo Airport, the airline's far-flung network covers scheduled domestic and international destinations and, in addition, seasonal holiday charter services are operated to a growing number of destinations in southern Europe.

SLOVAKIA

AIR TERREX SLOVAKIA ~ AIR SLOVAKIA

Air Terrex Slovakia was established as a wholly-owned subsidiary of the Czech carrier Air Terrex in 1993. After its buyout by Slovak investors in August 1994, the company was re-named Air Slovakia. Holiday charter operations commenced in June with aircraft leased from Czech and foreign airlines, including a 727, TU-154 and IL-62.

AIR TRANSPORT EUROPE (ATE)

Air Transport Europe is a privately-owned company formed in 1992, initially undertaking only air rescue and general charter work. ATE commenced holiday charter operations in 1996 from Bratislava and Kosice, with leased TU-154 and its own TU-134A aircraft.

SLOVENSKE AEROLINIE (SLOVAK AIRLINES)

Holding the status of Slovakia's national airline since its foundation in January 1997, Slovak Airlines initiated scheduled international services from the capital Bratislava on 1 May 1998. Its fleet of three new TU-154 aircraft, leased from the Slovak Government, was also used for regular holiday charters from Bratislava and Kosice. However the company suspended its activity in November 1998 after a new Slovak government was installed.

TATRA AIR

Established in November 1990 in co-operation with Slov-Air and Crossair, Tatra Air is Slovakia's airline specializing in regional scheduled operations since 2 April 1991. Adhoc charter flying was undertaken and, in 1993/94, a charter series was operated to Skopje in Macedonia. In 1998, the company's fleet consisted of two SF-340s and a Yak-40 on lease from the Slovak Government Flying Service, but the carrier suspended operations in 1999.

SLOVENIA

ADRIA AIRWAYS ~ INEX ADRIA ~ ADRIA AIRWAYS

In September 1961, Adria Airways was set up at its home base Ljubljana to specialize in inbound charters to Yugoslav resorts on the Adriatic coast and operations started in May 1962 with two DC-6B aircraft. At that time, Adria Airways was the only private airline in Yugoslavia licensed to operate international services, if only on a charter basis, alongside the national airline JAT. Approval for charter flights to the USA was granted in May 1965 and Adria airways launched transatlantic service to several US cities with large Yugoslav ethnic groups. In summer 1967, the carrier made use of a JAT Caravelle for IT charters from West German cities to Dubrovnik.

Adria Airways went bankrupt in 1968 but was reconstituted with the financial backing of the powerful Interexport Group. In line with this new link-up, the airline's name was changed to Inex Adria. The first DC-9-32 jet was introduced into service in April 1969 with four more aircraft added by 1975. Also, from April until October 1972, a DC-8-55 was used for long-haul charters across the Atlantic, while in 1976 and 1997 DC-9-51 jets were added.

By the mid-seventies, holiday charter traffic to Yugoslavia was booming and Inex Adria was able to expand its pattern of operation to cover a large number of cities in Western and Northern Europe. The opening of new civil airports at Pula and Split facilitated access to the popular coastal resorts on the Adriatic.

In May 1986, the airline's name reverted back to Adria Airways when its link-up with the Interexport Group came to an end. 1989 was a bad year for Mediterranean tourism. This was further aggravated by the political and economic problems of Yugoslavia. Europe-originating charter traffic to Yugoslavia was down by as much as 18% and the Adria Airways charter activity returned to the level of 1984. The carrier made strenuous efforts to win scheduled traffic rights considered an essential base for future development, as they were expected to balance out variations in seasonal traffic. Adria Airways was granted the right to operate domestic services in 1970 and regular 'public charter' flights were also instigated for Yugoslav expatriates working in West Germany.

Since 1984, Dash 7 aircraft have been in use for scheduled operations and also for weekend holiday charters to secondary airports like Portoroz, Maly Losinj and Brac. In April 1989, the first of five A320s entered service. Towards the end of the eighties, through co-operation with Yugoslav and foreign tour operators, Adria's holiday charter operations came to be extended into the winter season, covering selected coastal resorts on the Adriatic.

In 1984, Adria Airways was one of the few charter carriers to win traffic rights for the Seychelles and a holiday charter service started from Ljubljana on 20 December 1989. What was so remarkable about this long-haul service was the fact that it was supported by connecting traffic

originating in southern Germany, Austria and Italy. The deteriorating political situation in Yugoslavia eventually led to Slovenia declaring her independence from the Federation on 25 June 1991 and, as a result, a warlike situation arose which forced the carrier to suspend its operations. After the situation returned to normality, Adria Airways took on the role as Slovenia's national airline and began to build up a network of international scheduled services focused on the capital Ljubljana.

One of the notable side effects of the new political situation was that the popular resorts on the Adriatic coast came under the jurisdiction of Croatia. For Adria Airways, this signified the loss of its earlier traffic base in so far as international holiday charter operations were concerned. Prior to 1991, they used to form an essential part of the carrier's activity and the potential for international holiday charters to Slovenia was therefore limited. In co-operation with local tour operators, however, Adria began to build up a pattern of outbound 'public charter' and holiday charter services to destinations in southern Europe and North Africa, reaching as far as the Canary Islands. In 1996, Adria Airways carried 595,000 passengers and its fleet stood at three A320, two DC-9-30 and two Dash 7 aircraft.

SPAIN

AIR PLUS COMET

The failure of OASIS led to the formation of the successor company Air Plus Comet in late 1996. This made it possible to continue serving New York and Caribbean destinations, on behalf of selected tour operators, similar to the operations of the former company. The new carrier started operations on 1 March 1997 with one Airbus 310, on behalf of Pullmantur and Club de Vacaciones.

AIR ESPAÑA ~ AIR EUROPA

On 17 February 1984, Air España was founded with the aim of securing a share of the inbound holiday charter flights to Spain arranged by foreign tour operators. The company came to be aligned with the Air Europe-sponsored 'Airlines of Europe Group' which led to the name Air Europa being adopted. On 21 November 1986, IT charter operations were launched with a flight from London to Tenerife

The airline's activity proved successful but the collapse of the UK tour organiser ILG and Air Europe in early 1991 caused serious problems. Within a short span of time, however, Spanish investors took on the entire shareholding of the airline, thus enabling the carrier to continue normal operation without any interruption. Within the framework of the ongoing liberalization of air transport in Europe, the Spanish Government granted Air Europa a license for scheduled domestic services which began on 1 November 1993 and for international services from November 1995. Several of the long-haul charter services were switched to a 'scheduled' mode in 1996, including Varadero and Salvador do Bahía (Brazil) then, on 19 May 1997, Air Europa started charter flights to Mombasa and Male.

Air Europa is part of the Grupo Air Europa which works closely with the agency Halcon Viajes, and with the tour operator Travelplan which specializes in holiday charters to long-haul destinations. The airline has built up a fleet of Boeing 737-300, 737-400, 757-200, 767-200 and ATP aircraft, reaching a total of 26 aircraft in Summer 1996, with a medium age of about 5 years.

AIR SPAIN

Launched in May 1966, Air Spain only initiated IT charter operations on 26 March 1967 with a Birmingham-Palma flight. Initially, the fleet consisted of two Bristol Britannias but DC-8-21 jets were introduced also in November 1971. By 1973, all Britannia aircraft had been phased out and following merger talks with Aviaco which proved unsuccessful, Air Spain was disbanded in February 1975.

ANDALUSAIR ~ ANDALUCÍA INTERNATIONAL AIRWAYS ~ OASIS INTERNATIONAL

Andalusair was founded by private investors in 1986, specialising in sub-contract work from Malaga until 1988 when it was disbanded. On 26 May 1988, OASIS International took over from Andalusair and holiday charter operations began with two MD83 aircraft. The summer 1988 season saw an expanded service pattern covering cities in Germany, Switzerland, Scandinavia and the UK.

The acquisition of an Airbus A-310 in 1992 permitted OASIS to initiate long-haul services in April from Madrid to Santo Domingo, Cancun and Varadero, followed by New York, Orlando, Punta Cana, Isla Margarita and Cartagena de Indias. In 1994, the carrier's fleet stood at six MD83, one MD87 and one A-310 aircraft and, during the period 1994/95, OASIS carried 1,064,566 passengers.

Towards the latter part of 1996, the airline ran into financial problems. Declared insolvent on 10 December 1996, its A310 was subsequently impounded at New York and the carrier ceased flying.

In early 1999, the name Andalusair was resurrected when a new carrier commenced ITC operations on 1 May, from its Malaga base, to the UK and Ireland, using an A320 leased from TransAer. However the carrier suspended operations at the end of July 1999.

AVIACO

The origins of Aviaco go back to 18 February 1948 when the company was founded in Bilbao, initially involved in the development of a network of secondary domestic and international services. After Spain's Instituto de Industria (INI) took a 67% share in the company in 1954 and Iberia the remainder, a close working relationship developed between the two airlines.

In 1972, Aviaco assumed the role of Iberia's 'charter arm' and the first inbound holiday charters were started from the UK to Spain. Using a fleet of Caravelle jets, Aviaco also made use of Iberia aircraft in line with traffic demand. The carrier's charter business was successful and developed to such an extent that an extensive pattern of charter services covered most of Europe. The airline's highest level of IT activity was reached in 1984 with 2.1 million charter passengers carried.

The increasingly fierce competitive situation in Spain that evolved because of the formation of several privately-owned charter companies, prompted the Iberia Group to re-define Aviaco's role. Large-scale withdrawal from the charter market followed and emphasis came to be placed on Aviaco's involvement in the area of domestic scheduled services. Aviaco was fully intergrated into Iberia in 1999.

B C M AIRLINES

The charter carrier BCM Airlines came into existence in 1996 to succeed failed Centennial and to continue IT charter operations in a similar manner. The carrier's first A320 aircraft was delivered on 14 November 1996 making BCM the first privately-owned Spanish airline to use this type of aircraft and, by mid-1997, three A320s were in service.

In line with a special agreement, BCM began to operate scheduled services on behalf of Iberia. However, faced with financial difficulties, BCM suspended its activity on 28 January 1998 and was acquired by the Grupo Viajes Iberia on 20 March 1998. Subsequent to this, on 12 April 1998, a successor company was formed under the name of Iberworld, taking over some of the assets of the former BCM and operations started with an Airbus A320, supplemented by a second aircraft in May 1998.

CANAFRICA ~ AIRSUR

Canáfrica was formed in April 1985 and launched international holiday charter operations on 1 May 1986, focusing on the important UK, Irish, German and Swiss markets. Then, in June 1988, the carrier's name was changed to Airsur, with a fleet consisting of a single examples of the DC-9-14, MD83 and DC-8-61 aircraft. The airline was in operation until 16 June 1990 when it was subsequently liquidated.

CENTENNIAL

Centennial was launched by private investors in 1993, taking over some of the staff of the defunct Spanish carrier Meridiana. With a fleet of three MD83 jets, Palma de Majorca was chosen as the main base and Centennial commenced international charter operations on 2 April 1993. By Summer 1995, Centennial had seven MD83s in its fleet and 45 destinations throughout Europe were served by IT charter flights mainly from Palma de Majorca.

In summer 1996, Centennial was also operating international scheduled services linking Dusseldorf, London, Manchester, Prague and Vienna with Palma de Majorca. Towards the end of that summer season, financial problems surfaced which caused Centennial to suspend operations on 25 October 1996 and the company was wound up shortly after.

EUROPEAN REGIONS AIRLINES (ERA)

Private investors launched ERA in 1996 as a niche airline to serve regional routes and offer a higher quality service than competing carriers. Vitoria was chosen as the airline's base for scheduled services which commenced on 21 December 1998. After the delivery of its second EMB RJ145, ERA began IT charter operations from Paderborn, Dusseldorf and Frankfurt to Palma. In summer 1999, weekend charters were also flown from both Geneva and Zurich to several destinations in Spain.

FUTURA (CÍA. HISPANO-IRLANDESA DE AVIACIÓN)

This company was registered on 28 December 1989, with Aer Lingus and the Banco de Santander holding a major share. Futura initially had one 737-400 at the start of international IT charter operations on 17 February 1990 using Palma de Majorca and Tenerife-Sura as its main base airports.

On 2 May 1997, the carrier commenced scheduled service on the Palma-London (-Gatwick) route under the name of Futura Direct. For the Summer 2000 season, Futura had a fleet of fourteen 737-400/800 aircraft in service.

HISPANIA

Former employees of failed Transeuropa formed Hispania in 1982, in the form of a co-operative. Four Caravelle 10R jets formed the fleet when IT charter operations started on 28 April 1983 mainly from West Germany and the UK to Spanish destinations. After the addition of a fleet of five leased 737-300s in March 1987, Hispania expanded its international charter network, its activity proving very successful.

In the financial year 1985/86, Hispania carried over 600,000 passengers, resulting from fleet modernisation and wider acceptance by European tour operators. Known for the quality of its service, Hispania won a substantial contract from the UK tour operator Thomson for the Summer 1987 season and throughout that summer, 40 European cities were linked with Spain. By Summer 1988, the company's fleet had grown to seven 737s and one DC-8, and a 757 was acquired in November 1988 for winter long-haul IT charters mainly from Helsinki and Tampere to the Canary Islands. Plans were made to replace the older aircraft in Hispania's fleet with new 737-300s and 757s in the spring of 1989.

Several interested parties, including Aer Lingus, wanted to buy into Hispania. This was considered a favourable move by the Spanish authorities since they were keen on expanding Spanish airlines' share in the European holiday charter market and joint ventures with foreign airlines were favoured. However none of these plans went through. Similarly, a take-over bid by Air Europe in June 1989 did not materialise either. The airline made plans for scheduled service on popular holiday routes to Spain, thus hoping to cater for the surging demand in 'seat-only' arrangements. This, however, could not be put into effect since the authorities did not favour additional Spanish airlines operating international scheduled services since this was, at that time, the monopoly of state-owned Iberia.

Financial problems surfaced which eventually led Hispania's fleet to be repossessed. Operations were suspended on 15 July 1989 and the company was declared bankrupt shortly after.

IBERWORLD

The assets of the failed charter carrier BCM were sold to the Majorca-based tour operator Viajes Iberia on 20 March 1998. The new in-house carrier subsequently formed, adopted the name Iberworld and operations commenced with A320 aircraft on 12 April 1998. For the summer 2000 season, Iberworld had five A320s in use on European charter routes while its single A310 operated to Caribbean points mainly from Madrid.

LAC ~ LÍNEAS AÉREAS CANARIAS

To meet the latent demand for travel between the islands of the Canary Islands archipelago, LAC was formed in November 1985, supported by local shareholders. Only non-scheduled inter-island services could be operated with two Viscounts since the operation of scheduled services was the monopoly of Iberia.

In November 1987, LAC entered the field of international charter operations with two leased MD83 jets, mainly from northern Europe to the Canary Islands then, in April 1990, LAC was merged with other Spanish companies to form Meridiana. A resumption of service under the original name of LAC was planned for December 1996 when a 727-200 was delivered to Palma de Majorca but technical problems, however, delayed a resumption of service.

LTE ~ LUFTTRANSPORT ESPAÑA

The West German airline LTU was involved in the formation of LTE on 29 April 1987. LTE initiated IT charter operations on 1 November 1987 with flights from Helsinki and Hamburg, and the carrier's annual operating pattern has developed in such a way that, during the winter season, holiday charter flights are operated to the Canary Islands and in summer to the Balearic Islands.

LTE has periodically operated charter flights on behalf of LTU and in 1992, the LTU Group acquired a 100% stake in LTE. Unlike several of the private Spanish air carriers, LTE has not yet ventured into the area of scheduled services.

The LTE fleet comprised three 757s by 17 April 1989 and has remained unchanged since then. From November 1987 until the end of August 1996, LTE carried over 5.6 million passengers and in 1996 alone, a total of 650,000 passengers was achieved.

MERIDIANA (CÍA. ESPAÑOLA DE AVIACIÓN)

In a bid to profit from increasing air transport liberalisation in Europe and the adoption of more liberal rules in Spain, Meridiana was established on 9 April 1990 through the merger of LAC, Universair and a taxi company named Euravia. The intention was to start scheduled services between selected Spanish and foreign cities and, in addition, holiday charter flights to Spanish destinations, using MD-83 and BAe 146-300 aircraft.

On 1 March 1991, Meridiana was merged with the Italian airline Alisarda and the common name of Meridiana was adopted on 1 September 1991. The Spanish part of the airline suspended operations on 16 October 1992.

NORTJET

Nortjet was the commercial name of the company Euskal Air formed in 1989, and International charter operations to Spain started in April 1989 from several cities in central Europe. The first of three 737-400s was delivered in April 1990 and a leased BAe146 was in use from October 1990 onward. Nortjet ceased operations on 6 February 1992 and its aircraft were repossessed by GPA.

SPANAIR

Formed in December 1986 as a joint venture between the Spanish tour operator Viajes Marsans (51%) and SAS Leisure (49%), Spanair commenced IT charter operations on 31 March 1988. The carrier's year-round flight pattern consists of IT charters mainly to the Balearic and Canary Islands, both from cities throughout Europe and from the Spanish Mainland. The first long-haul charter services started in 1991 to New York, Cancun and Puerto Plata, and Spanair ventured into the field of scheduled operations when a Madrid—Barcelona service was launched on 7 March 1994.

There is close co-operation with a number of leading tour operators in Europe, notably with the Scandinavian tour operator Vingresor for which, in 1988, Spanair provided over 10% of the capacity requirements.

When Spanair launched its charter operations in 1988, the fleet during the first summer season consisted of four MD83 aircraft. In February 1991, the first of two 767s was introduced into service, and by Summer 1995, Spanair's fleet had grown to sixteen MD82/83s and two 767s. Spanair carried 3,304,052 million passengers in 1995, with scheduled services accounting for 35.4% of the total. The airline's charter production figures in 1994 showed a 25% share for Spain, 17% for the UK and Ireland (Eire), 14% for Germany, 10% for both Italy and Norway and 9% for Sweden. At the time of the demise of OASIS, Spanair considered taking over the failed charter carrier's Airbus 310 aircraft but it did not fit into its fleet of Boeing and Douglas jets.

SPANTAX

This company was originally founded on 6 October 1959 as 'Aero Taxis de España' for general charter work in the Spanish Sahara region in support of oil drilling work. The name Spantax was adopted in 1960. Also in that year, the carrier started to fly Spanish tourists from the mainland to the Canary Islands.

In 1962 when Spain became increasingly popular as a tourist destination, Spantax took the decision to enter the international IT charter business. At that time, Spantax had a fleet of four DC-4s and the acquisition of two DC-7C aircraft from Sabena enabled Spantax to launch international holiday charters to Spain in Summer 1963. CV-990 jets considered ideal for the long-haul charter routes between Northern Europe and the Canary Islands, were introduced into the fleet in February 1967, and two DC-8-61 aircraft were in service by 1973 which enabled Spantax to extend operations to New York. In 1975, 1,592,965 passengers were carried and the fleet consisted of twelve CV 990s, three DC-8-61s and two DC-9-14s.

Several Scandinavian tour operators partially boycotted Spain for a time, and this affected Spantax badly. Furthermore, the competitive situation in the UK almost excluded Spantax from that market. By 1977, however, Spantax had managed to regain some of the lost ground and was again running IT charters from major European cities. The operating pattern of Spantax consisted of holiday charter flights to the Balearic Islands, in particular to Palma de Majorca, throughout summer, and to the Canary Islands in winter. Spantax had a close working relationship with the Spanish tour operator Club de Vacaciones and was thus involved in the early development of outbound charter travel from Spain.

The second fuel crisis, prompting yet another sharp rise in fuel costs, hit the airline hard since, at that time, Spantax had Europe's largest fleet of fuel-thirsty CV-990 jets in its fleet. July 1978 saw the start of IT service from Tokyo to Palma and Madrid, then the longest route served by a European charter carrier, in operation until 1980. The Madrid—Las Palmas G.C.—Santiago de Chile long-haul route was started on 7 May 1980, in co-operation with the tour operator Viajes Fortuna, and it was planned to include a stop at Montevideo but this was refused by the Government of Uruguay.

In Summer 1980, 16 European airports were served, and Zurich become the busiest foreign station with up to 13 flight departures a week. In that year, Spantax carried over two million passengers and thus became Spain's premier charter company. Financial problems hit Spantax due to its use of the costly CV-990 jets but, by 1983, most of these aircraft had been withdrawn, and only five aircraft remained in service. However the loss of so much capacity caused a considerable loss of business to competing charter carriers. The accident at Malaga in 1982, involving its DC-10 airliner, is claimed to have been 'the beginning of the end' of Spantax and German tour operators refused to deal with the carrier. Its image problem badly affected the company's standing in several other European countries and, to remedy the situation, Spantax switched to 737 and MD83 aircraft from November 1983 onward but the financial situation overall grew worse. Douglas and other parties in Europe offered financial support to help overcome the carrier's problems and there was talk about Lauda Air acquiring a share. On 29 March 1988, however, the company suddenly ceased operations and was subsequently liquidated. Over a period of 23 years, Spantax had carried a remarkable 24 million passengers.

TAE ~ TRABAJOS AÉREOS Y ENLACES

TAE was formed in April 1967 by the AZNAR Shipping Line, fully owned by the concern, using a fleet of two DC-7 aircraft for IT charter work effective that month. To meet foreign carriers' competition, one BAC 1-11 jet was acquired in March 1969 but, by February 1970, TAE had run into financial difficulties and was forced to suspend its activity.

It was only on 1 April 1973 that TAE resumed its holiday charter operations. Having been re-financed, TAE acquired a fleet of three DC-8-33 and two Caravelle 10B aircraft and, by 1975, TAE carried 412,617 passengers. Some 90% of its charter traffic originated from West-Germany, Dusseldorf being the principal departure city. In addition, the Netherlands and Sweden were important markets, with all inbound charter flights serving Palma de Majorca exclusively.

In late 1979, plans were announced for the replacement of its DC-8-33 with the -55 version. TAE had, at that time, almost given up the UK market for competitive reasons and concentrated its IT charter activity on Germany. On 12 January 1980, TAE was due to start a Las Palmas G.C.—Banjul service which could be used by West-German tour operators for routing passengers to the Gambia by way of the Canary Islands.

TAE ceased operations in November 1981, allthough the company had intended to resume international IT charter services for a third time but this did not materialise.

TRANSEUROPA

Established in July 1965, Transeuropa commenced adhoc charter work in September of the same year. In 1966, international IT charter services started with a fleet of three DC-7 aircraft, supplemented by two Caravelle jets from 1969 onward. Recommendations were made to merge all the privately-owned charter carriers in Spain into one company, because of their critical financial situation, but this did not materialize. In the case of Transeuropa, Iberia eventually took a 60% share and Aviaco 40%. After INI bought out this air carrier, Transeuropa was closed down in 1982.

UNIVERSAIR

In 1986, Universair was formed by the Spanish hotel group Hola which had extensive business interests in the Balearic Islands. Other shareholders were Air Belgium, the Belgian tour operator Sun International and the UK charter carrier Orion Airways. Universair started international IT charter operations to Palma on 5 July 1987 with a 737-300 seconded by Air Belgium and by 1988, the fleet had increased to three 737s. In 1990, the company was merged with other Spanish carriers to form Meridiana.

VIVA (VUELOS INTERNACIONALES DE VACACIONES S.A.)

On 24 February 1988, VIVA was set up as a joint venture by Iberia and Lufthansa, each airline holding 48% of the shares. The initial fleet comprised four 737-300 aircraft and VIVA's first commercial IT charter flight took place on 15 April 1988 from Nuremberg to Palma de Majorca.

Until the end of 1990, the company's chosen activity was IT charter flying while, on several occasions, also operating scheduled flights on behalf of Iberia. Lufthansa's share was relinquished on 14 September 1990 and VIVA thus became a fully-owned subsidiary of Iberia. When air transport liberalisation in Europe was gaining momentum, Iberia took the decision to change VIVA's operating mode from 'charter' to 'scheduled', the intention being for VIVA to take over the operation of some of Iberia's European routes with predominantly tourist traffic. VIVA's lower cost structure made it possible to offer scheduled services at lower fares, a move intended to compete more effectively with the growing number of Spanish and non-Spanish charter carriers.

VIVA's first regular scheduled flights commenced in November 1990 and this led to a scaling down of its charter operations to a minimum. After joining IATA as a fully-fledged member, VIVA's scheduled flights in Summer 1991 were operated under its own name and new links were established between Spain and Turkey, Tunisia, Egypt and Israel, within the framework of new strategic plans set up by the Iberia Group. In February 1995, however, VIVA ceded to Iberia its scheduled services to North African and Middle Eastern destinations as well as its Malaga pattern of scheduled flights to European cities. April 1996 saw the airline giving up all its scheduled operations in favour of Iberia and VIVA's status reverted back to that of a charter carrier. This change was not popular with VIVA staff in view of the fact that profits had been achieved on many routes, which Iberia had previously been unable to do. In 1995, VIVA carried 962,001 passengers and had a fleet of nine 737-300 aircraft. In the end it was decided to close down the carrier and its integration into Iberia was completed by March 1999.

SWEDEN

AIR OPERATIONS OF EUROPE ~ AIR OPERATIONS INTERNATIONAL

Set up in 1992, Air Ops started charter operations with two TriStars in May 1993. Apart from holiday charter work from Sweden, the carrier also operated from the UK mainly on the basis of providing back-up capacity for other charter carriers.

The company ran into financial problems and services were suspended in 1995. with all aircraft remaining idle throughout the Winter of 1995/96. In January 1996, the company was offered for sale by its owners, the Dutch Bank ING and eventually, Air Ops was sold back to its original founder. After financial re-structuring, the air carrier was re-born on 17 April 1996 as 'Air Operations International'. With a fleet of three TriStars, two of them based at London-Gatwick and one in Germany throughout Summer 1996, the carrier planned to operate holiday charter services under its own name. Operations were however suspended again on 2 May 1996.

BLUE SCANDINAVIA ~ BRITANNIA SWEDEN AB

A large-scale re-organisation of Transwede took place in 1996 when the Norwegian airline Braathens acquired a share in the Swedish airline. On 28 October 1996, the new charter carrier Blue Scandinavia was created as a separate company within the Transwede Group to operate holiday charters on behalf of the Transpool group of tour organisers. In Summer 1997, the airline's fleet comprised three 757s and one TriStar, and additional aircraft in the form of a 727, 737 and M83 were leased in to handle peak season traffic. In early December 1997, the airline's name was changed to Britannia Sweden AB, after the British travel group Thomson acquired Fritidsresor, the owner of Blue Scandinavia.

EUROFLIGHT

This carrier operated a series of charter flights with Beech 1900 aircraft, between June and the end of September 1994, from Luleå in northern Sweden to Murmansk in Northern Russia, for small enthusiast groups venturing on fishing tours on the Kola Peninsula.

FALCON AVIATION ~ FALCON AIR

After its formation in 1996, Falcon Aviation specialized in air taxi work, then the acquisition of three Electra Turboprop aircraft in 1986 allowed the carrier to venture into the air freight business. Falcon was acquired by Sweden's Post Office in 1987/88 to take over responsibility for the overnight mail delivery system within the country. The Electra aircraft were replaced by three new 737-300QC aircraft between June and December 1991 and, after a licence for IT holiday charter services was granted in June 1994, operations were launched in co-operation with Swedish tour operators. The name Falcon Air was adopted in November 1997.

INTERSWEDE

Founded in 1971, Interswede acquired two DC-8-51 jets in December of that year. Its technical base was set up at Malmo and IT charter operations commenced on 7 February 1972. However they did not turn out to be a success and Interswede ceased all flying on 28 February 1972.

LINJEFLYG

In the years following its creation in 1957, Linjeflyg operated scheduled domestic services in Sweden, focused on the capital Stockholm. The airline entered the jet era with F-28s which were placed into service on 11 May 1973 and these aircraft were also used for special IT charter operations from Winter 1973/74 onward. The first services operated were to Geneva and Munich for skiing holidays. The range of the F-28 jet only allowed Linjeflyg to operate holiday charters to medium-haul destinations and it was only when the longer range 737-500 aircraft were added to the fleet in June 1990 that Linjeflyg could extend its charter routes to further away destinations in southern Europe. 737 jets were first used to Malaga, Rome and Zakynthos in Summer 1990. On 1 January 1993, SAS took over Linjeflyg and all its operations were integrated into the SAS system.

NORDAIR SWEDEN

The Danish charter company Nordair formed Nordair Sweden in April 1961 for ITC operations. This was done to meet an increasingly difficult situation created by Sweden's authorities with regard to international holiday charter operations.

NORDIC EAST ~ NORDIC EUROPEAN AIRLINES

Founded in 1991, Nordic East commenced IT charter operations from Sweden in the summer season of 1991. The Scandinavian country's membership of the European Union allowed the carrier to operate holiday charter flights from Germany in Summer 1995.

As a result of the deregulation of domestic air transport in Sweden, Nordic East started a domestic service from Stockholm to Ostersund in November 1995, followed by service on the Stockholm—Brussels route on 29 September 1996. To highlight the company's future commitment to international operations in the liberal air transport market promulgated by the EC, the company's name was changed to Nordic European Airlines in July 1996. For its Summer 1997 operations, Nordic operated a diverse fleet of aircraft, including Boeing 737/400s and 500s and one TriStar. The carrier was sold to a Swedish/Greek consortium in early 1997 with operations ceasing in March 1998.

NOVAIR ~ NOVA AIRLINES AB

Formed in early 1997 by its owner tour operator Apollo Resor, Novair had an initial fleet of one TriStar and A320 each to launch holiday charter flights on November 1997 to the Canary islands, London and Phuket. Novair has been a very successful operator so far and all the major cities in Sweden, Norway and Denmark serve as departure points for IT charter flights. The fleet composition has changed to three 737/800s and two TriStars, but two Airbus A330s, the first of which was placed into service in the 1999/2000 winter season, are intended to replace the TriStar fleet. Novair carried 465,000 passengers in 1999.

OSTERMANAIR

Ostermanair started holiday charters in the autumn of 1963, using a DC-6 and two DC-7 aircraft. On 30 November 1965 the carrier was merged with Aero-Nord to form Internord.

SKYLINE

In 1971, the charter carrier Skyline was formed and Malmo was chosen as its base. Two Viscount 784 aircraft were bought, supplemented by two Viscount 814s in late 1975. IT charter operations started in 1972, mainly to Germany, Austria and England but the charter carrier suspended its operations in 1977.

SAS ~ SCANDINAVIAN AIRLINES

On 1 January 1993, Linjeflyg was merged with SAS and the existing charter contracts with tour operators were taken over. Since then, SAS has continued to operate a limited pattern of seasonal holiday charter services, both during the summer and winter, from several major cities in Denmark, Norway and Sweden, using some of its spare aircraft capacity on Saturdays and Sundays. In Summer 1997, SAS served a total of 12 destinations with MD80 series aircraft and the new MD90.

STERLING AIRWAYS AB

Denmark's Sterling Airways formed the wholly-owned subsidiary company Sterling Airways AB in late 1970, coinciding with the decision to enter the holiday charter market in Sweden. The new company took over a DC-6B of its parent and acquired an Electra airliner from defunct Falconair.

SUNWAYS AB SWEDEN

Sunways AB was the Swedish branch of the Turkish carrier of the same name. It was established in 1994 to operate holiday charters on behalf of its affiliated tour organiser Express Resor. With a fleet of four 757-200s, Sunways AB successfully established itself in major traffic generating markets of northern Europe. In close co-operation with the Turkish airline Sunways Airlines, some two million passengers were carried between April 1996 and March 1997. Unexpectedly, the airline terminated its operations at the end of September 1997 because of financial problems within the parent Tursem Group.

TRANSAIR ~ TRANSAIR SWEDEN

Formed in 1951 as a successor to Nordisk Aero Transport (NAT), Transair initially undertook contract flying for Swedish newspaper companies out of Stockholm. A DC-3 was introduced on 6 April 1953, then Transair received its first C-46 on 1 April 1957, fitted out for 56 passengers, followed by additional aircraft later in the year. This allowed the launch of holiday charters in Summer 1957 on behalf of the Swedish tour operator Vingresor, from Transair's home base at Malmo. Outbound and inbound connections were provided for Stockholm and this facility was extended for Gothenburg and Oslo in Summer 1965.

The C-46 fleet grew to six aircraft but they proved costly to run and Transair faced financial difficulties as a result. A new management structure was set up in 1959 and the company's affairs subsequently improved for the better. The three DC-6B airliners acquired from SAS were

introduced into service from February 1960 onward and more aircraft were added in 1961, replacing C-46 aircraft formerly used for passenger charter work. The DC-6 proved popular with holidaymakers since it was no longer necessary to make several technical stops on the longer charter routes to holiday destinations in southern Europe as used to be the case with the C-46. Transair carried over 70,000 passengers in the Summer 1960 season.

In Summer 1961, Transair operated IT charter flights from Copenhagen for the first time. However, a proposed charter series from Malmo to Nairobi was not approved by the Swedish authorities since SAS was providing scheduled service to that destination at that time. The Transair fleet had grown to nine DC-6B, ten C-46 and one DC-3 aircraft in 1963. It was in that year that SAS acquired Transair but this ownership was short-lived as SAS sold the charter airline to the Nyman & Schultz travel group in June 1964. In November 1964, Transair started to replace its DC-6B fleet with DC-7B airliners which reached a total number of ten in subsequent years. At the beginning of the sixties when scheduled airlines started to introduce new jet aircraft, charter carriers found it necessary to look for suitable jet equipment in order to remain competitive and meet travellers' preference for jet travel. Transair bought three Boeing 727-100 aircraft named 'Sunjets' and the first two were delivered in November 1967. The 727s came to be used from Stockholm, Gothenburg and Malmo to all the major holiday destinations across Europe, and Transair also initiated jet service from Sweden's smaller provincial cities like Luleå, Umeå and Jonkoping. Since the range of the 727 was limited, technical stops were routinely made at Billund, Bordeaux or Nantes on the longer charter routes to the Canary Islands.

As a result of a special agreement in 1968, Transair came to operate its 727s on behalf of Scanair. This co-operation contract was renewed on 25 September 1974, and SAS finally bought the 727 jets on 1 October 1975, thus effectively taking over Transair. On 6 September 1981, Transair operated its final IT charter flight on the Malmo—Rhodes route and was subsequently placed into liquidation.

The Swedish charter carrier Transair wanted to become involved in Spanish charter air transport in view of the burgeoning holiday traffic to that country. There were no objections from the Spanish authorities concerning this venture and interested parties were found to invest in the proposed company. Initially, operations were planned from Spain to South America and, later on, also to Cuba, but Iberia objected to the formation of this new carrier and, as a consequence, plans for Transair de España did not materialize.

TIME AIR SWEDEN

Formed in 1990, Time Air used a fleet of 737, TriStar and DC-8-61 aircraft for IT charter operations from Sweden and Finland from March 1991 until 28 February 1993, when the carrier suspended its international services due to financial problems.

TRANSWEDE ~ TRANSWEDE AIRWAYS AB ~ TRANSWEDE LEISURE AB

This carrier's history goes back to 1976 when it was set up as a charter company under the name of Aerocenter Trafikflyg. Renamed Swedair in March 1983, the carrier also operated under contract to SAS then, in early 1985, the name Transwede was adopted.

The possibility arose to operate IT charter flights on behalf of a new tour operator based in Western Norway. Transwede acquired a Caravelle jet and operated its first holiday charter services from Haugesund and Stavanger to Palma on 31 March 1985. By April 1986, four Caravelle aircraft were in use to serve an expanding charter network and a maintenance agreement was concluded with Finnair. In September 1986, Transwede took delivery of its first MD83 jet and by September 1987, three aircraft were in service. The range of this aircraft permitted non-stop flights from Stockholm to Las Palmas in the Canary Islands, a decisive factor determining the success of any charter carrier. Transwede's activity in the field of holiday charter operations expanded after close co-operation was established with the Swedish tour operator Fritidsresor.

The addition of MD87 aircraft in June 1988 enabled Transwede to launch trans-Atlantic charter operations to Fort Lauderdale, Florida, with the right to carry traffic in both directions. In 1989, long-haul charters were started to Barbados and Miami, with the aircraft usually making technical stops at Reykjavik (Keflavik) and Gander as required.

Transwede succeeded in establishing itself as one of Scandinavia's leading charter carriers. In addition, it ventured into the field of scheduled international operations when, on 31 January 1991, a Stockholm—London (-Gatwick) service commenced. After the Swedish Government adopted deregulation rules for domestic air services, Transwede entered the scheduled domestic market in mid-1992.

In 1993, Transwede took delivery of Fokker F-100 jets and carried a total of 1.3 million passengers in that year, including some 600,000 on holiday charter flights. In August 1996, the Stockholm—London service came to be operated on a joint basis with Finnair.

1996 saw a change in Transwede's company structure as a result of the Norwegian airline Braathens taking a 50% share. The scheduled sector was allocated the name 'Transwede Airways AB', and the charter sector 'Transwede Leisure AB'. Further re-organisation took place in October 1996 when a new air carrier was formed under the name of Blue Scandinavia, taking over the bulk of the holiday charter work. Transwede has continued to operate a limited number of holiday charter flights for which F-100 and 737-500 aircraft are used .

SWITZERLAND

AERO JET

Beginning in Summer 1992, Aero Jet used a single Caravelle jet for IT charter operations from Sion. Because of operational restrictions imposed by the Swiss authorities with regard to the use of Caravelle jets on account of their noise emission, effective from 1 April 1995, the company had difficulty retaining its operator's licence. Aero Jet was able to operate its full summer 1995 program but, unable to secure finance for the acquisition of a 737 towards the end of 1995, the carrier suspended operations and was placed into liquidation.

AFRICAN SAFARI CLUB (ASC)

This charter carrier was set up in 1967. In Summer 1997, ASC had departures from Basel and Zurich in Switzerland; from Berlin, Frankfurt, Munich in Germany and from Vienna in Austria. Flights were mostly operated nonstop to Mombasa, the carrier's prime destination in Africa, but on selected dates a stop was made at Luxor, Egypt, which offered the alternative of combining a seaside holiday on the Indian Ocean with a visit to upper Egypt and a cruise on the Nile

AIR ALPES

This company was set up on 27 February 1996 and chose Sion as its main base. Using ATR 42 turboprop aircraft, IT charter services commenced on 26 May 1996 on the Sion-Tunis route and in Winter 1996/97, ski charter flights were operated from Rotterdam and Mönchengladbach to Sion. However the company suspended operations effective 1 March 1997 and went into liquidation.

AIR CITY GENÈVE ~ AIR CITY S.A.

The executive charter company Air City Genève was formed in early 1987 by private investors and Geneva was chosen as its main operating base. To expand its range of activity, the Sion-based company Jonathan Airways was bought out later in the year and the new name Air City S.A. was adopted. March 1988 saw the introduction of a 99-seat Caravelle 10B3 for adhoc passenger charters and, after operating on behalf of Air Inter for a couple of months, regular IT holiday charters commenced in the middle of the year. The addition of a second Caravelle in May 1989 led to an expanded IT charter program, and the operations base was transferred to Basel/Mulhouse. In 1989, 102,000 passengers were carried and, between March 1988 and October 1990, the passenger total reached over 300,000. In summer 1990, Air City began to offer 'seat-only' arrangements on some of the routes served by regular holiday charter flights. Financial difficulties arose as did problems over the use of the Caravelle jets, forcing Air City to suspend operations at the end of the Summer 1991 season.

AIR ENGIADINA

Formed on 22 April 1987, Air Engiadina was conceived as a regional airline to link secondary cities in central Europe from Switzerland not served by the national airline Swissair. Service to a number of foreign destinations has meanwhile been started and Air Engiadina has been instrumental in placing the Swiss capital Bern on the air route map as its DO-328 airliners are ideal for operations from this airport.

Air Engiadina initiated holiday charter operations in Summer 1995 after acquiring its third Dornier 328. In 1999, the airline carried a total of 125,000 passengers, and 7,000 on charter flights. The company is now known as KLM alps/Air Engiadina.

BALAIR ~ BALAIRCTA ~ BALAIRCTA LEISURE

Balair was originally launched as a scheduled airline on 2 September 1925 under the name of Basler Luftverkehrs-Aktiengesellschaft, and became known under its present name on 1 April 1926. The company's independent activity came to an end when it was merged with Ad Astra on 1 January 1931 but, after World War II, the name Balair reappeared in June 1948 when a pilot school was set up at Basel.

In the early fifties, Basel assumed a leading role as Switzerland's principal gateway airport for British charter carriers. This increasingly caused concern because the continuously growing inbound charter traffic was handled almost exclusively by foreign air carriers. A momentous decision was taken to alter Balair's sphere of activity by expanding into holiday charter operations, an important move to secure a share of the incoming traffic and to initiate IT charter operations from Switzerland on behalf of the country's major tour operators. Balair initiated IT charter flights in June 1957 with a 36-seat Viking, from Basel to Scandinavia, in co-operation with the local tour operator ESCO Reisen. The initial success of Balair's ITC operations led to the acquisition of a second Viking in May 1958 and, in that summer, IT charters were flown to holiday destinations across Europe and as far afield as the Canary Islands and the Middle East.

A new management structure was created in 1959 and Swissair acquired a 40% share in Balair which resulted in close and long-term co-operation with the Swiss national airline. April 1959 saw the addition of the first of two DC-4 aircraft from Swissair, but by 1961, the competitive situation for Balair had reached the point that, due to jet aircraft being used also for IT charters by other charter airlines, it became necessary to start modernising the fleet. Swissair transferred two DC-6B airliners, the first of which was delivered in December 1961, followed by a second aircraft in 1962. At that time, Basel still handled about a third of Balair's charter traffic. By 1963, the DC-4 aircraft began to be withdrawn and a 44-seat turbo-prop F-27

came to be phased in which proved a popular aircraft with tour operators. Balair's operating pattern had developed in a way that outbound IT charters were flown on behalf of several Swiss tour operators and inbound charters mainly from the UK to Switzerland.

In 1965, Balair carried 129,000 passengers. A series of long-haul charters was operated to Johannesburg, followed by IT charters to Bangkok from December then, in 1966, Balair commenced IT charter operations to Nairobi/Mombasa. 1967 proved eventful for Europe's air charter business as a whole in that the political situation in Greece, coupled with the outbreak of the Arab/Israeli war in October, effectively ended holiday charter flights to the Middle East, impacting negatively on traffic to that region. The crash of a Globe Air Britannia in April 1967 produced so much adverse publicity for charter companies in general that Balair's traffic was also affected. When Globe Air closed down in October of the same year, Balair took over some of the failed airline's contracts with Swiss tour operators. On 28 March 1968, Balair initiated jet operations with a CV-990 on lease from Swissair, followed by its own DC-9-33 jets in May 1970. Balair's charter activity shifted away from Basel to Zurich which became the focus of all long-haul operations. On 1 April 1971, a DC-8-55 was acquired from Swissair to replace the CV-990, followed a year later by a DC-8-63.

Meanwhile, long-haul IT charters developed so rapidly that this sector of Balair's operations reached 50% of the company's activity by 1972 but, in turn, the low level of profitability on short to medium-haul operations caused concern. Serious problems arose from the steep rise in aviation fuel prompted by the Arab/Israeli war of 1973. The introduction of night curfew restrictions at Swiss airports introduced from 1 November 1974, combined with recurring ATC problems in western Europe due to congestion, exerted a negative impact on Balair's performance. Charter companies generally came to face stronger competition from scheduled airlines, not only because of lower promotional fares on long-haul routes but also because of the widespread deployment of jet aircraft. On the positive side, Balair's growing long-haul charter traffic required more extensive use of the large-capacity DC-8-63s which were successfully deployed on the New York and Los Angeles routes from Zurich. However the July 1974 political crisis in Cyprus, involving Greece and Turkey, caused widespread disruption and cancellation of the airline's charter programme to that region. A DC-10 was added in February 1979. That year saw the adoption of the US Government 'deregulation policy' which, looked at in retrospect, also affected Balair's long-haul service pattern to the USA in line with new bilateral air transport agreements between Switzerland and the States. Furthermore, Balair had to revise its operating pattern to the Caribbean, even cancelling service to selected destinations because of losing traffic to British Airways and Air France, as a result of tour operators switching their capacity requirements to scheduled airlines because of their ongoing policy to offer lower tariffs approaching charter levels.

Balair placed new MD81 aircraft into service in 1982 and, by 1985, the carrier's charter traffic had developed in such a way that only the short to medium-haul routes showed increases whereas long-haul operations only flourished to selected destinations. March 1986 saw Balair introducing an Airbus 310 to North America and on high-traffic charter routes in the Europe/Mediterranean region, replacing DC-8-63s. Intense competition from numerous foreign charter carriers reduced Balair's overall share in Swiss charter traffic to 34% by 1987, and in line with other European charter companies' concern for the quality of service offered on charter flights, Balair introduced the 'Relax Class' on long-haul services in Winter 1989/90. In the case of flights to Caribbean destinations, a new marketing initiative allowed passengers to fly out to one destination and return from another. The addition of larger capacity aircraft has prompted Balair to focus its IT charter operations on Zurich, although some services to popular holiday destinations with high demand have periodically also been operated from Basel and Geneva.

Since the overall activity of both Balair and CTA were closely integrated with that of parent Swissair, the two separate companies were merged into one unit named BalairCTA in May 1993, combined charter operations having started at the beginning of 1993.

Adverse conditions for IT holiday charter travel, coupled with the fierce competitive situation with regard to foreign charter companies serving Switzerland, prompted Balair/CTA to terminate independent operations at the end of the Summer 1995 season. Long-haul IT charter operations have since continued to be operated with Airbus A310 aircraft, under the Swissair banner, using the BB prefix to retain international traffic rights. The Balair/CTA short to medium-haul fleet was combined with that of Crossair at the start of the Winter 1995/96 season and BalairCTA Leisure was set up on 1 November 1997. In September and October 1999, the carrier's Airbus A310s were replaced with two new 767-300ER aircraft, first introduced on the Zurich-Sharm el Sheikh charter route on 6 October 1999, and fleet modernization has continued with the addition of two new 757-200ER aircraft beginning on 28 April 2000

CHARTER - LEISURE

In line with streamlining its involvement with the leisure sector, Swissair created its Charter-Leisure subsidiary in the autumn of 1995, to function as a separate unit for the operation of holiday charter flights. Reverting to the name of Balair, this unit was to take over the charter operations from Swissair which had been in charge of this sector when Balair/CTA was merged into the parent company.

Swissair reportedly was unable to operate its long-haul charter services profitably. The new company is expected to be able to be more cost effective and thus become more competitive vis-à-vis the numerous foreign charter carriers seeking a bigger share of the Swiss outbound market. Cost savings are also expected since crews will not be bound by employment contracts with Swissair.

CROSSAIR

Created on 14 February 1975, Crossair was conceived as an airline for short-haul operations to complement the route network of Switzerland's national airline Swissair. Scheduled operations started from Zurich on 2 July 1979, with Crossair's initial fleet comprising Swearingen Metroliner feeder aircraft, with the larger SF-340s phased in from June 1984 onward.

In addition to serving a growing short-haul network, Crossair commenced IT charters in Summer 1981. The addition of SF-340 airliners to

the fleet in June 1984 made it possible to expand the network of holiday charter services to more destinations in France, Italy, Spain, Yugoslavia and Greece. Crossair is the only airline contracted by tour organisers to operate Summer IT charters to provincial destinations in France, including Lannion, Dinard, Biarritz, Rennes and Vannes, cities which do not normally form part of the network of Europe's holiday charter services.

In June 1990, delivery of the BAe 146 'Jumbolino' jets commenced and these were first used on IT charter flights from Zurich. 1993 saw the delivery of four Avro RJ85 jets then, in 1994, Crossair also started to use its new SF-2000 airliners on holiday charter routes.

When Balair/CTA was wound up towards the end of 1995, Crossair was given the responsibility for operating short to medium-haul IT charters within the Swissair Group. For this purpose, MD82/83 jets were taken over to join the airline's fleet of SF-340, SF-2000 and BAe 146 aircraft. All these changes occurred at a time when the demand for foreign holidays experienced a downward trend and Crossair's BAe 146 jets were phased out when the last Avro RJ85 was delivered on 23 July 1996. In 1996, Crossair's charter passenger traffic reached 745,329 out of a total of 3,974,676 passengers carried.

CTA ~ COMPAGNIE DE TRANSPORTS AÉRIENS

Swissair was involved with the formation of CTA on 28 September 1978 as a successor to the failed charter company SATA, and CTA initiated IT charter operations on 2 November of the same year with a fleet of three Caravelle jets. The charter route network was subsequently extended to cover most of Europe's popular holiday destinations and a daily charter service to London (Gatwick) was in operation throughout Summer 1980. In the early period, the carrier's activity was focused on the weekend, with 60% of all flights operated from Friday to Sunday night but, in later years, considerable improvement was made with regard to balancing the carrier's activity more evenly throughout the week. The company was a successful venture and passenger traffic increased from 161,770 in 1979 to 272,957 in 1983, then to 322,000 in 1992, the last year of CTA's independent activity.

The CTA Caravelle jets proved popular with tour operators and passengers alike, enabling the carrier to offer direct charters to some of the smaller holiday destinations around the Mediterranean. Competitive aspects, however, coupled with the need to comply with rules relating to noise abatement, made it necessary for CTA to replace its Caravelles with modern aircraft. MD87s were chosen and the first aircraft was delivered on 7 April 1988, and introduced on the Zurich-Antalya charter route on 30 April. At the start of the Summer 1989 season, CTA had phased out its Caravelles and was only using MD87s.

Excellent results were achieved in 1990 but the Gulf War crisis put an end to a hitherto positive development of the company. An especially negative impact was the sharp increase in fuel costs which CTA was able to pass on to tour operators only from December 1990, having had to absorb all the additional costs itself before then. Switzerland's difficult holiday market situation affected IT charter demand generally. Coupled with the fact that Swissair owned both Balair and CTA, the parent company decided to streamline the activity of its charter subsidiaries by effectively merging the two units effective May 1993. The name chosen for the new company was BalairCTA.

EDELWEISS AIR

On 19 October 1995, Edelweiss Air was formed to specialise in IT charter operations on behalf of Kuoni, one of Switzerland's leading tour operators, and Helvetic Tours. The airline commenced operations on 10 February 1996 with a Zurich-Larnaca holiday charter flight then, after the addition of the second MD83, Edelweiss Air expanded its summer programme to 16 destinations in Europe and North Africa. In Winter 1996/97, holiday charter flights were focused on destinations in the Canary Islands, North Africa and the Middle East.

On 29 March 1997, a third MD83 was introduced into service which allowed an expansion of the charter service pattern to 27 destinations. Meanwhile the tour operator Kuoni has increased its share in the airline to 62%. At the start of the Summer 1999 season, the carrier introduced new A320 aircraft to replace its MD83 jets.

GLOBE AIR

The formation of Globe Air on 9 March 1957 was in line with efforts of the Bernese Oberland tourism authorities aimed at winning a larger share in Switzerland's tourism. The carrier acquired a 49-seat Ambassador, a popular twin-engined propeller aircraft, in November 1960 and initiated IT charters from Switzerland to Spain and Madeira and from the UK to Switzerland, in January 1961 after receiving its AOL. By June 1962, the carrier owned three Ambassadors for use on medium-haul charter routes throughout Europe and the Mediterranean region.

The Globe Air fleet came to be modernised with the introduction of turboprop Herald airliners from 11 May 1963 onward. It was of significance that the Herald's performance made it possible to operate from smaller airports at Swiss cities like Bern, Lugano, Sion, Samedan and Interlaken.

From 1964 onward, Globe Air also operated inbound charter flights to Switzerland. The carrier was given permission by the Swiss Air Force to use Interlaken, a conveniently situated gateway to central Switzerland and the Bernese Oberland, and direct IT charter flights were operated from London. For the Winter 1966/67 season, Globe Air used its Herald airliners for ski charter operations to Interlaken and Sion from a number of major cities in Denmark, the UK, (West-) Germany, France and Sweden. In the span of two years, Globe Air succeeded in securing a 50% market share in Switzerland. From a passenger total of 35,879 in 1963, this figure had reached almost 100,000 in 1964.

In a policy change, Globe Air decided to venture into the long-haul holiday charter business and ordered two Britannia turboprop airliners, the first of which was introduced into service from Basel on 4 April 1964. In that summer, Globe Air aircraft served a total of 20 destinations in all

parts of Europe, primarily in co-operation with the tour operator Hotelplan. The arrival of a second Britannia in March 1965 allowed an expansion of service to Colombo, Lourenço Marques, San Juan P.R. and Montego Bay.

Globe Air's success prompted the company to consider acquiring Comet 4 jets from BOAC but this plan did not materialize. The crash of a Britannia airliner in April 1967, and the resultant bad publicity, affected the company in a way that it was forced out of business. Operations were suspended on 17 October 1967 when the operator's license was withdrawn, followed by a declaration of bankruptcy two days later.

PHOENIX AIRWAYS

Phoenix Airways was formed in 1970 by Swiss and German partners. After receiving its operator's certificate on 17 April 1971, Phoenix started IT charter operations later in that month from its home base at Basel, using a single BAC 1-11 jet. A 707 joined the fleet in November 1972 but financial problems led to the collapse of Phoenix and the withdrawal of its operating licence on 18 March 1974.

SATA ~ S. A. DE TRANSPORT AÉRIEN

Although formed on 1 July 1966, SATA did not enter the IT charter market until March 1970, using a Convair CV-640, a Viscount and a Caravelle. In the early years, the company's IT charter activity was focused on Geneva in western Switzerland but later on, Basel and Zurich were also served as departure points for holiday charter flights. By March 1973, five Caravelles were in operation then, on 28 June 1974, a DC-8-63 entered service which allowed SATA to start long-haul charters to New York, Los Angeles, Fort-de-France and Pointe-a-Pitre in the French West Indies. In the autumn of 1975, IT charter flights started to Lima, La Paz and Bangkok and in December 1976, SATA commenced service to Santo Domingo and Port au Prince in the Caribbean.

Because of this expansion into the long-haul business, SATA was considered a serious competitor to Balair. SATA's traffic increased from 120,000 passengers in 1970 to over 404,000 in 1976. By that time, the fleet consisted of three DC-8 and four Caravelle jets. As a result of a Caravelle crash at Funchal in December 1977, the company drifted into a financial crisis which eventually forced it to terminate its activity in October 1978, after the authorities extended its operating license on 23 August 1978.

SPEEDWINGS

The charter carrier Speedwings commenced IT charter operations on 27 March 1997 from its home base Geneva, using a 737-200, on the Geneva-Oporto route. Holiday charter flights were operated exclusively for tour operators offering package tours from the western part of Switzerland, but the company's activity did not prove successful and all operations were suspended at the beginning of June 1997.

SUNSHINE AVIATION

The charter carrier Sunshine Aviation was established in March 1985 with base airports at Locarno and Lugano in Switzerland's Ticino region. Throughout the Summer of 1987 and 1988, Sunshine Aviation operated a network of IT charter services to secondary destinations in the Mediterranean as far as Malta and Sfax in Tunisia. The company functioned until 1994 when it was disbanded.

TEA BASEL ~ TEA SWITZERLAND

TEA Basel was set up on 18 May 1988 to form part of the long-term plans of Belgium's charter company TEA for a pan-European airline consortium. In line with Swiss legal requirements, two thirds of the company's share capital was held by Swiss nationals, the remainder by TEA Belgium.

The company's main base was set up at Basel although all of its IT charter operations were, from the beginning, focused on Zurich. With a fleet of two 737-300s, TEA Basel began holiday charters on 23 March 1989 on the Zurich-Lisbon route and co-operated with most of the well-established tour operators of Switzerland. After the collapse of TEA Belgium in September 1991, TEA Basel was acquired by private investors and became 100% Swiss-owned. The air carrier's name was later changed to TEA Switzerland on 1 April 1994.

A fifth 737-300 delivered in November 1994 had additional fuel tanks for long-haul operations and by 1996, TEA had a fleet of six 737-300s. The charter carrier's passenger total grew from 140,000 in 1989 to 521,000 in 1995. The UK-based low cost airline easyJet acquired a 40% stake in TEA in March 1998 which led to a policy change for TEA. The intention was to move TEA out of the IT charter business and set up the Swiss company as a low cost airline. At the end of March 1999, TEA terminated its charter activity and moved into the scheduled sector as of 1 April, known since as easy Jet Switzerland.

TELLAIR

Intent on boosting foreign tourism to the Bernese Oberland, the regional tourist industry favoured the creation of a charter carrier which would make up for the loss of the capacity formerly offered by Globe Air. Tellair was set up on 18 March 1968 to fill this gap. British Eagle held a 33 1/3% share in this new venture and was under contract to offer operational and technical support. However the demise of this British airline in November 1968, affected Tellair, preventing the start of operations. A new partner was found in Caledonian Airways and an operating license was granted on 25 March 1969. Tellair started IT charter flying on 29 March on the Zurich-Al Hoceima route using two Britannia aircraft leased from Caledonian Airways and a Convair 440.

The Swiss authorities advised Tellair in October 1969 that its operating license would be extended only on condition that the company became the owner of the two Britannias it had in use. Since it was impossible to find suitable investors at such relatively short notice, the air carrier was forced to suspend operations on 31 October. The company was liquidated in August 1970

TURKEY

ACTIVE AIR

Formed in 1990, Active Air started charter operations between Turkey and several western European countries in early 1996. Its fleet consisted of three TU-154 aircraft on lease from Vnukovo Airlines. However the carrier ceased operations late in 1996.

AIR ALFA

Set up in 1992, Air Alfa started charter operations between Turkey and western Europe using 727-200 equipment. In 1993, operations were suspended but resumed in February 1994, in line with a new marketing strategy. In mid-December 1996, Air Alfa was acquired by Kombassan Holding, one of Turkey's largest service industry concerns which continues to provide a sound financial background for the air carrier. Sultan Reisen and TransAtlas Touristik, Germany-based tour operators, have a close working relationship with the airline. In 1996, Air Alfa carried over one million passengers, with a fleet of one 727-200, three A300B4 and two A321-200 aircraft.

AIR ANATOLIA

In March 1998, Air Anatolia came into existence as the successor to GTI Airlines, the former in-house airline of the German tour operator GTI German Travel International. The carrier focuses on service between cities in Germany, the Netherlands and Turkey. In 1999, the airline had three Airbus A300s in use.

AIR ROSE

The new charter carrier Air Rose started its activity on 21 May 1999 with one 737, focusing on the Turkey/German and Swiss markets. In July 1999, a leased 737-700 was also introduced to handle additional business.

AKDENIZ AIRLINES

Formed in 1988, Akdeniz Airlines launched charter operations between Turkey and western Europe in May 1995 with a fleet of three A300 aircraft. Operations continued until November 1995 when the company folded.

ALBATROS AIR

Albatros Air was set up in 1992 and commenced charter operations in Summer 1993 with a fleet of two 727-200 aircraft. The airline was active in the charter market until 1995 when it suspended operations and was disbanded.

ANADOLU

Anadolu leased a BAC 1-11 jet from Tarom for charter operations in summer 1987. However the airline returned the aircraft in August 1987 and its operations were terminated.

BIRGENAIR

Formed in 1988, Birgenair operated charter flights between Turkey and several western European countries for Turkish expatriate workers and foreign tourists. In 1989, its fleet consisted of only one DC-8-61 but, by 1995, in line with a modernization programme, 737s, 757s and 767s had been added. The crash of one of its 757s in early February 1996, on departure from Puerto Plata in the Dominican Republic, prompted the withdrawal of operating rights for Germany, as a result of which the airline was forced to suspend operations on 8 March 1996. It was planned to resume operations in summer 1997 but this did not materialize.

BOGAZICI (BHT)

Formed as a subsidiary by THY in December 1986, BHT commenced charter operations in July 1987, using 727-200 and DC-10 aircraft of its parent company. The carrier was only in operation until October 1989 when it was wound up and THY took over its charter operations.

BOSPHORUS AIR

Founded by private partners in 1991, Bosphorus Air used two 737-300s leased from JAT in 1992. It was also intended to use a DC-10 of the same carrier for the peak summer season but this plan could not be realized. The company worked closely with a UK tour operator which specialized in package tours to Northern Cyprus, but the carrier suspended operations in January 1994.

BURSA AIRLINES

Bursa Airlines was a privately-owned airline which was granted a license by the Turkish Government for scheduled and charter operations in 1977. Between March and June 1980, Bursa Airlines acquired one DC-8-21 and two DC-8-52 aircraft for charter operations between Turkey and central European countries. However this did not prove successful and, by early 1981, all the aircraft had been retired and the company folded shortly afterwards.

CEBIAIR

Created in 1997, Cebiair commenced operations with one Airbus A300 on a back-up basis for other charter carriers.

GREEN AIR

Green Air was a joint venture between Turkish partners (51%) and Aeroflot (49%). IT charter operations commenced on 19 April 1990 with a flight from Nuremberg to Istanbul, followed by service between additional cities in Germany and Britain and the Turkish destinations of Ankara, Antalya and Izmir. The carrier's initial fleet consisted of three TU-154 and two TU-134 aircraft leased from Aeroflot, and an IL-86 widebody airliner was used from July 1991 during the peak summer season on high density charter routes between Turkey and central Europe. Within two years of starting operations, Green Air had carried 576,412 passengers. The dissolution of the Soviet Union in late 1991 and the subsequent disbanding of the Aeroflot organization prompted the latter to withdraw from its partnership with Green Air, forcing the Turkish company to suspend operations.

GTI AIRLINES

Specializing in package holidays to Turkey, the tour operator German Travel International (GTI) set up its own partner airline GTI Airlines in mid-1996. The airline received its operator's licence on 18 September 1996 and commenced charter operations on the 26th of that month with a flight from Dusseldorf to Antalya. Initially using one 310-seat Airbus A300B4. In Summer 1997, GTI Airlines operated a charter service pattern linking 13 German cities with holiday destinations in Turkey, but financial problems caused the GTI tour operator to be sold to a group of Turkish financiers and the in-house airline suspended operations. It was succeeded by Anatolia Airlines in March 1998.

HOLIDAY AIRLINES

Formed in 1994, Holiday Airlines commenced charter operations in mid 1994 with an initial fleet consisting of one A310 and two A320s. However, the company ran into financial problems later in 1994 and one A320 each was held at Dusseldorf and Hanover airports which resulted in a suspension of all operations during the Winter 1994/95 period. When services resumed in summer 1995, the carrier had a mixed fleet of two A300, two TU-154, one 727-200 and one Yak-42 aircraft. By summer 1996, the fleet had changed to four A300s, one L10, one 727 and two 737s. Holiday Airlines continued its activity until October 1996 when the German authorities withdrew the carrier's operating rights, forcing the company to suspend operations entirely.

INTERSUN HAVACILIK ~ SUNWAYS AIRLINES

The charter company Intersun Havacilik, also known as Sunways Airlines, was set up by the Turkish Tursem Group in 1994. Operations commenced in summer 1995, with emphasis on holiday charters to Turkey. Together with its Swedish partner Sunways AB, the airline worked closely with tour operators of the Tursem Group in Denmark, Finland, Germany, Norway, Sweden and the UK, with a fleet of four MD83 airliners was in use. Intersun successfully established itself in the Turkish market but, because of the unexpected bankruptcy of the Tursem Group, the airline was forced to suspend operations in early September 1997.

ISTANBUL AIRLINES

Formed in December 1985, Istanbul Airlines started charter operations on 14 March 1986. A privately-owned company, Istanbul Airlines has succeeded in establishing itself in the highly competitive charter market of Turkey, carrying migrant workers and holidaymakers. There is a close working relationship with the tour operators Öger Tours, UFO Reisen, TT Turkei Flugreisen, Halley Tours, President Holidays and Prestige Travel.

Initially, the carrier used two Caravelle 10R jets and two BAC 1-11s on lease from Tarom, with the Caravelle jets forming part of the fleet from 1986 until 1992. Marmara Air, a Turkish charter carrier planning to commence flying in 1986, was merged into Istanbul Airlines before actually launching operations, and new 737 aircraft were acquired in October 1988 and placed into service on 1 November. During the summer 1996 season, Istanbul Airlines had a total of 17 aircraft in use, including a leased TriStar, two 757-236ERs, six 737-400s, seven 727-200s and one 727-200 freighter, and the network covered 57 cities throughout Europe and the Middle East.

In addition to international charter flights, Istanbul Airlines has operated domestic services on selected routes since 1 April 1996 and also took control of the charter carrier Pegasus in 1997. In 1986, its first full year of operation, Istanbul Airlines carried 105,122 passengers which compares with 2,399,350 million in 1997. With an overall market share of 10%, the company is in first place among the private airlines of Turkey.

KHTY - KIBRIS TURKISH AIRLINES

Since its formation on 4 December 1974, KHTY has provided essential air service between Northern Cyprus and the Turkish mainland, using leased aircraft from its parent Turkish Airlines. In 1995, KHTY commenced international holiday charter operations connecting Northern Cyprus (Ercan) and points in the UK, the Netherlands, Denmark and Germany, a few countries which granted the necessary traffic rights. All international flights serving Ercan require a compulsory stop on the Turkish mainland.

NESU AIR

Formed in 1983, Nesu Air launched international charters only on 18 March 1988 with an Istanbul-Hamburg flight. A mixed fleet of leased 727-200 and TU-134 aircraft was in use, and as the activity of the air carrier progressed, additional aircraft were leased in. The company was badly hit by financial problems in the wake of the Gulf War crisis of late 1990 and all operations had to be suspended in early 1991.

NOBLE AIR

The airline Noble Air was formed in 1989 to operate charter flights for Turkish emigrants and to carry tourists to Turkey, in co-operation with Turkish tour operators and services started on 18 March 1989 with two 727-200 aircraft. The company's link with the UK tour operator Mosaic Holidays was aimed especially at promoting tourism to Northern Cyprus.

Noble Air marketed itself with quality service. Early success led to plans for the addition of an Airbus 310 for the 1990 summer season but this did not materialize. The Gulf war crisis affected Noble Air in a way that it saw its traffic base decimated. Its precarious financial situation was further aggravated by problems of the UK company Polly Peck which was, like Noble Air, also owned by the entrepreneur Asil Nadir. The company ceased flying in December 1991 and plans to resume service in March 1992 could not be put into effect.

ONUR AIR

The Turkish tour operator group Ten Tour was involved in the formation of Onur Air in April 1992. With an initial fleet of three A320 aircraft, operations were launched on 14 May 1992 on the Istanbul-London charter route. Onur Air has a close working relationship with tour operators forming part of the Ten Tour Group, including Inter Travel (Switzerland), Nazar (Germany), Marmara (France), Bosphorus (Belgium), Sunquest (UK), I Viaggi del Turchese (Italy), Royal Vacaciones (Spain), and On Travel (Russia).

By mid-1997, Onur Air had built up a fleet of 16 aircraft, including five A320s, three A321s and A300s, with five new MD88 aircraft were placed into service in February 1997. Onur Air has one of the youngest air fleets of the privately-owned air carriers of Turkey. From May 1992 until the end of 1996, 6.3 million passengers were carried.

PEGASUS AIRLINES

Pegasus Airlines came into being on 1 December 1989 as a joint venture between Turkish investors and Aer Lingus, the Irish airline retaining its share until 1994. 85% of the company is owned by the Cukurova Group. Charter operations commenced on 1 April 1990, catering both for Turkish migrant workers and for European tour operators arranging package tours to Turkey. The carrier's aircraft are usually leased out to tour operators on a seasonal basis which reduces operational risks for the carrier. Since initiating service in 1990, Pegasus has considerably expanded its activity to cover seven countries in Europe, as well as Israel, using a fleet of eight 737-400 aircraft in Summer 2000. In 1997, the administrative control of Pegasus passed over to Istanbul Airlines.

SULTAN AIR

Founded by private investors in July 1989, Sultan Air commenced international charter service on 2 August of that year with two Caravelle jets leased from Transwede. However the carrier later suspended operations from September 1990 until April 1991. Subsequently, Sultan Air managed to gain a firm foothold in the highly competitive Turkey charter market, and a significant increase in traffic led to Sultan Air using a fleet of two A300, two 737-300, four 737-200 and one IL-86 aircraft in the peak period of Summer 1993. Passenger traffic rose from 33,083 in 1989 to 464,336 in 1992. Financial problems, however, caused Sultan Air to suspend operations in October 1993.

SUNEXPRESS

Excellent growth prospects for tourism to Turkey prompted Lufthansa and Turkish Airlines to form SunExpress in April 1990 as a joint venture, and Antalya in southern Turkey was chosen as the company's base. In addition to operating holiday charter flights to Turkey on behalf of tour operators, SunExpress is also involved with the transport of Turkish expatriates working in central European countries. With an initial fleet consisting of two 148-seat 737-300 jets, operations commenced on 4 April 1990 between Germany, Austria and Antalya/Izmir in Turkey. The SunExpress service pattern continued until May 1991 when, as a result of new marketing policies, the network was extended to cover additional cities in Italy and Spain. Summer 1993 saw the start of service from the Netherlands, Switzerland and Israel, followed by Finland, Norway, Sweden and the UK in Summer 1994. In 1995, the Czech Republic (Ostrava, Brno), Slovakia (Bratislava) and Hungary (Budapest) also came to be served and future plans call for service to destinations in Russia.

75% of all SunExpress flights are on a full-charter basis, 23% are part charter and 2% of the capacity is sold on a seat-only basis. On 13 September 1993, the airline welcomed its millionth passenger since the start of operations. The carrier's quality of onboard service, regularity of operations and overall reliability have produced good traffic results, with the annual passenger total of some 360,000 in 1992 increasing to over 900,000 in 1995.

From the start of operations in 1990, Germany has been the airline's top traffic-generating market in Europe and high demand for capacity in Summer 1996 required the use of three 737-300s, two 737-400s and a leased Airbus 320. SunExpress serves several major cities in Turkey but Antalya is the focal point and prime destination. Over the last decade, the southern part of Turkey has developed into a sought-after holiday sojourn in summer. It has also been realised that there is great potential for winter tourism, even in combination with skiing holidays in the Taurus Mountains. Since Winter 1991/92, SunExpress has been actively involved in the promotion of Antalya as a winter destination. This has proved so successful that a record 290,000 passengers were carried by the airline in Winter 1995/96. In addition, a promotion of south-west Turkey started in Winter 1993/94 with a boost in flights offered to Dalaman. On 13 September 1993, the one millionth passenger was welcomed since the start of operations. The ownership of SunExpress changed in 1995 when Condor acquired Lufthansa's 40% share in this German/Turkish joint venture.

TALIA AIRWAYS

Turkish and German investors established Talia Airways in March 1987, catering both to the migrant workers and leisure tourism markets, with operations focused on the UK, West-Germany, France and Scandinavia. Talia had one 727-200 when services started in July 1987 between Istanbul and Munich and, in Winter 1987/88, the airline served one of Europe's longest charter routes linking Helsinki with Ercan, Northern Cyprus, via Antalya. The air carrier's future plans called for the lease of up to six 737s starting in November 1988, to target a passenger total of 800,000 by 1990. Talia, however, ran into financial problems which led to the withdrawal of its operating license in May 1988.

TOP AIR

Top Air joined the list of private Turkish airline companies in 1996. It acquired two 727-200s from THY and initiated international charter operations in April 1996. The carrier acquired three 727s at the end of March 1996 for international charter operations and lease to other carriers but, at the end of December 1996, these aircraft were withdrawn from service and the company reverted to its former activity as an air taxi operator.

TOROS AIR

Privately owned Toros Air was founded in 1986 and charter operations started with one 727-100 in August 1987 on the Ankara-Istanbul-Dusseldorf route. The company's operational standards came under scrutiny after the crash of a 727 at Ankara in August 1989, prompting several European states to cancel the carrier's traffic rights in the light of this event and low customer confidence. In November 1989, it was announced that the Turkish authorities intended to extend the carrier's licence provided that a sound financial base could be arranged. Unable to meet this requirement, Toros Air remained grounded and was finally wound up at the end of 1989.

TURKISH EUROPEAN AIRWAYS ~ TUR AVRUPA

As part of the pan-European group of airlines created by TEA Belgium, Turkish European Airways was established in 1987, with the Belgian parent company holding a 49% share. Operations commenced in April 1988 with 727-100/200s, covering several countries in Europe, Northern Cyprus and Israel. After TEA terminated its involvement with the air carrier in mid-1989, the company's name was changed to TUR Avrupa but the Gulf crisis of early 1991 caused problems, as its traffic base was seriously eroded. A financial crisis arose as a result of which operations had to be suspended in December 1993.

TURKISH AIRLINES (THY)

Turkish Airlines' history goes back to 1933 when the airline was established by the government, under the control of the Ministry of Defence. In 1955, the airline was re-organised while remaining under complete government control. THY is well established as a leading scheduled airline and has, in the last decade, expanded its route network to cover important cities throughout Europe and in other parts of the world.

This is in line with government directives towards closer commercial contacts with various nations. The changed political situation resulting from the break-up of the Soviet Union has prompted the Turkish Government to seek closer links with the newly independent nations of Central Asia and THY has, therefore, forged new links with their capital cities since 1991. The airline's activity has seen remarkable growth throughout the nineties, with a total of over nine million passengers carried in 1995. The airline's traffic development has profited from the ongoing influx of foreign tourists to Turkey, and THY is in the process of modernizing its fleet to handle future expansion of its domestic and international operations. As a result, the average age of its air fleet stood at 3.3 years in 1995, and it was planned to increase the number of aircraft to 100 by the year 2000. The present boom in tourism to Turkey has also involved THY in the operation of special holiday charter flights from a number of important cities in Europe. The airline is facing strong competition from Turkey's privately-owned airlines since, according to Government policy decisions, they are increasingly granted scheduled rights for international and domestic destinations. The migration of large numbers of Turkish nationals to central European countries, which started in the sixties, also led to THY operating special flights between major cities in Turkey and West-Germany. The first such operation was on 12 September 1969 on the Istanbul-Hanover route. In the nineties, the status of these special charters flights was changed to a 'scheduled' one.

UKRAINE

AEROSVIT AIRLINES

Formed in 1994, Aerosvit serves a network of scheduled routes using 737-200s from Kiev to several cities in other CIS states. On the international scene, the company operates holiday charters in co-operation with Ukrainian tour operators.

AIR UKRAINE

As the successor airline to Aeroflot's Ukraine Directorate which used to be one of the largest units within the former organisation, state-owned Air Ukraine operates an extensive network of domestic and international scheduled and charter services focused on Kiev (Borispol) Airport. Air Ukraine's international operations are complemented by those of Ukraine International Airlines.

DNIPROAVIA

Based at Dnepropetrovsk, one of the Ukraine's most important industrial and commercial cities, Dniproavia serves an extensive network of domestic and international scheduled and charter services, using Yak-40 jets for the short to medium-haul routes and Yak-42 jets for the longer routes.

UKRAINE INTERNATIONAL AIRLINES (UIA)

After receiving its registration certificate in October 1992, Ukraine International Airlines (UIA) commenced scheduled international service on 28 November 1992. UIA links Kiev, its main base, with a select number of Western European gateway cities using a fleet of 737 aircraft. The airline is intent on establishing itself as a quality carrier, with its professional service aimed at a discerning business clientele. On the routes connecting Dnepropetrovsk and Odessa with Vienna, there is co-operation with Austrian Airlines and on the Kiev-Zurich route with Swissair, and both these airlines now hold a financial stake in UIA. In February 1998, UIA began to place new 737-300s into service. In addition to its scheduled activity, UIA also operates international holiday charters from the Ukraine and for foreign visitors to the Ukraine. In summer 1995, UIA operated series of charters to Simferopol from Frankfurt, Hanover and Munich, and to Odessa from Zurich, in co-operation with the tour operators DER Tour (Germany) and Mittelthurgau (Switzerland). The Summer 1997 charter plan called for a total of 75 flights compared with 47 flights in Summer 1996.

UNITED KINGDOM

ACE SCOTLAND

Set up in July 1966, ACE Scotland operated IT charters from Glasgow to Mediterranean resorts, with a Lockheed Constellation L-749 until 14 September 1966 when the company ceased trading and went into liquidation.

AFRICAN AIR SAFARIS (AAS) ~ AIR SAFARIS

African Air Safaris (AAS) was formed on 29 November 1954, as a successor to its forerunner company named Meredith Air Transport. AAS became involved in IT charter work in 1958 when services were initiated with two Vikings from London-Gatwick to continental destinations. In November 1959, the company changed its name to Air Safaris, and the addition of two Hermes 4 aircraft allowed the carrier to operate an expanded network of holiday charter services from 1960 onward. In November 1960, Air Safaris took over the air transport branch of Don Everall as well as the Falcon Airways fleet of Hermes airliners. Financial difficulties, however, led to the suspension of flight operations on 31 October 1961 and the airline's operating permit was revoked in January 1962.

AIR CONDOR

Air Condor was set up in early 1960 and was involved with IT charter operations from Southend and Manchester throughout that summer season. Both Viking and Bristol Wayfarer aircraft were in use but the company ceased flying in November 1960 and went into receivership one month later.

AIR EUROPE

The fuel price rise in the wake of the 1973 Middle East War, the collapse of Court Line in 1974 and the depressed economic situation of the time created a general reluctance among UK air carriers to invest in new equipment while older aircraft were being phased out, without this lost capacity being replaced. It was against this background that Air Europe was created on 18 July 1978, as a partner of the Intasun Group, at the right moment when tour operators again considered adding IT charter capacity in line with growing demand. The new airline commenced IT charter operations on 4 May 1979 on the London-Gatwick-Palma route and, in the first Summer season, 29 destinations were served from London. Later on, Manchester and Cardiff also became departure cities.

Air Europe became a successful and popular airline and enjoyed the distinction of being 'charter airline of the year' on four occasions, i.e. in 1983, '84, '85 and '88. On 6 April 1983, 757s were placed into service on the Gatwick-Faro route and were subsequently, were used on the new long-haul routes to Orlando, Acapulco, Goa, Male and Bangkok. Holidaymakers' growing demand for low fare travel, without the traditional package tour arrangements, prompted Air Europe to venture into the field of scheduled service. The first route served was London—Palma in May 1985, followed by London—Gibraltar on 1 November of the same year. The airline intended to further its involvement with the scheduled sector by providing service from London to major cities throughout Europe, offering quality service for business and leisure travellers alike. This led to the formation of the Airline of Europe Group in 1989, a nucleus of airlines trading under the common name of 'Air Europe'. Those airlines eventually forming part were Air Europa, NFD, Norway Airlines and Air Europe Italy (w.e.f. December 1989), envisioning a target date of 1 January 1993 for a comprehensive European service pattern to be in operation. Plans also called for the formation of similar associated airline ventures in France and in the Netherlands. In this connection, Air Europe intended to acquire the French air carrier Corsair but this did not work out. As part of these pan-European plans, it was intended to have a pool of aircraft available for all the affiliated companies to use in line with their seasonal capacity requirements.

By 1989, Air Europe was firmly established as a major charter airline while also serving a growing number of scheduled destinations. The fleet consisted of nineteen aircraft whose average age was 1.5 years, comprising six 757s, seven 737-300s, five 737-400s and one 747 leased from Tower Air from 1 May 1989. Ambitious plans called for Air Europe's fleet expansion to 130 aircraft by 1994, all to be available for use by the member airlines of the Airlines of Europe Group.

The Gulf War crisis in the last quarter of 1990 and in early 1991 caused a sharp fall-off in traffic demand. The situation was further aggravated by the high cost of aviation fuel and rising interest rates. All these factors contributed to financial problems within the ILG Group which, in turn, affected Air Europe as well. The final straw was when the Swiss financier who had invested heavily in the ILG Group, went into receivership and Air Europe was forced to suspend operations on 8 March 1991. At that time, the airline was running about 400 charter and scheduled flights a week out of London-Gatwick alone. In retrospect, ILG invested heavily to create a pan-European airline under a common banner. Air Europe's venture into the scheduled business was costly and significantly contributed to the debts incurred. Nevertheless, the airline had a fleet of 29 aircraft and carried 3.5 million passengers a year, achieving the status of being one of the pillars of the British air transport establishment.

AIR FERRY

Air Ferry was established in July 1962 to operate IT charters on behalf of the tour operators Leroy Tours and Lyons Tours, using a fleet of two Vikings and a DC-4 from its base at Manston in Kent. ITC operations started on 30 March 1963 to a large number of destinations across Europe as far as the Canary Islands. In seven months of operation, some 120,000 passengers had been carried and, by 1964, Air Ferry's fleet had grown to five Vikings and three DC-4s. In October of that year, the company was bought out by the Air Holdings Group but operations in its own name, continued until the end of October 1968. In its final summer season, the airline had two leased Viscounts in use.

AIR GREGORY

Air Gregory operated IT charters from Newcastle in summer 1965, using a single DC-3.

AIR INTERNATIONAL CHARTER

This carrier was set up in May 1971 and had its base at London-Stansted. IT charter operations commenced on 4 September 1971, with one Viscount, to Frankfurt and Vienna in co-operation with the tour operator Arrow Travel. ITC flying continued in summer 1972 but all operations came to a stop in November 1972. Plans were made for the use of 1-11 jets in summer 1973 but this did not work out and the company was finally disbanded in June 1973.

AIR KRUISE

Air Kruise was among the earliest independent charter carriers having been founded in 1946. Using two DC-3 aircraft, IT charter operations were operated in the summer 1955 season from Lydd in Kent, Birmingham and Manchester, mainly in co-operation with the tour operator Blue Cars. Numerous European continental destinations were served until 1958 when the company was merged into Silver City Airways.

AIR LINKS ~ TRANSGLOBE

Air Links was established on 21 August 1958 but only commenced IT charter operations in Summer 1961 using a DC-3 from its London-Gatwick base. The carrier introduced four-engined Hermes 4 aircraft in December 1962 which, in turn, were replaced with Argonauts from March 1964.

On 1 August 1965, the company's name was changed to Transglobe. Using Britannia aircraft, Transglobe operated IT charter flights throughout Europe from London-Gatwick, Manchester and Glasgow then, in May 1966, ITC operations commenced to North America. A switch to CL-44 turboprop airliners was made in April 1968 but the company's operations were later suspended on 28 November 1968.

AIR MANCHESTER

The Manchester-based tour operator Sureway Travel was behind the venture to create an airline subsidiary for its IT charter work. Aptly named Air Manchester, the carrier relied on BAF to operate its single BAC 1-11 in Summer 1982 but the charter carrier's activity was terminated in November 1982.

AIR SCANDIC

Registered on 30 October 1997, Air Scandic took delivery of its first A300B4 — ex Finnair — at Manchester on 26 April 1998 and initiated IT charter flying from Manchester and Newcastle in May 1998.

AIRTOURS INTERNATIONAL

The tour operator Airtours formed Airtours International on 10 October 1990 to provide the bulk of its seating capacity which, in earlier years, Dan-Air had been contracted for. IT charter operations started on 20 March 1991 on the Manchester-Rhodes route, and the initial fleet consisted of five MD83 jets, increased in subsequent years in line with capacity requirements. July 1993 saw the acquisition of Inter European Airways which also involved taking over that charter carrier's fleet and by Summer 1994, two 767s were in use on transatlantic charter routes and the carrier operated 449 charter flights/week to 68 destinations, using 18 UK departure airports. In Winter 1994/95, the tour operator Airtours initiated short and medium-haul day trips to a number of popular tourist destinations across Europe, opening up a new field of activity for its in-house carrier. It is reported that the airline achieved high rates of aircraft utilisation, with an average of 15.5 hrs in Summer and 10.5 hrs in Winter, and higher load factors than other comparable UK airlines.

AIR TRANSPORT CHARTER

Air Transport Charter was set up in July 1946 and was initially based at Jersey C.I. Throughout the summer of 1950, charters were flown to continental European destinations, then operations were transferred to Blackbushe Airport in October 1950 from where holiday charters continued to be flown until October 1952.

AIR UK

Air UK appeared on the UK air transport scene on 16 January 1980 as a new airline formed by the merger of Air Anglia and British Island Airways. Conceived as a local and regional airline, Air UK expanded its network of scheduled air services to a large number of regional cities throughout Britain and on the continent. Its fleet of F-28 jets, F-27, Herald and Bandeirante turboprop airliners was used for scheduled operations whereas four BAC 1-11 jets were allocated to the operation of international IT charter services. These continued until June 1987 when a subsidiary company named Air UK Leisure came to be set up to specialize in this line of business.

AIR UK LEISURE

Air UK, one of Britain's leading regional airlines, had a 30% stake in the charter carrier Air UK Leisure formed in June 1987. With an initial fleet of three 737-200s, operations commenced on 1 May 1988 from its base at London (Stansted) to Rome, Gerona and Faro. On 2 May, IT charters started from Manchester to Rhodes and from East Midlands to Palma. One of the company's major share-holders was Viking International, claimed to be Europe's largest broker in the air charter market, holding a stake of 40%. On 7 October 1988, the airline introduced new 737-400 aircraft to replace its older 737s. The airline ceased operating under this name at the end of March 1996 and its programme of summer 1996 IT charters was taken over by its affiliate Leisure International Airways.

AIR ULSTER

Air Ulster was the operating name of Belfast-based Ulster Air Transport. Set up in 1967, the carrier took over the assets of Emerald Airways and commenced operations in February 1968. It was only in Summer 1969 that the company operated a programme of IT charters, using a DC-3 but financial difficulties forced the company out of business in January 1970.

AIRWAYS INTERNATIONAL CYMRU

Founded in 1986, Airways International Cymru was based at Cardiff, Wales, from where IT charters were flown with a mixed fleet of BAC 1-11 and 737 aircraft. To overcome financial problems, merger talks were held with Paramount in 1987 but this did not work out and operations were suspended in January 1988. A successor airline was set up under the name of Amber Air.

AIRWORLD AVIATION

The tour operators Sunworld and Iberotravel were involved with the formation of Airworld in October 1993, to fill a gap created by the merger of IEA with Airtours International in July 1993. IT charter operations commenced on 29 April 1994 with an initial fleet of two A-320 aircraft. As a result of the tour operator Sunworld acquiring the charter airline Flying Colours in June 1998, Airworld was merged into that airline and lost its separate identity at the start of the Winter 1998/99 season.

AIR 2000

The tour operator Owners Abroad was involved in the formation of Air 2000 in 1986 and 757s were chosen as the ideal type of aircraft for its planned network of IT charter services across Europe. Flying commenced on 11 April 1987 from its Manchester base and in Summer 1990 from London-Gatwick. Air 2000 also ventured into long-haul operations in December 1987.

In early Summer 1989, ITC operations to Orlando from Glasgow's airport at Abbotsinch ran into controversy when flights had to make a technical stop at Prestwick Airport, in line with existing law requirements, before crossing the Atlantic. A judicial review of this matter eventually established that this type of operation was no longer necessary and transatlantic flights could be operated non-stop from Glasgow itself. Although Air 2000 used 757s as its standard aircraft since starting operations, four Airbus 320s were added in mid-1992 to meet tour operators' requirements for smaller capacity aircraft. An announcement was made for a change of the airline's image to be distinctly different from other charter carriers, by offering schedule-airline style meals and on-board entertainment and, by 1993, the Air 2000 passenger total had grown to over 4.2 million, making it the UK's third largest airline. Meanwhile, on a regular annual basis throughout the Winter season, the charter carrier seconded some of its aircraft to its partner airline Canada 3000.

Air 2000 started scheduled services to Cyprus from London-Gatwick on 3 November 1993 and Birmingham on 4 May 1994 to Larnaca and Paphos, which were run in addition to its IT charter operations. In Summer 1996, Air 2000 operated IT charters from Ireland [Eire] for the first time. In June 1998, the airline's parent company First Choice acquired its rival tour operator Unijet. This led to the integration of Unijet's in-house airline Leisure International with Air 2000 at the start of the Winter 1998/99 season.

ALIDAIR

Set up in 1971, Alidair initially functioned as an air taxi company but its role changed after the acquisition of three Viscounts in April 1972, used for day trips from Castle Donington in the summer of that year. IT charter operations commenced from Southend in May 1973, and Birmingham, Castle Donington and Manchester became additional departure points in 1974. On behalf of Clarksons, springtime charters were flown in early 1974 and 1975 to Beauvais and Rotterdam.

ALL LEISURE AIRLINES (ALA)

Set up in May 1995 as a UK-based subsidiary of the Irish airline Translift Airways, All Leisure Airlines (ALA) operated IT charters from London (Gatwick), Manchester and Newcastle, using three A320 aircraft. ALA transferred its aircraft for the Winter 1995/96 season to the new US carrier Trans Meridian Airlines, based at Houston, as a result of taking a 40% share in that company. For Summer 1996, only one A320 aircraft was used out of London (Gatwick) and Translift handled ALA's flight operations. The air carrier ceased flying in January 1997.

AMBASSADOR AIRWAYS

The UK tour operator Best Leisure was involved in the formation of Ambassador Airways in February 1992, and IT charter work started on 21 May 1993 from Newcastle with an initial fleet of two 757s. In Summer 1994, the carrier used two A320, four 757 and two 737 aircraft, but the bankruptcy of its parent tour operator company led to the demise of Ambassador, its operations being terminated on 28 November 1994.

AMBER AIR

Intended as a successor to bankrupt Airways International Cymru, Amber Air appeared on the IT charter scene in May 1988. Throughout that summer season, the carrier used two 737-200s for IT charters from Cardiff and Manchester but, at the end of November 1988, the company was taken over by Paramount Airways.

AQUILA AIRWAYS

The wartime involvement with the Flying Boat Squadron of the RAF was of great use to B Aikman when he set up Aquila Airways on 18 May 1948. This company was unique among the British airlines of the time in that it employed a fleet of ex-BOAC 4-engined Sunderland flying boats. Starting in May 1949, a network of scheduled routes, mostly of a seasonal nature, was built up that was of special interest to tourists visiting mainly Southern European destinations, and plans were also made to operate aerial cruises around the Mediterranean on behalf of Thomas Cook from June 1949 but the demand was insufficient to support such a venture. In Winter 1951, the first Solent flying boat was introduced into service. Aquila Airways operated IT charters from Southampton to Palma, Biarritz and Montreux in 1957. Other services were run in 1957 on behalf of the French tour operator, Club Méditerranée from Marseilles to Palermo and Corfu, the sector Southampton-Marseilles being run as a scheduled service. The company continued its activity until 30 September 1958 when all flying operations came to an end. It was at this point in time that the future prospects looked dim and uncertain for a flying boat operator.

AUTAIR ~ AUTAIR INTERNATIONAL ~ COURT LINE

In 1960, Autair (Luton) was formed as the airline partner of Autair which came into being in 1953 for contract charter work using helicopters. Using three DC-3s, the airline commenced IT charter operations in 1961 from its Luton base and, in summer 1962, also from West-Berlin. Elizabethan, Herald and HS-748 airliners were acquired in 1963, also for use on charter routes and in the same year, the air carrier's name became Autair International. A single DC-4 was in the fleet from January until August 1965. In addition to IT and general charter work, Autair also built up a network of scheduled routes linking secondary destinations in Britain, in operation until 31 October 1969. By that time, all propeller and turboprop airliners had been disposed of.

The collapse of Treffield in June 1967 led to Autair taking over the contracts of the failed air carrier. The subsequent use of BAC 1-11 jets for the first time helped boost Autair's passenger total to 273,200 and additional HS-748 aircraft were added in March 1968. The name of the company was changed to Court Line as of 1 January 1970, in recognition of the fact that the airline formed part of the Court Line Group. The air carrier was extensively involved with IT charter work and had a long-term contract with the tour operator Clarksons. The boom in Britain's package tour business led to Court Line serving an extensive network of IT charters from a number of UK cities, in addition to Luton, and a notable event was the introduction of a Lockheed L-1011 TriStar on the Luton-Palma charter route on 2 April 1973. Court Line was the first airline to use this widebody type in Europe. TriStars were in service on heavy traffic routes within Europe but also came to be used on long-haul charters to the Caribbean from November 1973 onward. The airline expanded quickly to become Britain's largest in the field of leisure travel, carrying over 2.2 million passengers in 1973. However the UK cut-throat tour operator business entered a period of crisis which, together with a sharp fuel cost increase in October 1973, affected Court Line badly. To improve its fortunes, the tour companies Horizon Holidays and Clarksons were acquired by the airline in May 1973, but the economic situation in Britain had, by that time, worsened and accentuated Court Line's precarious financial situation. Eventually, the air carrier collapsed on 15 August 1974, leaving thousands of holidaymakers stranded. At that time, the fleet comprised two TriStars and nine BAC 1-11s.

BEA AIRTOURS ~ BRITISH AIRTOURS

In January 1969, BEA announced plans for the formation of a subsidiary charter carrier which would be using aircraft withdrawn from BEA's scheduled operations. This news was met with opposition from the British independent airlines as they were concerned about this new competitor entering their well-established sphere of activity. Furthermore, it was generally thought that BEA's entry into the field of IT charters, through its new subsidiary, would be a subsidised venture.

Support for BEA's involvement with IT holiday charter operations came from the Edwards Committee which recommended that BEA should be allowed to operate such flights. BEA made the point that there had been very strong interest from tour operators in this proposed new venture especially in view of the fact the average holidaymaker at that time was still relatively uneasy about charter operations generally and BEA's name and standing was seen as being synonymous with reliability. This remark did, however, upset the independent airline companies and caused a great deal of anger. BUA made representations to the authorities and highlighted the serious implications of BEA's entry into the IT charter business, with a planned capacity of 245,000 seats, in a market which had been developed by Britain's private airlines. BEA's proposed new venture was considered a development of such magnitude that it ought to be balanced by offering the independent airlines more opportunities in the scheduled sector. It was against this background that BEA's subsidiary BEA Airtours was founded on 24 April 1969. A fleet of nine Comet 4B jets was made

available, the jets having been released from BEA's scheduled front-line duty. The task was set for the new charter carrier to secure a 25% share of the UK IT charter market where BEA had formerly participated only periodically on a few selected routes.

BEA Airtours commenced IT charter operations on 6 March 1970 with a flight from London (Gatwick) to Palma. In its first year of operation, BEA Airtours carried over 650,000 passengers, almost one half of them during the peak period from July to September then, in February 1972, the first ex-BOAC 707s were received and introduced into service in April. BEA Airtours' performance out of Gatwick Airport, at that time, was highlighted by good punctuality compared with its numerous competitors. On 31 October 1973, the last Comet 4B flight took place, and from 1 November 1973, the airline's name was changed to British Airtours and the company was placed under the control of BEA's European Division.

British Airtours was granted a world-wide Air Operator's Certificate by the UK CAA which allowed the charter carrier to initiate trans-atlantic charters to North America in Winter 1972/73. By 1973, the fleet of 707s had grown to seven aircraft, and although there was evidence of the company's financial situation improving notably, the heavy increase in fuel costs from 1973 onward had a very negative impact. In 1975, the carrier came to work more closely with the tour operator Enterprise Holidays and in the following year, for the first time, British Airtours operated IT charters to all six continents, using a fleet of nine 707s. In addition, capacity was provided for British Airways scheduled and charter operations as required. Increased competition arose for British Airtours from the scheduled airlines' move towards lower promotional fares, aimed at combating competition from the charter sector. For the first time in 1978, inbound traffic was also carried from the USA to Britain, mainly from Los Angeles and Oakland whereas, in Europe, ITC operations to the UK were initiated from Sweden, West-Germany and Italy. One aircraft came to be dedicated to flights to the Far East.

A new era began when British Airtours introduced 737s, using four aircraft for Summer 1980 IT charters. In the course of that year, over a million passengers were carried in spite of very strong competition from other charter carriers. However long-haul services proved unsuccessful, mainly because of the lower fares offered by scheduled airlines causing a considerable loss of business. The company's 707s were sold as they were gradually replaced by 737s and two L-1011s were added for the Summer 1981 season. When British Airways PLC was incorporated on 13 December 1983, the assets and liabilities of British Airtours were transferred to the new company and in March 1984, it became the first UK charter carrier to introduce a 747 on routes to USA and Canada. Operations started from London (Heathrow) Terminal 4 on 12 April 1986. As a result of British Airways acquiring a controlling interest in B'CAL on 3 December 1987, the charter carrier Caledonian Airways came into existence, replacing British Airtours.

BERLIN REGIONAL UK ~ BERLIN EUROPEAN UK

Berlin Regional UK was formed on 4 December 1985 with the intention of building up a network of secondary routes from Berlin. The use of Jetstream J31 aircraft did not, however, prove successful and the airline's pattern of international services came to be scaled down. The company name was changed to Berlin European and with two 737s leased from Germania, the carrier started IT charter operations in April 1990. This activity continued until, on the re-unification of Germany, the air carrier suspended operations from Berlin and was acquired by Germania.

BKS AERO CHARTER ~ BKS AIR TRANSPORT ~ NORTHEAST AIRLINES

The company BKS Aero Charter was registered on 7 February 1952, initially based at Southend. Adhoc work was undertaken throughout 1952, followed by ski charters to Innsbruck in Winter 1952/53 under contract to a club of winter sports enthusiasts. In addition to scheduled domestic operations which started in May 1953, the same month saw the start of IT charters from Newcastle and Southend using DC-3 aircraft. The company's name was changed to BKS Air Transport at the end of 1953 and, by 1956, the BKS fleet consisted of five DC-3s and three Vikings.

Holiday charter operations from Southend continued until the end of the 1959 summer season, and from then on, BKS placed emphasis on developing Newcastle as a major base. Since mid-1958, Ambassador aircraft have also been deployed on the airline's charter routes, supplemented by Viscounts in 1961, turboprop HS-748s from April 1962 and Britannias from April 1964.

Meanwhile, London-Gatwick was added as a departure point for IT charter operations in June 1961 as was Teesside in summer 1965. Ambassador aircraft were later withdrawn from service in October 1967 and Britannias in February 1969, while BKS acquired a batch of Viscounts from BEA in 1968 and this was followed by the introduction of Trident jets into IT charter work on 9 April 1969 on the Newcastle-Palma route. By 1970 the fleet was made up of two Tridents and six Viscounts.

After becoming part of British Air Services in 1967, the airline changed its name to Northeast Airlines on 1 November 1970. Merged into the British Airways Regional Division at the end of March 1976, the name Northeast disappeared from the civil air transport scene.

BRITISH OVERSEAS AIR CHARTER

BOAC formed its wholly-owned subsidiary British Overseas Air Charter Ltd on 11 March 1971, for low fare charter operations on North Atlantic routes and to Southeast Asia. Starting in 1972, there was notable expansion of the carrier's charter activity across the North Atlantic where its traffic share doubled. In addition to the aircraft specially allocated to the charter carrier, all types of BOAC aircraft were used according to capacity requirements. The 'exempt charter' flights operated to the Southeast destinations of Bangkok, Kuala Lumpur and Singapore produced excellent traffic results but were affected by the new low fares to Australia offered by the scheduled carriers.

In 1973/74, talks were held with scheduled and charter carriers with regard to setting minimum charter rates for operations between Europe and the USA. At that time, the 'exempt charter' flights to Bangkok and Singapore were cancelled but continued to Kuala Lumpur. The company's name was changed to BOAC Ltd on 11 December 1989. It ceased trading at the end of March 1997.

BRITAVIA

Britavia came into existence in June 1949 as a result of a re-organization involving the forerunner company British Aviation Services. Also at that time, Britavia became the parent company of Silver City Airways. Six Hermes aircraft were acquired from BOAC for military trooping flights and they were introduced into service in July 1954. Britavia also used these airliners for IT charters from its Blackbushe Airport base in the summer seasons of 1957 and 1958 then, in mid-1959, Britavia passed over its Hermes fleet to Silver City Airways at Manston from where the type was used on IT charter routes in SCA colours. Britavia's involvement with IT charter work was terminated at the end of the summer 1959 season and the carrier's name finally disappeared.

BRITISH AIR FERRIES ~ BRITISH WORLD AIRLINES (BWA)

BAF was the name adopted on 1 October 1967 for BUAF - British United Air Ferries. It then became a unit functioning separately from BUA and, in 1975, the company switched the focus of its activity to scheduled operations and acquired a fleet of Herald airliners for this purpose. After transferring its scheduled service network to British Island Airways on 1 January 1979, BAF concentrated on general charter work in and a fleet of Viscount airliners was acquired from British Airways in early 1981 to be used for IT charter work. This was considered a surprising move since most holiday charter flights had been flown by jet aircraft for many years.

IT charter operations continued, together with a multitude of other tasks, until the Viscount aircraft were finally withdrawn from service in 1997. The company's name was changed to British World Airlines (BWL) on 6 April 1993 and London-Stansted Airport became the main operating base. BWL continues to operate IT charter services to France and Italy with a fleet of BAC 1-11s and 737s, from both London-Stansted and Gatwick airports.

BRITISH AIRWAYS

Periodically, British Airways has operated IT charter services, using spare capacity of its medium-haul air fleet for this purpose. Furthermore, its Concorde aircraft have been deployed to ferry Cunard passengers to various ports to join their cruise ships and, since December 1984, Concorde aircraft have also been used for Winter charters to Rovaniemi, Finnish Lapland.

The political situation in Berlin after the Second World War led to a very extensive involvement by BEA and British Airways in the operation of a scheduled service pattern focused on West-Berlin. In addition to this, British Airways commenced IT charter operations from West-Berlin in Summer 1983. This relatively late start was due to the fact that the airline's standard equipment on Berlin routes at that time, the BAC 1-11, did not have the required range to fly non-stop to Southern European holiday destinations. BA introduced its new 737s out of Berlin, on its scheduled routes, which enabled the carrier to operate holiday charters on behalf of local tour operators. The extent of these charter operations from its Berlin base was, however, much less compared with those of other UK air carriers like Dan-Air and Laker.

BRITISH CALEDONIAN CHARTER
CAL AIR INTERNATIONAL ~ NOVAIR

In the wake of the demise of Laker Airways, BCAL established British Caledonian Charter in December 1982, in a joint ownership with the Rank organization. The carrier initiated IT charter operations in March 1983 and carried over 420,000 passengers in the first summer season then, in 1984, BCAL gave up its share in the charter company. October 1985 saw the company's name changed to Cal Air International, and three DC-10s were in use on long-haul routes.

In line with plans for expanding IT charter operations in Europe, two 737-400s were acquired, the first of which was delivered in March 1989. The carrier operated holiday charters mainly on behalf of the tour operators Blue Sky, Wings and OSL. In December 1987, when British Airways took over BCAL, a large stake in the charter airline was acquired by BA as well. The Rank Organization became the sole owner of the charter carrier on 25 May 1988, prompting another name change to Novair.

Adverse economic conditions forced tour operators to cut back their IT charter capacity requirements for 1989 and this had a dramatic impact on Novair. Aggravated by ATC problems and costly delays, the carrier's financial state was made worse in the course of that year while favourable summer weather in northern Europe depressed the demand for foreign holidays. Novair was forced to suspend operations on 5 May 1990 after attempts by its owners to merge with, or sell to, another charter carrier proved unsuccessful.

BRITISH EUROPEAN AIRWAYS (BEA)

BEA occasionally operated IT charters during Summer and Winter periods. A major involvement was in 1974 when Vanguard aircraft were used for IT charters from Exeter.

BRITISH ISLAND AIRWAYS (BIA)

British Island Airways (BIA) was set up as a separate company in July 1970, after being part of the BUA Group. A network of short-haul routes was served mainly with Herald aircraft, then BIA acquired three BAC 1-11s in 1978 and ventured into the field of IT charter work. Merged with Air Anglia and British Air Ferries, BIA's name disappeared for a time when the new airline Air UK was created, owned by its parent British and Commonwealth Shipping.

It was in 1982 that BIA was re-established as a charter carrier based at London-Gatwick, commencing its activity at the time when Laker Airways went under. The airline prospered through its co-operation with smaller tour operators since its fleet of 89-seat BAC 1-11 jets aptly met their package tour capacity requirements. In addition to IT charter operations, BIA was contracted in winter 1984/85 to run air cruises to Egypt, involving intermediate stops at Vienna, Athens outbound and at Rome inbound. BIA came to be closely linked to the tour operator Island Sun which was acquired in May 1985.

For the summer 1987 season, BIA had a fleet of eight 1-11s in service, and the company continued to operate successfully until late 1989 when financial problems began to make an impact, attributed to the declining demand in the UK holiday charter market. Another negative factor was the fact that this carrier was not affiliated to a major tour operator which would have secured a more sound traffic base. BIA was forced to suspend its activity in February 1990 and subsequently went into receivership.

BRITISH UNITED AIRWAYS (BUA)

The name of British United Airways (BUA) was adopted by Airwork on 19 May 1960, with Hunting-Clan and several of its subsidiary air carriers merged into the new company. BUA became fully operational on 1 July 1960 and thus emerged as Britain's largest independent airline of that time. Holiday charter services were operated, using a varied fleet of aircraft, to destinations across Europe. BUA was the first airline to introduce the new BAC 1-11 twinjet into scheduled service on 9 April 1964, followed by their use also for IT charter work. The Caledonian Airways take-over of BUA became effective on 30 November 1970 and the new airline became known as Caledonian/BUA, re-named British Caledonian Airways in November 1971.

BRYMON AIRWAYS

The airline Brymon Airways was established in 1972 for the purpose of developing a scheduled service network from Plymouth and Exeter to regional destinations in the UK, to the Channel Islands and France. On a number of occasions, Brymon has also operated IT charter services albeit on a limited scale, and it was the first air carrier to operate ski charters out of London (City Airport) to Chambéry in the Winter of 1989/90.

CALEDONIAN AIRWAYS ~ CALEDONIAN/BUA
BRITISH CALEDONIAN AIRWAYS ~ CALEDONIAN AIRWAYS

Founded on 27 April 1961, Caledonian Airways launched charter operations on 29 November of that year. Initially, the air carrier used DC-7C airliners for its long-haul passenger charter flights. US presidential approval for charter operations to the USA was granted on 17 June 1963, and this was an important decision for Caledonian as it was the first non-US charter carrier to win such a licence. The carrier came to be extensively involved with trans-Atlantic charter work linking London, Manchester and Glasgow with New York, San Francisco and Toronto. Britannia airliners were introduced into IT charter work on 14 April 1965 on the London-Gatwick—Venice route, followed by service on the North Atlantic from 8 May 1965 onward. Caledonian phased its DC-7C aircraft out of service at the end of the Summer 1965 season, and this was followed by the introduction of 707 jets in time for summer 1968, mainly on North Atlantic charter routes.

Meanwhile, Caledonian Airways acquired BUA in November 1970 and this prompted the formation of a new airline named Caledonian/BUA. The company adopted the name British Caledonian Airways (BCAL) in November 1971 to highlight the proposed creation, then under way, of a 'second force' airline in Britain. In addition to serving a growing network of scheduled routes, BCAL also operated transatlantic affinity and European IT charters. The company decided not to take part in North Atlantic ABC charters in Summer 1978 in view of the low yield situation in that market at that time.

BCAL announced its take-over by British Airways on 16 July 1987, a move which, after extended negotiations, was completed in December. The company's charter activity was merged with British Airtours, reverting back to the former name of Caledonian Airways. British Airways sold Caledonian Airways to the tour operator Inspirations on 31 March 1995. However, BA did retain a link with the charter carrier since the latter operated scheduled services to selected destinations on its behalf. This contract was, however, lost to Flying Colours, from the start of the Summer 1997 season.

For the Summer 1999 season, Caledonian Airways used a fleet of eight TriStars, six A320s and two DC-10-30s for IT charter operations. On 1 September 1999, the carrier was merged with Flying Colours to form JMC Airlines but continued to operate in its own colours until March 2000.

CAMBRIAN AIRWAYS

This company's history goes back to April 1935 when it was registered as Cambrian Air Services. After the war, operations were resumed in January 1946 with general charter work. The company altered its name to Cambrian Airways on 23 May 1955, which followed the introduction of DC-3s and its move into scheduled services. On 2 February 1963, Cambrian started to introduce ex-BEA Viscount 700s into scheduled service, followed by IT charter operations from 25 May 1963 on behalf of a Cardiff-based tour operator, to Nice, Rimini and Valencia. The availability of this airliner subsequently led to a considerable expansion of IT charter work from Cardiff and Bristol. In November 1967, Cambrian Airways became part of the British Air Services group. BAC 1-11s entered service on 15 January 1970 and, in Summer 1970, also came to be used for IT charter work during the weekend. The airline created its affiliated tour operator Cambrian Air Holidays in 1970, the intention being to counter-balance the activity of the Clarksons/Hourmont Travel group. On 1 September 1972, the airline became an integral part of the British Airways Regional Division and Cambrian Airways thus lost its individual identity for good.

CAPITAL AIRLINES

This company was formed in 1988 and was based at Leeds/Bradford Airport. In addition to its scheduled services, Capital Airlines also operated IT charters during the weekend and at off-peak periods, the first service flown on 26 August 1989 with a BAe 146 on the Leeds/Bradford-Palma de Majorca route. The airline suspended operations on 28 June 1990.

CIRO'S AVIATION

Ciro's Aviation was formed in 1949 and was involved in the operation of holiday charters from London (Gatwick) throughout the Summer 1950 season using one DC-3. However the company folded in October 1950.

CONTINENTAL AIR SERVICES (CAS) ~ CONTINENTAL AIR TRANSPORT

Continental Air Services (CAS) came into existence in November 1957 in Jersey C.I. Initially operating from Rotterdam under contract to a shipping concern, the carrier's Viking aircraft also undertook IT charter work in 1958 from Rotterdam, on behalf of a Dutch tour operator, as well as from Blackbushe in England. In early 1959, CAS established its main base at Blackbushe Airport from where IT and student charters were flown, with Rotterdam and Southend also used as departure points in summer 1959. After an ownership change in December 1959, the airline's name was changed to Continental Air Transport and Southend became the carrier's main base in January 1960. With a fleet of seven Vikings and a DC-4, a more extensive IT charter pattern was in operation throughout summer 1960, with Southend and Manchester as the main departure points. Financial problems led to the carrier's suspension of service in October 1960.

DAN-AIR SERVICES

On 21 May 1953, Dan-Air Services was set up with a home base at Southend, initially, to undertake general charter work. It was only after the air carrier's move to Blackbushe Airport to the south-west of London, in January 1955, that IT charter operations were initiated in May of that year. When Blackbushe Airport closed down on 31 May 1960, Dan-Air established its main operating base at London's Gatwick Airport.

In 1959, three Ambassador aircraft joined the fleet and this type enjoyed great popularity with passengers. Their number had increased to eight aircraft by 1966 and they formed the backbone for the airline's ITC work then, in May 1966, Dan-Air placed two Comet 4 jets into service on holiday charter routes. The bulk of its IT charters was flown on behalf of the tour operators Clarksons and Horizon, but the demise of British Eagle in November 1968 brought Dan-Air additional IT charter contracts. 1969 saw the addition of BAC 1-11s and the Comet fleet increased to eleven aircraft.

Although, over the years, Dan-Air had also started a number of regional scheduled services, IT charter flying continued to form the bulk of the airline's activity. In March 1968, Dan-Air also started holiday charters from West-Berlin and this involvement continued until 1991 when, as a result of Germany's reunification, Dan-Air withdrew from the German market. In April 1971, Dan-Air started affinity group charter operations on North Atlantic routes for which 707 long-range jets were acquired then in 1974, the airline was granted a licence for affinity group charters to Hong Kong. Dan-Air's involvement with long-haul passenger operations continued until 1978.

In 1973, Dan-Air acquired three 727s which were used for IT charters both from the UK and West-Berlin. The airline operated Britain's largest network of IT charters in 1974, carrying over 2.1 million passengers, and 1975 saw the addition of six more BAC 1-11 jets used mainly on holiday charter routes. The phase-out of fuel-thirsty Comets was completed by November 1980 which coincided with the introduction of 737-200 aircraft in that month and new BAe 146 jets were introduced into ITC charter work in December 1984. Dan-Air was the UK's first charter carrier to introduce widebody Airbus A300 jets in May 1986 for service on high-traffic charter routes to Corfu, Faro and Palma de Majorca.

Dan-Air began to expand its international scheduled network to key cities in Europe, focused on London (Gatwick), from 1980. By 1989, the airline's annual passenger total reached a record 6.2 million but, hit by recession and a general slowdown in the tourism sector based on charter air travel, Dan-Air increasingly incurred financial difficulties which ultimately prompted its demise. On 23 October 1992, the decision was taken for the airline to become a subsidiary of British Airways and this deal was completed on 8 November 1992 when the name Dan-Air disappeared. Prior to this take-over, the company had decided to give up its involvement with IT charter work.

DEBONAIR

Debonair was registered on 1 October 1995 and initiated low-cost scheduled operations on 19 June 1996 from its base at London (Luton) Airport. Its route network was extended to a number of cities in continental Europe and a fleet of seven BAe 146 jets was used. In 1998, for the first time, Debonair became involved with holiday charter operations from the UK and Germany to a select number of holiday destinations in Europe, but financial problems led to bankruptcy in late September 1999.

DERBY AVIATION ~ DERBY AIRWAYS
BRITISH MIDLAND AIRWAYS (BMA)

On 16 February 1949, Derby Aviation was set up for adhoc charter work, but in 1953 the company initiated seasonal service on a number of holiday routes from Derby (Burnaston Airport) and other cities in the Midlands. In Summer 1958, the airline started IT charter operations with DC-3s then, on 12 March 1959, the company was re-registered as Derby Airways. IT charter flights in Summer 1959 were operated from Derby, Birmingham, Manchester and London-Gatwick. May 1962 saw the introduction of four-engined Argonaut airliners which came to be extensively used throughout Europe on charter routes with high demand.

The company adopted the name British Midland Airways (BMA) on 1 October 1964 and Derby's Burnaston Airport remained its main base until all operations were transferred, on 2 April 1965, to the newly commissioned Castle Donington Airport. It was from here that BMA gradually expanded its network of scheduled and charter routes with Argonaut aircraft used until June 1968. Viscounts were placed into service from January 1967, a 707 for transatlantic operations from April 1970, BAC 1-11s from May 1970 and Heralds from March 1973. The airline's involvement with IT charter work continued until April 1974 when the market situation prompted BMA to withdraw from this field. It was only in Summer 1982 when BMA resumed service on holiday charter routes. BMA has also made great efforts to expand into the field of scheduled services, providing links not only for important cities in the Midlands but also from London. The addition to its fleet of DC-9s, 737s, F-100s and A319/320s and, in 1999, of A321 aircraft, has allowed the airline to make use of spare capacity in the course of the weekend for IT charter operations.

DIAMOND AIRWAYS

The charter carrier Diamond Airways was set up by private investors and commenced IT charter operations from Cardiff, its main base, in May 1988 with two 737s.

DONALDSON INTERNATIONAL AIRWAYS

Although formed in 1964, Donaldson only commenced IT charter flying in April 1969 from London-Gatwick and Glasgow using three Britannia aircraft. The company also acquired two 707s, the first of which was introduced on transatlantic charter routes in May 1971 and, by the end of 1972, the fleet of 707s had increased to four aircraft. However a re-organization of the carrier took place in early 1973 which led to the sale of two 707s. A mixed pattern of European IT, North Atlantic and Far East charter operations continued until the airline terminated its operations on 8 August 1974, prompted by financial difficulties.

DON EVERALL AVIATION

The charter carrier Don Everall Aviation came into existence on 5 September 1951. The acquisition of a DC-3 enabled the carrier to commence international IT charter flying in May 1957 from Birmingham to several continental destinations and this charter work was extended with the phasing in of Viking airliners in May 1960. Don Everall Aviation terminated its IT charter operations in September 1960 and subsequently merged with Air Safaris in November 1960, although adhoc charter work continued until January 1961.

EAGLE AVIATION ~ EAGLE AIRWAYS ~ CUNARD-EAGLE AIRWAYS
BRITISH EAGLE INTERNATIONAL

Eagle Aviation was established on 14 April 1948 and became involved with general charter work and operations on behalf of British government departments. When policies changed with regard to the operation of scheduled services, granting the independent airlines a chance to enter this field, Eagle chose to take on new challenges and this was accompanied with a name change to Eagle Airways on 1 July 1953. The company's sphere of operation subsequently covered scheduled services, charters under contract to the UK Government and IT charters from Blackbushe Airport.

Eagle sought rights for transatlantic operations and, for this new area of activity, formed the wholly-owned subsidiary Eagle Overseas Airways on 11 December 1957 for charters to the Caribbean and North America. Transatlantic charters were operated by DC-6 and Britannia aircraft. The Cunard shipping concern acquired a 60% share in Eagle on 19 May 1960 and this led to the formation of a new company named Cunard Eagle Airways (Holdings) to group together all the separate Eagle companies then in existence.

As part of a general re-organisation, British Eagle International Airlines was formed on 9 August 1963 followed, at the end of December 1963, by the take-over of the Liverpool-based airline Starways. North Atlantic charter flying was resumed in Summer 1965 and a switch to jet operations commenced in April 1966 with the delivery of the first BAC 1-11 jet and its introduction into scheduled service on 9 May 1966. The 1-11 jets

came to be used on a wide network of seasonal scheduled and IT charter services radiating from several UK cities. In spite of returning to profitable operations in 1964, the airline's financial situation gradually deteriorated to the extent that it was forced to close down and its operations were terminated on 6 November 1968.

EAST ANGLIAN FLYING SERVICES (EAFS) ~ CHANNEL AIRWAYS

On 16 August 1946, EAFS (East Anglian Flying Services) was established, specialising in the operation of adhoc passenger flying from its Southend base, from which eventually a pattern of regular short-haul services evolved. Several types of aircraft were added to the fleet in the late fifties and early sixties, including Bristol Wayfarers in 1957, Vikings in 1958, DC-3s in 1960 and a DC-4 in April 1962. The availability of Vikings led to IT charter work beginning in May 1959.-

The company changed its name to Channel Airways on 25 October 1962 and, by acquiring the Southend-based air carrier Tradair in December 1962, Viscount aircraft were introduced into service. Subsequently, more Viscounts were acquired from BEA and Continental Airlines which allowed Channel Airways to become one of the larger airlines in Europe handling IT charter work. Also 58-seat Avro 748s were in use on holiday charter routes from 1 May 1966, mainly from Southend. The first BAC 1-11 jet was delivered on 14 June 1967, for scheduled and IT charter work, followed by the addition of Trident jets in June 1968.

The proximity of Southend Airport to its urban surroundings created problems over jet aircraft noise, coupled with operational problems on account of the relatively short runway, and this prompted Channel Airways to move the bulk of its IT charter operations to Stansted Airport in early 1968. In January 1970, the first Comet 4B was delivered and the acquisition of another four Comets led to Channel Airways expanding its IT charter operations from UK cities as well as out of West-Berlin from March 1971. However financial problems emerged later in that year and the company went into receivership at the beginning of February 1972 with flight operations suspended on 29 February.

EROS AIRLINES ~ EROS AIRLINE (UK)

Eros Airlines was established on 12 December 1957 in Cyprus but remained inactive until another company had been formed under the name of Eros Airline (UK) Ltd on 2 March 1962. Using a fleet of three Vikings from its London-Gatwick base, Eros operated IT and student charters throughout the Summer 1962 and 1963 seasons. Licensing problems forced the airline to cease trading in April 1964.

EURAVIA ~ BRITANNIA AIRWAYS

On 1 December 1961, Euravia was founded to specialize in IT charter flying mainly on behalf of the tour operator Universal Sky Tours with Luton Airport chosen as the company's base and operations commenced on 5 May 1962 with a Manchester-Perpignan-Palma de Majorca IT charter flight. Initially, the Euravia fleet consisted of three L-049 Constellations. In September 1962 when Euravia took over Skyways, three L-749 Constellations were added to the fleet and another two Constellations were acquired from defunct Trans-European Airways later in 1962. For the summer 1963 season, a fleet of eight Constellations was in service, thus meeting the increase in capacity requirements of the airline's tour operator partners.

On 16 August 1964, Euravia was renamed Britannia Airways, just a short while before the introduction of turboprop Britannia airliners on 6 December 1964. This initiated the gradual replacement of the Constellations in use so far. Britannia Airways became a wholly-owned subsidiary of the Thomson organization on 26 April 1965 which, since that time, has provided the financial background for the continuing success of the carrier. An event of significance for the entire IT charter business was the UK Government's approval, in 1965, for tour operators to offer eleven and twelve-day holiday package tours which was a move away from the traditional holiday trip of two weeks duration. For charter airlines, in turn, this meant better aircraft utilization especially during the low season. In summer 1965, Britannia had five Britannia turboprop airliners in use and this allowed the withdrawal of Constellations by August of that year. On 31 March 1968, Britannia commenced IT charter operations from London-Gatwick, in line with the policy of its parent tour operator Thomson to offer IT charter flights from more departure points throughout Britain. July 1968 saw Britannia becoming the first European charter carrier to take delivery of new 737-200 jets. The era of turboprop operations soon came to an end in December 1970 with the withdrawal of all Britannia aircraft.

In April 1971, Britannia entered the fiercely competitive North Atlantic affinity charter market and 707s were used to serve destinations in the USA and Canada. This involvement lasted until early 1973 when, as a result of a change in the rules covering transatlantic charters, it was decided to opt out of this business sector.

The demise of the charter carriers Court Line and Donaldson in 1974 brought additional business to Britannia Airways, which helped to strengthen its leading position among British charter carriers. By 1976, the airline was enjoying a market share of almost 30%. The 737 fleet reached a maximum of thirty-four aircraft during the summer season of 1982 then, on 8 February 1984, the first widebody jet in the form of a Boeing 767-200 was delivered to the airline's home base at Luton. In summer 1984, 767 aircraft were deployed from Luton and Manchester to the most popular destinations, allowing Thomson to offer more capacity in line with ongoing demand. The addition of 767 aircraft enabled Britannia to start long-haul charters to the Caribbean and Southeast Asia and, in 1984, Britannia's annual passenger total reached beyond four million, giving it a very prominent ranking among the leisure airlines of Europe.

Thomson acquired its rival tour operator Horizon Travel in October 1988, together with its in-house carrier Orion Airways. This added two 737-300s and two A300s to the Britannia fleet but the Airbus aircraft were soon disposed of. The Australian Government granted traffic rights

to Britannia Airways for IT charters to Australian destinations starting in Winter 1988/89. This was followed by approval for charters to New Zealand from Winter 1991/92. At the end of 1990, the first 757 aircraft were introduced into service which initiated a wide-ranging fleet change in that all the 737s were withdrawn by 1994. For that year's summer season, Britannia had a total of nineteen 757s and ten 767s in service.

The German tour operator Paul Gunther Tours contracted Britannia Airways, within the framework of the liberalization of air transport in the EU, to operate IT charter flights from Germany to the Dominican Republic. Initially, these plans were not approved by the authorities, due to objections raised by German charter companies. Eventually, the operations did go ahead, as planned, in November 1996 but the authorities refused permission for Britannia to operate non-stop from Germany to the Dominican Republic so that flights had to be routed from Berlin and Cologne/Bonn to Puerto Plata via Manchester. To overcome such problems in future, Britannia founded a fully-owned German subsidiary Britannia Airways GmbH in 1997. Further involvement with the tourism industry in Europe followed when Britannia took over the Swedish charter carrier Blue Scandinavia as a result of the Thomson organization acquiring that company's tour operator parent Fritidsresor.

In line with South Africa opening up to international tourism, Britannia started IT charters to Capetown and Johannesburg on 19 November 1997. For its Summer 1998 IT charter programme, Britannia Airways used a fleet of 757s and 767s and the carrier's charter service pattern covered most major cities in Britain. For the summer 1999 season, Britannia leased in four A320 aircraft for service on charter routes with lower capacity requirements.

Britannia Airways is the world's largest charter carrier whose passenger total reached 8.4 million in 1998. For the ninth year in succession, the company was privileged to win the TTG award for 'Top Charter Airline' again in 1999. A fleet of eighteen 757 and thirteen 767s served the airline's route network in the Summer of 2000.

EUROPEAN AVIATION ~ EUROPEAN AVIATION AIR CHARTER

Established in 1989 as European Aviation, the company specialised in the maintenance and sale of second-hand BAC 1-11s, and providing a lease service to various airline customers later on. Eventually, so many BAC 1-11s were acquired that it became the largest operator of the type in the world.

The company formed a subsidiary carrier under the name of European Aviation Air Charter which, from 1994 onward, became involved with the operation of IT services from London-Gatwick and Manchester.

EXCALIBUR

Excalibur was set up in January 1992 to succeed failed TEA UK, taking over staff of the former company. Financial backing came from the 3i Group and Air Malta, and operations started on 1 May 1992 with flights from London (Gatwick) and Manchester to Tenerife, with two A320 aircraft forming part of the initial fleet.

The carrier operated successfully and passenger numbers reached two million by June 1995. In the course of that summer, Excalibur initiated 'seat-only' operations from East Midlands to Alicante, Faro, Ibiza, Mahon and Palma. In early 1996, after being acquired by the tour operator Globespan, a policy change led to Excalibur giving up its medium-haul IT charters in Europe in favour of long-haul charters to North America, from London, Manchester and Glasgow. Furthermore, it was planned to operate charters to Australia in the Winter season of 1996/97, offering departures from Glasgow for the first time. Excalibur acquired two DC-10 aircraft for its long-haul operations, but a number of operational problems occurred early in the Summer 1996 season, causing much adverse publicity and a resultant loss of passenger confidence. This caused the carrier to suspend operations and liquidation followed on 26 June 1996.

FALCON AIRWAYS

Falcon Airways was set up in March 1959, initially using Viking and Hermes 4 airlines for IT charters from Blackbushe starting in May. All operations were transferred to London-Gatwick Airport as of 1 June 1960 but the carrier terminated its operations temporarily in November 1960. The acquisition of L-049 Constellations in early 1961 led to problems with the authorities and eventually only one aircraft was in service on IT charter routes from May 1961. A range of problems caused Falcon to terminate its activity on 21 September 1961 and, in January 1962, the airline went into receivership.

FLIGHTLINE

Since its formation in April 1989, Flightline has concentrated on IT charter operations from Bournemouth on behalf of the tour operator Palmair. With a fleet consisting of BAe 146 jets.

FLYING COLOURS AIRLINES

Flying Colours Airlines was set up in November 1995 and IT holiday charters were initiated on 6 March 1997 on the Manchester—Arrecife route. The initial fleet of four 757s was deployed from Manchester and London-Gatwick, supplemented by an A320 based at Glasgow. The carrier has operated in close affiliation with the tour operators Sunset Holidays and Club 18-30 forming part of the Flying Colours Group.

The tour operator Sunworld — a partner in the Thomas Cook Group — acquired the airline Flying Colours in June 1998. This led to the merger of its in-house carrier Airworld with Flying Colours at the start of the Winter 1998/99 season and the combined fleet stood at six A320, two A321 and six 757 aircraft. In Winter 1998/99, Flying Colours operated IT charters also from Amsterdam and Maastricht/Aachen. For the summer of 1999, Flying Colours had a fleet of twelve 757s and four A320s in service. On 1 September 1999, the new company JMC Airlines was formed through the merger of Flying Colours with Caledonian Airways although Flying Colours continued operating, with its own identity, until 25 March 2000.

GB AIRWAYS

GB Airways' history goes back to 1930 when it was set up as Gibraltar Airways. The airline was involved with IT charters from Summer 1989 until the end of the Summer 1995 season. Its commitment to scheduled operations, especially since becoming a British Airways franchise carrier on 1 February 1995, has committed the company's fleet to this type of work and IT charters are no longer operated.

GLOBE MEDITERRANEAN

Globe Mediterranean came into existence in early 1991 and was due to commence IT charters on 21 June 1991 from Manchester. Due to the late delivery of 737 aircraft which were planned to be used, the carrier ran into operational problems and was forced to suspend operations after only one week. Plans to resume service at a later date did not materialise and a creditors' meeting on 14 August 1991 led to the company being disbanded.

GO - FLY

In addition to its scheduled low-cost operations, GO-Fly has operated IT charter services from London-Stansted to Salzburg both in summer 1999, using 737s.

HIGHLAND EXPRESS

Highland Express terminated its scheduled operations between Scotland and Canada in mid-December 1987 and planned to start holiday charter services to Orlando, Florida, in January 1988. This did not work out, however, and the airline was disbanded shortly after.

HUNTING AIR TRANSPORT ~ HUNTING-CLAN AIR TRANSPORT

This company's history dates back to December 1945 when it was founded as Hunting Air Travel for general charter work. In August 1951, the company changed its name to Hunting Air Transport then, in October 1953, the Clan Shipping Line acquired a stake in the air carrier which resulted in the company's name changing to Hunting-Clan Air Transport. Beginning in May 1958, the airline started IT charter flying from London-Heathrow, and also from Manchester in 1959, to European destinations. The carrier merged with the Airwork group of companies to become British United Airways on 1 July 1960.

INDEPENDENT AIR TRAVEL ~ INDEPENDENT AIR TRANSPORT (IAT) ~ BLUE-AIR

Founded on 1 January 1953, Independent Air Travel acquired four Vikings in April 1956 for IT charters from Blackbushe and Bournemouth. That month also saw the carrier's name changed to Independent Air Transport (IAT). For the 1958 summer season, IAT had three DC-4s and six Vikings in service. In April 1959, the company's name became Blue-Air, prompted by the inquiry into the crash of one of its Vikings and the resultant adverse publicity. Operations were suspended in October 1959 and the company folded soon after.

INTER EUROPEAN AIRWAYS (IEA)

The Cardiff-based tour operator Aspro Travel formed Inter European Airways (IEA) in 1986 to handle its IT charter programme and operations commenced on 18 May 1987 from Cardiff with two leased 737-200 aircraft. After a break in Winter 1986/87, operations were resumed on 2 May 1988 with a Cardiff-Rhodes flight using two 737-300s and one 757 which was added in March 1990. In November 1993, IEA was absorbed into Airtours International.

INTRA AIRWAYS

Intra Airways came into existence on 1 January 1969, with Jersey serving as its base. Beginning in that first summer season, Intra operated IT charters to destinations in nearby France, followed by operations from Ostend in summer 1970 and from Brussels in summer 1971, to fly tourists to Jersey. By 1973, three DC-3s were in service. The lease of a Viscount from March 1976 onward led to Intra Airways operating more IT charters than in previous seasons. The carrier terminated its activity in 1978.

INVICTA

Manston-based Invicta was set up in November 1964 and initiated IT charters in March 1965 on the Manston-Basel route. With its fleet of two DC-4 and two Viking airliners, Invicta carried 120,143 passengers in its first year. In 1968, two Viscounts were added to the fleet and more UK cities, as well as West-Berlin, became departure points for IT charter operations. In January 1969, Invicta was merged with BMA.

INVICTA INTERNATIONAL AIRLINES

The name 'Invicta' reappeared in early 1971 when Invicta International Airlines was set up. Luton was chosen as its main base and holiday charters were flown using Vanguard aircraft. Two 720B jets were acquired in 1973 but only one aircraft was used by the airline for holiday charter operations. The company suspended its passenger services in October 1975.

JANUS AIRWAYS

The Midlands-based tour operator Hards Travel was involved in the formation of Janus Airways in 1982. Using two Herald aircraft, Janus initiated IT charter flights on 2 January 1983. In Summer 1984, using both Herald and Viscount aircraft, the carrier was operating series of charter flights from Coventry and Lydd to Beauvais as well as Ostend in connection with touring holidays on the continent. Operations were terminated in 1986.

JERSEY AIRLINES

Established in 1948, Jersey Airlines was re-registered as Airlines (Jersey) in December 1948, to focus its activity on scheduled inter-island services and links with mainland UK and France. In winter 1962/63, IT charters were operated on behalf of Lord Brothers from London-Gatwick to continental destinations using Bristol Wayfairer and Herald aircraft. Although becoming part of the Air Holdings Group in May 1962, the airline continued operating under its well-known identity until 1 August 1963 when the name of British United (C.I.) Airways was adopted.

JMC AIRLINES

The European Commission approved the merger of the Thomas Cook Group with Carlson Leisure Group in February 1999. This led to the formation, on 1 September 1999, of JMC Airlines by the intergration of the two charter carriers Flying Colours and Caledonian Airways. The new airline carries the same identity as its sister company JMC Holidays Ltd. Using its own AOC, JMC launched IT charter operations on 26 March 2000 and, with a fleet of sixteen 757, ten A320 and two DC-10-30 aircraft, the airline operated IT charters from nine UK cities throughout summer 2000.

LAKER AIRWAYS

On 8 February 1966, Freddie Laker, former MD of BUA, set up Laker Airways to specialize in IT charter work. Adhoc operations commenced on 29 July 1966 from London-Gatwick, the airline's base, with Britannia aircraft then, using new 1-11 jets, Laker began IT charters in March 1967 from London and Manchester. There was close co-operation with the airline's tour operator partners Lord Brothers (later re-named Laker Air Travel) and Wings. An innovative approach to the working relationship between the charter company and tour operators was that ITCs were handled on a 'time charter' basis whereby Laker Airways aircraft flew a guaranteed number of hours, within a specified period of time, according to the contract with a tour operator. IT charter operations from West-Berlin commenced in 1969. Operations were expanded following the demise of Treffield in June 1967 and after taking over the Liverpool-based tour operator Arrowsmith.

The initial Laker Airways fleet consisted of two Britannias, followed by three BAC 1-11 jets in 1967 and two 707s acquired from defunct British Eagle in 1969. The 707s were used to launch North Atlantic charter operations in 1970 to New York and Toronto and also to provide extra capacity on high traffic charter routes in Europe. In 1976, the airline carried 1,024,753 passengers and its aircraft averaged a daily utilization of 8.6 hrs, second only to Britannia Airways.

Laker Airways was one the first European airlines to introduce the DC-10 at the start of the winter 1972/73 season to Spain's Balearic and Canary Islands and also to North America. The airline's success in the North Atlantic market was due to the popularity of the 'Affinity Group' charter travel formula and, by 1979, Laker Airways was carrying about 750,000 passengers between Britain and North America. In line with promoting low cost air travel, Laker devised the 'Skytrain' concept for travel between the UK and the USA, as a no frills, scheduled walk-on service. Obtaining the necessary licenses took the airline several years and involved a great deal of legal wrangling on both sides of the Atlantic. The London~New York 'Skytrain' service eventually commenced on 26 September 1977, followed by a similar London~Los Angeles service on

26 September 1978. By that time, the Laker Airways fleet consisted of four DC-10-30s, two 707s and five 1-11s and the operating pattern covered IT charters in Europe, ABC flights to North America and the 'Skytrain' service to New York and Los Angeles. However popular the 'Skytrain' turned out to be, the IATA airlines vigorously objected to this type of service from the beginning. Seeking to exclude Laker Airways from their North Atlantic domain, the scheduled airlines decided to offer promotional fares almost as low as those applicable under the 'Skytrain' travel formula. A fiercely competitive situation arose which gradually developed into a serious financial crisis for Laker Airways, which was aggravated by a general downturn in the airline business caused by faltering economic growth and significant oil price rises. The airline was unable to opt out of this dilemma. Operations had to be suspended suddenly on 25 February 1982 and the company went into receivership.

LANCASHIRE AIRCRAFT CORPORATION (LAC)

LAC was founded in WW II for general charter work, but it was in the summer 1952 season that holiday charter flights were first operated with York aircraft and, from 1953 onward, with newly acquired DC-3s. Summer 1956 saw the expansion of LAC IT charter operations to continental destinations from London-Gatwick, Southend, Manchester and Blackpool. For operations in summer 1957, all the LAC aircraft were re-painted in the colours of Silver City Airways which signified the end of LAC passenger charter operations under the original company's name.

LEISURE AIR ~ LEISURE INTERNATIONAL AIRWAYS (LIA)

On 18 February 1992, Leisure International Airways (LIA) was formed as a subsidiary company to Air UK Leisure, to concentrate on the operation of long-haul IT charter services, using 767ER aircraft. The company commenced long-haul charters in April 1993, covering destinations in North America and the Caribbean, and a London~Lagos service was operated in Winter 1993/94 with a new service to Las Vegas started in January 1996.

Air UK Leisure was merged into LIA on 1 April 1996 and the company completed its move from London-Stansted to Gatwick Airport. It was fully owned by the tour operator Unijet and, as a result of Unijet being acquired from the tour operator group First Choice, LIA was merged into Air 2000 at the start of the Winter 1998/99 period.

LLOYD INTERNATIONAL

Set up on 18 January 1961, Lloyd International had close links with the shipping business. Initially one DC-4 was available for air freight services to the Far East, operated in the form of 'tramp flights', then the carrier commenced IT charter flights in June 1961. A DC-6C was then introduced in 1964, followed by Britannia aircraft in July 1965. 8.497 passengers were carried by IT charter flights in 1965. For the Summer 1966 season, Lloyd International won a contract from a Berlin tour operator for IT charters which dovetailed with a series of weekend flights out of Glasgow. The acquisition of 707 equipment also allowed the company to start North Atlantic charter flights in April 1970 but financial problems forced the airline into receivership in June 1972.

LOGANAIR

Loganair was founded on 1 February 1962 and initially concentrated on scheduled short-haul operations in Scotland and the carrier also operated IT charters at off peak times. After joining the Airlines of Britain Group at the end of 1987, Loganair began operating on a number of regional routes throughout the UK using BAe 146 jets, This involvement came to a close when Loganair became a British Airways franchise partner on 11 July 1994.

LONDON CITY AIRWAYS (LCA)

London City Airways (LCA) was formed to provide scheduled service from London to nearby continental destinations out of the new City Airport. In addition to its scheduled work, LCA also operated IT charters to Zurich on behalf of the tour operator Falcon, throughout the Summer of 1989.

MAITLAND AIR CHARTER ~ MAITLAND DREWERY AVIATION

Maitland Air Charter was created in 1959 then, in March 1960, the name of the air carrier was changed to Maitland Drewery Aviation. IT charters were operated from April 1960 until August 1961 from both the carrier's London (Gatwick) base and also from Manchester and West Berlin using Viking and Viscount aircraft. In December 1961 however, all operations came to an end and the company folded.

MEDITERRANEAN EXPRESS

Mediterranean Express was set up in 1987 for IT charter work from the UK to Italian destinations, with a fleet of two BAC 1-11s. The first service was on 15 June 1987 on the London Luton-Naples route, but the company ran into financial problems which prompted the UK CAA to revoke the carrier's operating license in February 1988.

181

MEREDITH AIR TRANSPORT

Set up in 1952, Meredith Air Transport operated IT charters from December 1952 until early 1953 using a single DC3. However the company suspended its operations in May 1953, after selling its sole aircraft to Davies and Newman, the founders of Dan Air.

MONARCH AIRLINES

Monarch Airlines was founded on 1 June 1967 to specialize in IT charter work, and since that time there has been a close working relationship with the affiliated tour operator Cosmos. The initial fleet consisted of two Britannia 312 aircraft and the first commercial service took place on 5 April 1968 from Luton to Madrid. Monarch managed to take over some charter work from failed British Eagle in November 1968, including staff and, by the end of 1968, the carrier's fleet had grown to eight Britannias. In 1969, the second year of operations, the carrier's passenger total had risen to over 250,000, the growth in traffic having been influenced by the demise of several charter companies. The jet age began for Monarch on 15 September 1971 with the delivery from Northwest of their first Boeing 720B which was introduced into IT service on 13 December 1971 on the Luton-Tunis route. The addition of more 720Bs to the fleet led to the withdrawal of Britannias and the last aircraft were phased out in 1975. In summer 1972, the first IT charters were flown from Birmingham and Teesside, after having been focused exclusively on Luton until then.

From June until August 1974, Monarch operated trans-atlantic charters from Birmingham to Toronto, Calgary and Vancouver. Due to the collapse of Court Line in August 1974, Monarch acquired two 1-11 jets in March 1975 to handle the additional traffic arising out of this. In summer 1976, London-Gatwick was added as a departure point for holiday charter flights and the airline, now an all-jet operator, had three 720B and 1-11 jets each in service. Also in that summer, Monarch operated its first long-haul charters with a flight series to St. Lucia in the eastern Caribbean. The passenger total in 1976 rose to over 750,000. At the end of 1977, another two 720Bs were acquired followed by the addition, in 1978, of two 707s which were in service until 1979.

1980 saw the addition of two 737s fitted with long-range fuel tanks, as part of a fleet modernization programme. Monarch also set up an operations base at Berlin-Tegel Airport from where IT charter flying commenced on 30 March 1981 and continued until June 1983. It was Britain's first charter company to order Boeing 757s, with the first aircraft delivered in March 1983 and the 720B fleet subsequently disposed of. Monarch's passenger total stood at 1.1 million in 1980 and, by 1983, passenger traffic had risen to just under two million. In that year, the carrier formed its subsidiary company Monarch Air Travel which handled 'seat-only' sales and by mid-1985, Monarch's fleet consisted of four 737s and 757s each. In Winter 1987/88, Monarch operated to Male (Maldives) and in May 1988 to Orlando for the first time and by mid-summer 1988, the 757 fleet had grown to eight aircraft. Monarch also became the first charter carrier to introduce A300/600 Airbus aircraft in 1990.

A winter charter series to South Africa was planned, beginning in November 1991, but this did not materialize because the authorities in South Africa were not prepared to grant a license for more than two months ahead. For summer 1994, two A320 aircraft were added to support the three leased ones already in use then, in the autumn of 1995, new long-haul charter services were advertised, due to be operated for the tour operator Voyages Jules Verne, to Lusaka effective 12 December 1995, to San Jose C.R. effective 14 December 1995 and to Damascus effective 14 February 1996. Other long-haul destinations were Agra (India) from 1 October 1996, Harare from 5 November 1996 and to the Comores on 4 November 1997. As part of the fleet modernization under way, two new Airbus A321 and A330 aircraft each were added to the fleet from March 1999 onwards.

ORION AIRWAYS (1)

Formed on 26 January 1956, Orion Airways commenced IT charter operations in August 1957 from Blackbushe Airport. The carrier's base was transferred to London-Gatwick as of 1 June 1960, from where an extensive network of holiday charter routes was served, with three Vikings, throughout the summer 1960 season. Operations were terminated on 7 November 1960 and the company was wound up shortly after.

ORION AIRWAYS (2)

The tour operator Horizon Travel created Orion Airways in January 1979 as a wholly owned subsidiary company, choosing East Midlands Airport as its base. Operations started on 28 March 1980 from Birmingham, East Midlands, Luton and Manchester, with three 737-200s. Although Orion commenced ITC operations at a time of economic recession and the air charter business generally was penalized by relatively high fuel costs, the airline managed to operate successfully, carrying its millionth passenger in September 1981. On 26 March 1985, Orion started to phase in new 737-300 aircraft and, from April 1987 onward, was one of the first UK carriers to use two Airbus A300 aircraft obtained from Lufthansa. Orion was among the first British charter carriers to be granted a license for scheduled services between the UK and Spain. The company was merged with Britannia Airways on 26 January 1989.

OVERSEAS AVIATION

Formed in 1957, Overseas Aviation started operations from its main base airport at Southend on 1 March 1958. Throughout that summer, IT charters were also flown from West-Berlin, Frankfurt and Munich, then Manchester joined the list of departure airports in summer 1959. June 1960 saw Overseas Aviation move to its new base at London-Gatwick from where an extensive network of charter routes was served. The carrier took delivery of its first ex-BOAC Argonaut aircraft in November 1958 and subsequently built up a sizeable fleet of this type. However financial problems forced Overseas Aviation to suspend operations on 15 August 1961 and the company was subsequently wound up.

PARAMOUNT AIRWAYS

On 8 July 1986, Paramount Airways was set up with the intention of specializing in IT charter flying from Bristol, Cardiff and England's Southwest. The initial fleet consisted of two MD83 aircraft leased from GPA, and operations commenced on 1 May 1987 with IT charter flights from Bristol to Malaga and Tenerife. Paramount was given wide publicity over the deployment of MD83s for IT charters from the UK to Goa, India, during the Winter 1987/88 season.

In November 1988, Paramount took over Amber Air including that carrier's fleet and route licenses. In addition to its MD83 aircraft, Paramount also acquired a 737-200 for use on IT charters from (West-) Berlin for the Summer 1989 season. Due to financial problems however, Paramount was put into administration on 7 August 1989, although operations were maintained until the end of the 1989 Summer season when the air carrier disappeared from the holiday charter scene.

PEACH AIR

Formed in 1996 as a subsidiary company of Caledonian Airways, with a close link to the seatbroker specialist Goldcrest. Peach Air commenced IT charter flying on 1 May 1997 from London-Gatwick, and selected provincial cities in the UK and from Ireland [Eire]. Peach Air had an initial fleet of two 737-200s leased from Sabre Airways and one TriStar on lease from Atlanta Air Icelandic. The carrier ceased operations with effect from 1 November 1998.

PEGASUS

Pegasus came into existence early in 1958 using Viking aircraft from Luton and Blackbushe airports on IT charter routes. Operations were transferred from Blackbushe to London-Gatwick at the end of May 1960 due to the closure of Blackbushe airport, and IT charter flying continued throughout the Summer of 1961, with Gatwick, Manchester and Glasgow serving as departure points. At the end of October 1961 however, operations ceased due to the carrier's unsatisfactory financial situation.

PRINCESS AIR

The Southend-based travel agency and tour company Burstin Travel set up Princess Air in 1989 to handle its IT charters from Southend during the day and freight charters at night. Operations with a BAe 146 airliner commenced on 6 April 1990 from Southend to Palma de Majorca and a network of services based on Southend was in operation until early 1991. By that time, Princess Air had encountered financial problems due to a downturn in demand for freight charters and, on 27 February 1991, Princess Air was grounded and subsequently wound up.

SABRE AIRWAYS

Sabre Airways was formed by Air Foyle on 17 December 1994 as a successor company to failed Ambassador Airways. IT holiday charters commenced in the same month with 737s, and later ex-Dan Air 727-200s with the company taking over the former Ambassador Airways' contracts with tour operators. Sabre Airways expanded its network of holiday charter services in Summer 1997 and introduced the 737-800 into the fleet, as a replacement for the 727s.

SILVER CITY AIRWAYS (SCA)

Silver City Airways (SCA) was formed on 25 November 1946 and General charter work was undertaken which led to the operation of the first-ever cross-Channel car ferry in July 1948. After incorporating Air Kruise in 1958 and taking over Britavia's Hermes aircraft, SCA entered the holiday charter business in June 1959. A fleet of DC-3 and Hermes aircraft was used for IT charter work from Manston until 1960. Operations were then switched to London (Gatwick) for the Summer 1961 season then, in January 1962, SCA became part of the BUA Group. It retained its identity until October 1962 which coincided with the end of the IT charter season.

1973 saw the re-appearance of Silver City's name when a carrier was created to use the well-known name of earlier years. With a fleet of Vanguard aircraft, SCA again undertook charter operations but at the end of the year, this venture was terminated and the company's name disappeared for good.

SKYWAYS

Between its formation in early 1946 and March 1950, Skyways was involved with the operation of adhoc and general charter work. For a time, Skyways provided DC-4 aircraft to BOAC prior to the corporation phasing in their own Argonaut equipment. The end of the Berlin Airlift and its contract flying on behalf of BOAC left Skyways in a precarious situation which led to its voluntary liquidation in March 1950.

Almost immediately, a new Skyways emerged with a reduced fleet of six DC-3s but lack of work again prompted a temporary shut-down of the company in February 1952. One month later, Skyways was bought out by LAC. Retaining its identity, Skyways was involved with general charter work using the LAC fleet of York aircraft and, after the acquisition of Hermes aircraft from BOAC, Skyways became involved with IT charter work in Summer 1955. By 1960, the York and Hermes airliners had been withdrawn from passenger service and ex-BOAC L-749 Constellations were in use for IT charter operations across Europe, focused on London-Gatwick.

In addition, Skyways operated holiday charters from Lympne throughout the Summer 1962 season. Since the Luton-based charter carrier Euravia was in need of additional aircraft to meet its associated tour operator's capacity requirements, Skyways — together with its Constellation fleet — was taken over as of 1 September 1962.

STARWAYS

Formed on 7 December 1948, Starways used Blackpool as a base until 1949, when it moved to Liverpool. 1951 then saw the start of IT charter operations with a DC-3. Two DC-4 aircraft were used in Summer 1958 for holiday charter flights from Belfast, Glasgow, Liverpool and Manchester, and a Viscount was then acquired in February 1961.

Holiday charter routes continued to be served until the end of the Summer 1963 season. By then, negotiations had been under way for the carrier's merger with British Eagle. Skyways subsequently suspended operations at the end of December 1963 and was integrated into British Eagle as of 1 January 1964.

SWISS UNIVERSAL AIR CHARTER

Starting in July 1957, a Viking of Independent Air Travel came to be used by Swiss Universal for IT charter flights between Blackbushe and Basel. A similar arrangement continued after this aircraft joined the fleet of Overseas Aviation. When the latter company folded in August 1961, this led to the suspension of the Swiss Universal operations.

TEA UK

TEA UK was established in 1988 to form part of the pan-European airline consortium under the umbrella of TEA Belgium. Taking over from the failed charter carrier Mediterranean Express, TEA UK commenced operations on 21 March 1989 on the Birmingham-Grenoble route.

However the company was badly affected by the downturn in the UK holiday charter business of 1989, causing financial problems. Operations did, however, continue as before but plans for additional aircraft were abandoned. The carrier continued its activity until the collapse of its parent company TEA Belgium in September 1991. The impact of this was such that TEA UK ceased trading on 27 September 1991 and was declared bankrupt on 16 October of the same year.

TRADAIR

Tradair was a Southend-based charter company formed on 22 November 1957 and, with the use of two Viking aircraft, IT charters were flown mainly from Southend in the course of the Summer 1958 season. For Summer 1959, Tradair had seven Vikings in service for an extended pattern of holiday charter services, later supported by two Viscounts which were purchased in January 1960.

Financial problems hit the air carrier late in 1961 and a receiver was appointed in early November. Tradair was, however, able to maintain its operations for a short while and became a subsidiary of Channel Airways at the end of December 1961.

TRANSAIR

Transair's history goes back to 12 February 1947 when it was founded for general charter work. DC-3s were in use for Summer 1953 IT charters from London-Croydon, then a Viscount was placed into service in October 1957. May 1958 saw the carrier moving its base to London-Gatwick. and, by that time, the fleet comprised twelve DC-3s and two Viscounts. Transair became a part of BUA on 1 July 1960.

TRANS EUROPEAN AVIATION ~ TRANS EUROPEAN AIRWAYS

Formed in 1959, Trans European Aviation initiated IT charter flying with an L-049 Constellation from London-Gatwick in July 1961. At that time, the company changed its name to Trans European Airways.

In the course of Summer 1962, holiday charter services were also in operation from West-Berlin but, as a result of financial problems, the air carrier went into receivership on 27 July 1962 and operations were suspended in August.

TRANSMERIDIAN

After its formation on 5 October 1962, Transmeridian operated adhoc freight and passenger charter flights with DC-4 Skymaster equipment. In April 1963, IT charter flying started from Luton and continued through the Summer seasons of 1963 and 1964.

TREFFIELD AVIATION ~ TREFFIELD INTERNATIONAL AIRWAYS

Formed in September 1965, Treffield Aviation was re-named Treffield International Airways in November 1966. On 27 April 1967 it was awarded its Air Operators Certificate and IT charters followed from Castle Donington, the company's main base, and also from Liverpool, London-Gatwick, Manchester and Bristol/Cardiff, with Viscounts leased from Channel Airways.

A Britannia aircraft was introduced from 5 May 1967 for IT charter flights from Gatwick. However technical problems arose in early June, badly affecting the regularity of flight operations, and this prompted the airline's tour operator partner Hourmont Travel to cancel its ITC contract in mid-July 1967. Financial problems forced Treffield to close down on 23 June 1967.

TYNE TEES AIR CHARTER

Tyne Tees Air Charter was set up on 21 December 1960 and used DC-3 aircraft from March 1962 for IT charter work from Newcastle and Manchester. Operations continued until January 1965 when the company was liquidated.

VIRGIN ATLANTIC

In the late eighties, Virgin Atlantic operated IT charter services from London (Gatwick) to Orlando and Los Angeles. These services were switched to a 'scheduled mode' in 1991.

VIRGIN SUN

In 1998, the charter company Virgin Sun was formed to operate IT charters on behalf of the tour operator Virgin Holidays from London-Gatwick and Manchester. Operations started on 1 May 1999 using two leased A-320 aircraft.

WESTPOINT AVIATION ~ BRITISH WESTPOINT AIRLINES

The history of this Exeter-based air carrier goes back to December 1960 when it came into existence as F & J Mann Airways. Adhoc passenger and cargo charter flying was initiated in March 1961, and it was at this time that the company's name was changed to Westpoint Aviation. With two DC-3 aircraft, the carrier operated IT charter services, mainly from London-Gatwick, from July 1961 until Summer 1963. The company later changed its name to British Westpoint Airlines in October 1963. Due to financial problems, the carrier later suspended all operations in May 1966.

WILLIAM DEMPSTER

The charter company William Dempster originated in 1948 and used Blackbushe Airport as its main base. After acquiring two Tudor 5 aircraft in April 1950, the carrier launched a low fare service between Blackbushe and South Africa. The company's operating base was transferred to Stansted Airport in 1951 and, for a short period starting in August 1952, IT charters were flown to continental destinations with a recently acquired DC-3. Late in 1953 however, all services were suspended.

WORLD WIDE AVIATION

Formed in July 1960, World Wide Aviation was based at London-Gatwick and, using DC-4 aircraft, the air carrier started IT charter operations in July 1961. After the demise of Overseas Aviation in August 1961, World Wide took over some of the tour operator contracts of that airline, including those from West-Berlin. Prompted by financial difficulties, the company suspended operations in October 1961, but continued a nominal existence until July 1962.

YUGOSLAVIA

AIR COMMERCE

Air Commerce operated charter services from Zurich to Ohrid and Skopje in Macedonia and to Sarajevo in Bosnia from December 1991 until April 1992. Its fleet consisted of two TU-154 aircraft which were disposed of in early 1998 when a leased L-410 came to be acquired.

AIR YUGOSLAVIA

The Yugoslav national airline JAT (Jugoslovenski Aero Transport) founded Air Yugoslavia as a wholly-owned charter subsidiary on 1 April 1969 and, from the beginning, the carrier has made use of JAT aircraft for its charter work. Initially, Air Yugoslavia operated charters to selected destinations in Australia and in the USA, but these services were switched to a scheduled mode in 1975/76 and taken over by JAT.

When Yugoslav nationals increasingly sought employment in other central European countries, this opened up a new field of activity for Air Yugoslavia. By 1971, regular charter flights were in operation between Belgrade, Zagreb and several cities in West Germany, complementing the scheduled services of JAT. Also at that time, Air Yugoslavia commenced holiday charter operations from numerous cities in western and northern Europe to resorts on the Adriatic coast and, by 1989, Air Yugoslavia's share in foreign tourists' travel to Yugoslavia had grown to 250,000.

In addition to inbound charters to Yugoslavia, Air Yugoslavia also operated outbound IT charters to southern European holiday destinations, mainly in co-operation with JAT's own tour operator Airlift. Air Yugoslavia's charter activity continued successfully until mid-1991 when civil strife erupted among the constituent republics of the Yugoslav Federation and the tourist industry practically ground to a halt. The charter carrier's activity was at a standstill, as was JAT's, as a result of a UN blockade imposed on Yugoslavia which effectively closed the country's air space to civil flying.

When the UN embargo was lifted in October 1994, JAT and Air Yugoslavia resumed their operations albeit on a limited scale. Because Yugoslavia now only consisted of Serbia and Montenegro, JAT's traffic base was reduced in size to a fraction of what it was before 1991. Air Yugoslavia's market was equally curtailed in that it had lost access to most of the long Adriatic coast, and the most popular resorts, apart from a small area wedged between Croatia and Albania, with Tivat serving as a gateway airport.

Until 1991, Air Yugoslavia operated 'public charter' flights for Yugoslav migrant workers employed in West Germany. When operations to Germany were resumed in October 1994, JAT took over all services which were then operated in a scheduled mode. Meanwhile, Air Yugoslavia started 'public charter' flights between Belgrade and Trieste/Milan and 1996 saw the resumption of holiday charter operations by Air Yugoslavia to Tivat, on the Adriatic coast of Montenegro, from German cities. In addition, adhoc charters for Yugoslav workers in Central Europe are operated according to demand. Outbound holiday charters from Yugoslavia are also operated.

GENEX AIRLINES ~ AVIOGENEX

The Generalexport organisation founded Genex Airlines, later re-named Aviogenex, on 21 May 1968 for the purpose of operating tourist charter flights. The air carrier's close working relationship with the tour operator Yugotours, also a partner in the same trading group, has been instrumental in the success of its activity. The Aviogenex fleet initially consisted of two TU-134 jets which were replaced with more modern TU-134As in later years, and a switch to western aircraft was made in 1983 when two 727s were introduced in, followed by 737s in 1987/88.

When the Yugoslav Federation was dissolved in 1991 and international tourism to the country collapsed, Aviogenex was forced to discontinue its IT charter operations. Some of its aircraft were leased out to other air carriers but adhoc charter flights continued to be operated for Yugoslav expatriate workers in central Europe.

MONTENEGRO AIRLINES

Montenegro Airlines was founded in 1994 and has its main base at Podgorica (formerly Titograd). Operations started in April 1997 with one F-28 jet. Although catering mainly for Yugoslav workers resident in Central European countries, inbound holiday charters are also operated to Tivat on Yugoslavia's Adriatic coast.

BIBLIOGRAPHY

BOOKS

Banks Howard ....The Rise and Fall of Freddie Laker, Faber and Faber London 1982

Block John............................Mijn Verhaal, Uitgeverij Balans Amsterdam 1992

Bongers Hans M. ....Es lag in der Luft, Econ Verlag Dusseldorf 1971

Borner Walter........................Balair :: Geschichte der Schweizer Charter-Gesellschaft, AS Buchkonzept Zurich 1991

Braunburg Rudolf...................Interflug, ADV-Mediendienste Augsburg 1992

Buraas Anders ....The SAS Saga, Norbok Oslo 1979

Cuthbert Geoffrey...................Flying to the Sun - Britannia Airways, Hodder and Stoughton London 1987

Eglin Roger/Ritchie, Berry........Fly Me, I'm Freddie, Weidenfels and Nicolson London 1980

Finnis Malcolm ....Twilight of the Pistons - Air Ferry, MF Eastbourne 1997

Foldes Laszlo ....Five Decades of Flight - Malev 50 Years, Gábor Peterffy Budapest 1996

Grange C Perez/Pecker Beatriz..Crónica de la Aviación Española,SILEX Madrid 1983

Haapavaara Heikki ....Time flies - Finnair 75 Years, Finnair Group Helsinki 1998

Heuberger Günter ....Die Luftverkehrsabkommen der Schweiz, Schultheiss Polygraphischer Verlag Zurich 1992

Hull Norman...........................Eagles Over Water, Baron Birch 1998 The Story of Aquila Airways

Iarossi Marco ....Charter, EDAI Florence 1997, 1998

Jacquat Charles ....Le Goût du Risque, Geneva 1982

Krauthauser J/Kappner Ulrich ..Fliegen ist für alle da LTU, Nara-Verlag Allershausen 1996

Lúvíksson Steinar J.................Fimmtíu Flogin Ár

Sæmundsson Sveinn...............Atvinnuflugssaga Islands, Frjálst framtak Reykjavik 1989

MacDonald Hugh ....Aeroflot - Soviet Air Transport since 1923, Putnam London 1975

Merton Jones A. C..................British Independent Airlines since 1946, LAAS International London 1976

Mézière Henri/Sauvage J.M ....Les Ailes Françaises - l'aviation marchande de 1919 à nos joursÉditions Rive Droite Paris 1997

Michels Jurgen/Werner Jochen Luftfahrt Ost 1945 1990, Bernard & Graefe Verlag Bonn 1994

Penrose Harald.......................Wings across the World: An Illustrated History of British Airways, Cassell London 1980

Pompl Wilhelm ....Luftverkehr, Springer-Verlag Berlin 1998

Przychowski Hans von ....Luftbrücken nach Berlin, Brandenburgisches Verlagshaus Berlin 1994

Public Relations Braathens ......På Norske Vinger Braathens 50 Years History, Braathens Oslo 1996

Public Relations ....Channel Airways 25 Years, Channel Airways Southend 1971 Channel Airways

Public Relations ....Finnair 50 Years, Finnair Helsinki 1973

Public Relations ....JAT 20 Years, Informator Belgrade 1967

Public Relations ....This is JAT, JAT Belgrade 1990

Public Relations ....Sabena Revue: 50 Years of Sabena, Sabena Brussels 1973

Public Relations ....Tails of Success - 25 Years of Transavia, Transavia Amsterdam 1991

Public Relations ....Tarom 1954 -1999, Tarom Bucharest 1999

Seifert Karl-Dieter...................Weg und Absturz der Interflug, Brandenburgisches Verlagshaus Berlin 1994

Share Bernard ....The Flight of the Iolar: The Aer Lingus Experience, Gill and Macmillan Dublin 1986

Simons Graham M. ....Colours in the Sky - Court Line, GMS Enterprises Peterborough 1997

Simons Graham M. ....The Spirit of Dan-Air, GMS Enterprises Peterborough 1993

Sobelair ....SOBELAIR 1946 -1986 40 jaar/ans, Brussels 1987

Sobelair ....SOBELAIR 1946 -1996 50 jaar/ans, Brussels 1996

Stigø Sven ....25 Timer i Døgnet i 25 År: 25 Years of Sterling Airways, Dansk Reklame Produktion Copenhagen 1987

Van Laere Nicole ....Dat is Vliegen - Delta Air Transport, Lannoo Brussels 1997

Wegg John............................Finnair - The Art of Flying since 1923, Finnair Helsinki 1983

BIBLIOGRAPHY

Wesselink Theo/Postma Thijs ..Martinair 1958 - 1983, De
Bataafsche Leeuw Dieren 1983
Wölfer Joachim ....Deutsche Passagier-Luftfahrt von
1955 bis heute, Mittler Berlin 1995
(no author) ....Alitalia, R & S Milan 1973

AIRCRAFT REFERENCE GUIDES

Avrane A/Gilliand M/Guillem J ..Sud Est Caravelle Jane's Publishing
Co. London 1981
Chillon J/Dubois J-P/Wegg J ....French Post War Transport Aircraft
Air Britain (Historians) Tonbridge
1971
Church Richard J. ....The ONE-ELEVEN Story: Air Britain
(Historians) Tonbridge 1994
Klee Ulrich Ed. ....jp airline fleets international
Bucher Glattbruck, annual
Eastwood Tony/Roach John ....Jet Airliner Production List
tahs West Drayton October 1999
Volume 1 - Boeing
Eastwood Tony/Roach John ....Jet Airliner Production List
tahs West Drayton September 1998
Volume 2
Eastwood Tony/Roach John ....Piston Engine Airliner Production
List second edition tahs West
Drayton November 1996
Eastwood Tony/Roach John ....Turbo Prop Airliner
tahs West Drayton June 1998

MAGAZINES / NEWSPAPERS

Aero International
Aeronautical Journal, The
Aeroplane, The
Aéroports Magazine
Aerospace International
Air-Britain Digest
Air-Britain News
Aircraft Illustrated
Airline 92
Airliners
Airlines & Airliners
Airlines International
Air Pictorial

Airports Int'l Magazine
Air Transport World
Airways
Annals of Tourism Research
ASTA Travel News
Aviation Civile
Avion Revue
Aviation News
Avmark Aviation Economist, The
Balkan News International
BEA Magazine
Business Week
CAPC magazine
Chartered Institute of Transport Journal, The
DVWG
Eastern Mediterranean Tourism Travel
l'Echo Touristique
Economist, The
EIU Travel and Tourism Analyst
l'Expansion Voyages
Flight International
Freesun News
FVW International
Gatwick Life
Gatwick Skyport
Greek Tourist News
Hellenic Travelling
IATA Review
ICAO Bulletin
Interavia
Internationales Archiv für Verkehrswesen
International Herald Tribune
ITA Press
Jetstream
Journal of Air Law and Commerce
Journal of Industrial Economics, The
jp4 Aeronautica
La Gazette Touristique de Tunisie
Le Monde "Affaires"
Luftfahrt
Lufthansa Bordbuch
Lufthansa Jahrbuch

BIBLIOGRAPHY

Royal Aeronautical Society Journal, The
Sky Port Gatwick Edition
Spiegel, Der
Time
Tourism Management
Touristik Aktuell
Travel Express
Travelnews
TTG - Travel Trade Gazette
WATN
Welt am Sonntag, Die
Wings Magazine
Zeitschrift für Verkehrswissenschaft

AIRPORT PUBLICATIONS

Aeroporto di Bologna
Bremen JET
Catullo News
Dortmund Flughafen Report
Düsseldorfer Flughafen Nachrichten
Flugblatt Stuttgart Airport
Follow Me Hamburg Airport
Luftverkehr Hanover Airport
Salzburg Airport Magazin
Schipholland
VIA Dresden

ANNUAL REPORTS
AIRLINES

Aer Lingus
Aeroflot
Air Atlantis
Air France
Austrian Airlines
Balair

British European Airways
British Overseas Airways Corporation
British Airways
British Eagle
C T A
Finnair
Globe Air
K L M
Martinair
Sabena
Scandinavian Airlines   System
Scanair
Sobelair
Swissair
Virgin Express

AIRPORT AUTHORITIES

A D V (Germany)
AENA (Spain)
Aer Rianta
Amsterdam Schiphol Airport
A N A   (Portugal)
B A A   (United Kingdom)

CIVIL AVIATION AUTHORITIES

BAZL   (Switzerland)
Ilmailulaitos (Finland)
Luftfartsverket (Norway)
Luftfartsverket (Sweden)
Rijksluchtvaartdienst (Netherlands)
Statens Luftfartsvæsen (Denmark)

ORGANIZATIONS

B I A T, I A T A & I C A O

SCOVAL
PUBLISHING LTD